TExES English Language Arts and Reading 7–12
231
Teacher Certification Exam

Sharon A. Wynne, M.S.

XAMonline, INC.
Boston

Copyright © 2017 XAMonline, Inc.

All rights reserved. No part of the material protected by this copyright notice may be reproduced or utilized in any form or by any means, electronic or mechanical, including photocopying, recording or by any information storage and retrievable system, without written permission from the copyright holder.

To obtain permission(s) to use the material from this work for any purpose including workshops or seminars, please submit a written request to:

> XAMonline, Inc.
> 21 Orient Avenue
> Melrose, MA 02176
> Toll Free 1-800-301-4647
> Email: info@xamonline.com
> Web www.xamonline.com
> Fax: 1-617-583-5552

Library of Congress Cataloging-in-Publication Data

Wynne, Sharon A.
    English Language Arts and Reading 7-12 (231): Teacher Certification / Sharon A. Wynne.
    ISBN 978-1-60787-606-9
    1. English Language Arts and Reading 7-12 (231). 2. Study Guides. 3. TExES
    4. Teachers' Certification & Licensure. 5. Careers

Disclaimer:

The opinions expressed in this publication are the sole works of XAMonline and were created independently from the National Education Association,
Educational Testing Service, or any State Department of Education, National Evaluation Systems or other testing affiliates.

Between the time of publication and printing, state specific standards as well as testing formats and website information may change that is not included in part or in whole within this product. Sample test questions are developed by XAMonline and reflect similar content as on real tests; however, they are not former tests. XAMonline assembles content that aligns with state standards but makes no claims nor guarantees teacher candidates a passing score. Numerical scores are determined by testing companies such as NES or ETS and then are compared with individual state standards. A passing score varies from state to state.

Printed in the United States of America   œ-1

TExES English Language Arts and Reading 7–12 (231)
ISBN 978-1-60787-606-9

TEACHER CERTIFICATION STUDY GUIDE

About the Test

Test Name	English Language Arts and Reading 7-12
Time	5 hours
Test Code	231
Number of Questions	100 multiple choice questions 2 constructed-response questions
Format	Computer Assisted Test (CAT)

The TExES English Language Arts and Reading 7–12 (231) test is designed to assess whether an examinee has the requisite knowledge and skills that an entry-level educator in this field in Texas public schools must possess. The 100 multiple-choice questions and the two constructed-response questions are based on the English Language Arts and Reading 7–12 test framework. Questions on this test range from grades 7–12.

The test may contain questions that do not count toward the score. The number of scored questions will not vary; however, the number of questions that are not scored may vary. Your final scaled score will be based only on scored questions.

Domain	Doman Title	Approx. Percentage of Test	Standards Assessed
I.	Integrated Language Arts, Diverse Learners and the Study of English	15%	English Language Arts and Reading 7–12 I, VII
II.	Literature, Reading Processes and Skills for Reading Literary and Nonliterary Texts	40%	English Language Arts and Reading 7–12 I–IV
III.	Written Communication	30%	English Language Arts and Reading 7–12 I, V–VI
IV.	Oral Communication and Media Literacy	15%	English Language Arts and Reading 7–12 I, VIII–IX

The Standards

English Language Arts and Reading 7–12 Standard I
English language arts teachers in grades 7–12 know how to design and implement instruction that is appropriate for each student, reflects knowledge of the Texas Essential Knowledge and Skills (TEKS), integrates all components of the English language arts (i.e., writing, reading, listening/speaking, viewing/representing) and is based on continuous assessment.

ENGLISH LANG. ARTS & READING

TEACHER CERTIFICATION STUDY GUIDE

English Language Arts and Reading 7–12 Standard II
English language arts teachers in grades 7–12 understand the processes of reading and teach students to apply these processes.

English Language Arts and Reading 7–12 Standard III
English language arts teachers in grades 7–12 understand reading skills and strategies for various types of nonliterary texts and teach students to apply these skills and strategies to enhance their lifelong learning.

English Language Arts and Reading 7–12 Standard IV
English language arts teachers in grades 7–12 understand an extensive body of literature and literary genres and provide students with opportunities to read diverse types of literature and to view literature as a source for exploring and interpreting human experiences.

English Language Arts and Reading 7–12 Standard V
English language arts teachers in grades 7–12 understand that writing is a recursive, developmental, integrative and ongoing process and provide students with opportunities to develop competence as writers.

English Language Arts and Reading 7–12 Standard VI
English language arts teachers in grades 7–12 understand how to write effectively for various audiences and purposes and provide students with opportunities to write in a variety of forms and contexts.

English Language Arts and Reading 7–12 Standard VII
English language arts teachers in grades 7–12 understand the structure and development of the English language and provide students with opportunities to develop related knowledge and skills in meaningful contexts.

English Language Arts and Reading 7–12 Standard VIII
English language arts teachers in grades 7–12 understand oral communication and provide students with opportunities to develop listening and speaking skills.

English Language Arts and Reading 7–12 Standard IX
English language arts teachers in grades 7–12 understand how to interpret, analyze and produce visual images and messages in various media and provide students with opportunities to develop skills in this area.

Domains and Competencies

The content covered by this test is organized into broad areas of content called **domains**. Each domain covers one or more of the educator standards for this field. Within each domain, the content is further defined by a set of **competencies**. Each competency is composed of two major parts:

- The **competency statement**, which broadly defines what an entry-level educator in this field in Texas public schools should know and be able to do.

- The **descriptive statements**, which describe in greater detail the knowledge and skills eligible for testing.

TEACHER CERTIFICATION STUDY GUIDE

Table of Contents

DOMAIN I.   INTEGRATED LANGUAGE ARTS, DIVERSE LEARNERS, AND THE STUDY OF ENGLISH

COMPETENCY 001   THE TEACHER UNDERSTANDS AND APPLIES KNOWLEDGE OF RELATIONSHIPS AMONG THE LANGUAGE ARTS AND BETWEEN THE LANGUAGE ARTS AND OTHER ASPECTS OF STUDENTS' LIVES AND LEARNING 1

A.   Understands the continuum of language arts skills and expectations for students in grades 8–12, as specified in the Texas Essential Knowledge and Skills (TEKS) 1

B.   Understands the importance of integrating the language arts to improve students' language and literacy 8

C.   Understands the interrelationship between the language arts and other areas of the curriculum and uses this knowledge to facilitate students' learning across the curriculum 9

D.   Understands relationships among reading, writing, speaking, listening, and complex thinking and uses instruction to make connections among them in order to improve performance in each area 9

E.   Understands and teaches how the expressive uses of language and the receptive uses of language influence one another 10

COMPETENCY 002   THE TEACHER IS AWARE OF THE DIVERSITY OF THE STUDENT POPULATION AND PROVIDES INSTRUCTION THAT IS APPROPRIATE FOR ALL STUDENTS 11

A.   Knows how individual differences may affect students' language skills 11

B.   Designs learning experiences and selects materials that respond to and show respect for student diversity 17

C.   Knows strategies for providing reading, writing, and oral language instruction for all students, including English Language Learners and students with reading, writing, or oral language difficulties and/or disabilities 19

D.   Understands basic processes of first- and second-language acquisition and their impact on learning in the English language arts classroom 20

TEACHER CERTIFICATION STUDY GUIDE

E. Understands how a first language or dialect differences may affect students' use of English and knows strategies for promoting all students' ability to use standard English 20

F. Promotes students' understanding of the situational nature of language use and the value of knowing and using standard English while fostering pride in their own language background and respect for the language backgrounds of other people 21

COMPETENCY 003 THE TEACHER UNDERSTANDS THE STRUCTURE AND DEVELOPMENT OF THE ENGLISH LANGUAGE AND PROVIDES STUDENTS WITH OPPORTUNITIES TO DEVELOP RELATED KNOWLEDGE AND SKILLS IN MEANINGFUL CONTEXTS 22

A. Demonstrates knowledge of major historical, regional, and cultural influences on the ongoing development of the English language 22

B. Understands and teaches how to research word origins and analyze word formation as an aid to understanding meanings, derivations, and spellings . 23

C. Understands and teaches relationships among words and issues related to word choice 24

D. Knows and teaches rules of grammar, usage, sentence structure, punctuation, and capitalization in standard English and is able to identify and edit nonstandard usage in his or her own discourse and the discourse of others 27

E. Knows how to provide explicit and contextual instruction that enhances students' knowledge of and ability to use standard English 37

F. Knows and teaches how purpose, audience, and register affect discourse .. 37

G. Demonstrates an understanding of informal and formal procedures for monitoring and assessing students' ability to use the English language effectively 39

H. Uses assessment results to plan and adapt instruction that addresses students' strengths, needs, and interests and that builds on students' current skills to increase proficiency in using the English language effectively 40

TEACHER CERTIFICATION STUDY GUIDE

DOMAIN II. LITERATURE, READING PROCESSES, AND SKILLS FOR READING LITERARY AND NONLITERARY TEXTS

COMPETENCY 004 THE TEACHER UNDERSTANDS READING PROCESSES AND TEACHES STUDENTS TO APPLY THESE PROCESSES 41

A. Understands and promotes reading as an active process of constructing meaning 41

B. Understands reader response and promotes students' responses to various types of text 42

C. Knows how text characteristics and purposes for reading determine the selection of reading strategies and teaches students to apply skills and strategies for reading various types of texts for a variety of purposes 44

D. Knows how to use and teaches students to use word analysis skills, word structure, word order, and context for word identification and to confirm word meaning 45

E. Demonstrates an understanding of the role of reading fluency in reading comprehension and knows how to select and use instructional strategies and materials to enhance students' reading fluency 46

F. Knows and applies strategies for enhancing students' comprehension through vocabulary study 47

G. Understands and teaches students comprehension strategies to use before reading, during reading, and after reading 48

H. Understands the role of visualization, metacognition, self-monitoring, and social interaction in reading comprehension and promotes students' use of these processes 49

I. Understands levels of reading comprehension and strategies for teaching literal, inferential, creative, and critical comprehension skills 50

J. Knows how to intervene in students' reading process to promote their comprehension and enhance their reading experience 50

K. Knows how to provide students with reading experiences that enhance their understanding of and respect for diversity and guides students to increase knowledge of cultures through reading 52

L. Knows how to use technology to enhance reading instruction 52

M.	Demonstrates an understanding of informal and formal procedures for monitoring and assessing students' reading, such as using reading-response journals	53
N.	Uses assessment results to plan and adapt instruction that addresses students' strengths, needs, and interests and that builds on students' current skills to increase their reading proficiency	54

COMPETENCY 005 THE TEACHER UNDERSTANDS READING SKILLS AND STRATEGIES FOR VARIOUS TYPES OF NONLITERARY TEXTS AND TEACHES STUDENTS TO APPLY THESE SKILLS AND STRATEGIES TO ENHANCE THEIR LIFELONG LEARNING ... 55

A.	Demonstrates knowledge of types of nonliterary texts and their characteristics	55
B.	Understands purposes for reading nonliterary texts, reading strategies associated with different purposes, and ways to teach students to apply appropriate reading strategies for different purposes	56
C.	Knows strategies for monitoring one's own understanding of nonliterary texts and for addressing comprehension difficulties that arise and knows how to teach students to use these strategies	57
D.	Demonstrates knowledge of skills for comprehending nonliterary texts and knows how to provide students with opportunities to apply and refine these skills	58
E.	Understands types of text organizers and their use in locating and categorizing information	58
F.	Demonstrates knowledge of types of text structure and strategies for promoting students' ability to use text structure to facilitate comprehension of nonliterary texts	59
G.	Knows strategies for helping students increase their knowledge of specialized vocabulary in nonliterary texts and for facilitating reading comprehension	59
H.	Knows how to locate, retrieve, and retain information from a range of texts, including interpreting information presented in various formats, and uses effective instructional strategies to teach students these skills	60
I.	Knows how to evaluate the credibility and accuracy of information in nonliterary texts, including electronic texts, and knows how to teach students to apply these critical-reading skills	61

TEACHER CERTIFICATION STUDY GUIDE

J. Demonstrates an understanding of the characteristics and uses of various types of research tools and information sources and promotes students' understanding of and ability to use these resources 61

K. Understands steps and procedures for engaging in inquiry and research and provides students with learning experiences that promote their knowledge and skills in this area 62

L. Demonstrates an understanding of informal and formal procedures for monitoring and assessing students' reading of nonliterary texts 63

M. Uses assessment results to plan and adapt instruction that addresses students' strengths, needs, and interests and that builds on students' current skills to increase their proficiency in reading nonliterary texts 64

COMPETENCY 006 THE TEACHER UNDERSTANDS LITERARY ELEMENTS, GENRES, AND MOVEMENTS AND DEMONSTRATES KNOWLEDGE OF A SUBSTANTIAL BODY OF LITERATURE 65

A. Demonstrates knowledge of genres and their characteristics through analysis of literary texts 65

B. Demonstrates knowledge of literary elements and devices, including ways in which they contribute to meaning and style, through analysis of literary texts 68

C. Demonstrates knowledge of major literary movements in American, British, and world literature, including their characteristics, the historical contexts from which they emerged, major authors and their impact on literature, and representative works and their themes 72

D. Demonstrates knowledge of a substantial body of classic and contemporary American literature 83

E. Demonstrates knowledge of a substantial body of classic and contemporary British literature 95

F. Demonstrates knowledge of a substantial body of classic and contemporary world literature 101

G. Demonstrates knowledge of a substantial body of young adult literature 101

H. Demonstrates knowledge of various critical approaches to literature 113

TEACHER CERTIFICATION STUDY GUIDE

COMPETENCY 007 THE TEACHER UNDERSTANDS STRATEGIES FOR READING LITERARY TEXTS AND PROVIDES STUDENTS WITH OPPORTUNITIES TO FORMULATE, EXPRESS, AND SUPPORT RESPONSES TO LITERATURE 118

A. Demonstrates knowledge of various types of responses to literary texts and encourages a variety of responses in students 118

B. Knows strategies for motivating students to read literature and for promoting their appreciation of the value of literature 119

C. Knows how to draw from wide reading in American, British, world, and young adult literature to guide students to explore and select independent reading based on their individual needs and interests 122

D. Knows how to promote students' interest in literature and facilitate their reading and understanding.. 122

E. Uses technology to promote students' engagement in and comprehension of literature 122

F. Knows strategies for creating communities of readers and for promoting conversations about literature and ideas... 122

G. Understands and teaches students strategies to use for analyzing and evaluating a variety of literary texts, both classic and contemporary........... 122

H. Applies effective strategies for helping students view literature as a source for exploring and interpreting human experience 130

I. Applies effective strategies for engaging students in exploring and discovering the personal and societal relevance of literature...................... 131

J. Promotes students' understanding of relationships among literary works from various times and cultures 131

K. Promotes students' ability to analyze how literary elements and devices contribute to meaning and to synthesize and evaluate interpretations of literary texts.. 133

L. Knows effective strategies for teaching students to formulate, express, and support responses to various types of literary texts 135

M. Demonstrates an understanding of informal and formal procedures for monitoring and assessing students' comprehension of literary texts........... 136

ENGLISH LANG. ARTS & READING

N.	Knows how to use assessment results to plan and adapt instruction that addresses students' strengths, needs, and interests and that builds on students' current skills to increase their proficiency in comprehending literary texts	136

DOMAIN III.   WRITTEN COMMUNICATION

COMPETENCY 008   THE TEACHER UNDERSTANDS AND PROMOTES WRITING AS A RECURSIVE, DEVELOPMENTAL, INTEGRATIVE, AND ONGOING PROCESS AND PROVIDES STUDENTS WITH OPPORTUNITIES TO DEVELOP COMPETENCE AS WRITERS 137

A.	Understands recursive stages in the writing process and provides students with explicit instruction, meaningful practice, and effective feedback as they engage in all phases of the writing process	137
B.	Understands writing as a process that allows students to construct meaning, examine thinking, reflect, develop perspective, acquire new learning, and influence the world around them	138
C.	Applies writing conventions, including sentence and paragraph construction, spelling, punctuation, usage, and grammatical expression, and provides students with explicit instruction in using them during the writing process	139
D.	Applies criteria for evaluating written work and teaches students effective strategies for evaluating their own writing and the writings of others	140
E.	Structures peer conference opportunities that elicit constructive, specific responses and that promote students' writing development	140
F.	Understands and promotes the use of technology in all phases of the writing process and in various types of writing, including writing for research and publication	141
G.	Applies strategies for helping students develop voice and style in their writing	141
H.	Demonstrates an understanding of informal and formal procedures for monitoring and assessing students' writing competence	144
I.	Uses assessment results to plan and adapt instruction that addresses students' strengths, needs, and interests and that builds on students' current skills to increase their writing proficiency	144

TEACHER CERTIFICATION STUDY GUIDE

COMPETENCY 009 THE TEACHER UNDERSTANDS EFFECTIVE WRITING AND TEACHES STUDENTS TO WRITE EFFECTIVELY IN A VARIETY OF FORMS AND FOR VARIOUS AUDIENCES, PURPOSES, AND CONTEXTS 146

A.	Understands and teaches the distinguishing features of various forms of writing...	146
B.	Applies and teaches skills and strategies for writing effectively in a variety of forms and for a variety of audiences, purposes, and contexts	147
C.	Understands and teaches how a writer's purpose and audience define appropriate language, writing style, and text organization	152
D.	Provides students with explicit instruction, meaningful practice opportunities, and effective feedback as the students create different types of written works...	152
E.	Promotes students' ability to compose effectively	154
F.	Provides students with professionally written, student-written, and teacher-written models of writing..	157
G.	Demonstrates knowledge of factors that influence student writing.............	158
H.	Analyzes and teaches the use of literary devices in writing........................	158
I.	Teaches students skills and strategies for using writing as a tool for reflection, exploration, learning, problem solving, and personal growth......................	162
J.	Understands and teaches writing as a tool for inquiry, research, and learning	162
K.	Teaches students to evaluate critically the sources they use for their writing...	162
L.	Provides instruction about plagiarism, academic honesty, and integrity as applied to students' written work and their presentation of information from different sources, including electronic sources...	162
M.	Understands and teaches students the importance of using acceptable formats for communicating research results and documenting sources......	163
N.	Demonstrates an understanding of informal and formal procedures for monitoring and assessing students' writing development	164

ENGLISH LANG. ARTS & READING

TEACHER CERTIFICATION STUDY GUIDE

O. Uses assessment results to plan and adapt instruction that addresses students' strengths, needs, and interests and that builds on students' current skills to increase their writing proficiency 164

DOMAIN IV.   ORAL COMMUNICATION AND MEDIA LITERACY

COMPETENCY 010   THE TEACHER UNDERSTANDS PRINCIPLES OF ORAL COMMUNICATION AND PROMOTES STUDENTS' DEVELOPMENT OF LISTENING AND SPEAKING SKILLS ... 165

A. Understands similarities and differences between oral and written language and promotes students' awareness of these similarities and differences 165

B. Understands and helps students understand the role of cultural factors in oral communication 166

C. Facilitates effective student interaction and oral communication, including group discussions and individual presentations 167

D. Understands and teaches various forms of oral discourses and their characteristics and provides effective opportunities for practice 167

E. Understands and teaches skills for speaking to diverse audiences for various purposes and provides students with effective opportunities to apply these skills in a variety of contexts 169

F. Understands and teaches strategies for preparing, organizing, and delivering different types of oral presentations, including informative and persuasive messages and literary interpretations 169

G. Understands and teaches skills and strategies for using technology in oral presentations 170

H. Understands and teaches strategies for evaluating the content and effectiveness of spoken messages and provides effective opportunities for practice 171

I. Understands and teaches skills for active, purposeful listening in various situations and provides effective opportunities for practice 172

J. Demonstrates an understanding of informal and formal procedures for monitoring and assessing students' oral communication skills 172

ENGLISH LANG. ARTS & READING

TEACHER CERTIFICATION STUDY GUIDE

| K. | Uses assessment results to plan and adapt instruction that addresses students' strengths, needs, and interests and that builds on students' current skills to increase proficiency in oral communication .... 172 |

COMPETENCY 011   THE TEACHER UNDERSTANDS AND TEACHES BASIC PRINCIPLES OF MEDIA LITERACY AND PROVIDES STUDENTS WITH OPPORTUNITIES TO APPLY THESE PRINCIPLES IN INTERACTIONS WITH MEDIA 173

A.	Understands different types and purposes of media 173
B.	Analyzes and teaches about the influence of the media and the power of visual images 173
C.	Demonstrates awareness of ethical and legal factors to consider in the use and creation of media products 174
D.	Applies and teaches skills for responding to, interpreting, analyzing, and critiquing a variety of media... 175
E.	Understands and facilitates the production of media messages 175
F.	Guides students to evaluate their own and others' media productions 177
G.	Demonstrates an understanding of informal and formal procedures for monitoring and assessing students' media literacy 178
H.	Uses assessment results to plan and adapt instruction that addresses students' strengths, needs, and interests and that builds on students' current skills to increase media literacy... 179

RESOURCES 180

SAMPLE TEST 186

ANSWER KEY 215

SAMPLE TEST WITH RATIONALES 216

TEACHER CERTIFICATION STUDY GUIDE

DOMAIN I. INTEGRATED LANGUAGE ARTS, DIVERSE LEARNERS, AND THE STUDY OF ENGLISH

COMPETENCY 001 THE TEACHER UNDERSTANDS AND APPLIES KNOWLEDGE OF RELATIONSHIPS AMONG THE LANGUAGE ARTS AND BETWEEN THE LANGUAGE ARTS AND OTHER ASPECTS OF STUDENTS' LIVES AND LEARNING

A. **Understands the continuum of language arts skills and expectations for students in grades 8–12, as specified in the Texas Essential Knowledge and Skills (TEKS)**

Writing/purposes. The student writes in a variety of forms, including business, personal, literary, and persuasive texts, for various audiences and purposes. The student is expected to:

(A) write in a variety of forms using effective word choice, structure, and sentence forms with emphasis on organizing logical arguments with clearly related definitions, theses, and evidence; write persuasively; write to report and describe; and write poems, plays, and stories

(B) write in a voice and style appropriate to audience and purpose

(C) organize ideas in writing to ensure coherence, logical progression, and support for ideas.

Writing/writing processes. The student uses recursive writing processes when appropriate. The student is expected to:

(A) use prewriting strategies to generate ideas, develop voice, and plan

(B) develop drafts, alone and collaboratively, by organizing and reorganizing content and by refining style to suit occasion, audience, and purpose;

(C) proofread writing for appropriateness of organization, content, style, and conventions

(D) refine selected pieces frequently to publish for general and specific audiences

(E) use technology for aspects of creating, revising, editing, and publishing.

Writing/grammar/usage/conventions/spelling. The student relies increasingly on the conventions and mechanics of written English, including the rules of grammar and usage, to write clearly and effectively. The student is expected to:

(A) produce legible work that shows accurate spelling and correct use of the conventions of punctuation and capitalization such as italics and ellipses

(B) demonstrate control over grammatical elements such as subject-verb agreement, pronoun-antecedent agreement, verb forms, and parallelism

(C) compose increasingly more involved sentences that contain gerunds, participles, and infinitives in their various functions

(D) produce error-free writing in the final draft.

Writing/inquiry/research. The student uses writing as a tool for learning. The student is expected to:

(A) use writing to formulate questions, refine topics, and clarify ideas;

(B) use writing to discover, organize, and support what is known and what needs to be learned about a topic

(C) compile information from primary and secondary sources in systematic ways using available technology

(D) represent information in a variety of ways such as graphics, conceptual maps, and learning logs

(E) use writing as a study tool to clarify and remember information;

(F) compile written ideas and representations into reports, summaries, or other formats and draw conclusions

(G) analyze strategies that writers in different fields use to compose.

Writing/evaluation. The student evaluates his or her own writing and the writings of others. The student is expected to:

(A) evaluate writing for both mechanics and content

(B) respond productively to peer review of his or her own work.

Reading/word identification/vocabulary development. The student uses a variety of strategies to read unfamiliar words and to build vocabulary. The student is expected to:

(A) expand vocabulary through wide reading, listening, and discussing

(B) rely on context to determine meanings of words and phrases such as figurative language, idioms, multiple meaning words, and technical vocabulary

(C) apply meanings of prefixes, roots, and suffixes in order to comprehend words new to the student

(D) research word origins, including Anglo-Saxon, Latin, and Greek words

(E) use reference material such as glossary, dictionary, thesaurus, and available technology to determine precise meanings and usage

(F) identify the relation of word meanings in analogies, homonyms, synonyms/antonyms, and connotation/denotation.

Reading/comprehension. The student comprehends selections using a variety of strategies. The student is expected to:

(A) establish a purpose for reading, such as to discover, interpret, and enjoy;

(B) draw upon his or her own background to provide connection to texts;

(C) monitor reading strategies such as rereading, using resources, and questioning and modify them when understanding breaks down

(D) construct images such as graphic organizers based on text descriptions and text structures

(E) analyze text structures such as compare and contrast, cause and effect, and chronological ordering

(F) identify main ideas and their supporting details;

(G) summarize texts;

(H) draw inferences such as conclusions, generalizations, and predictions and support them from text

(I) use study strategies such as skimming and scanning, note taking, outlining, and using study-guide questions to better understand texts

(J) read silently with comprehension for a sustained period of time.

Reading/variety of texts. The student reads extensively and intensively for different purposes in varied sources, including world literature. The student is expected to:

(A) read to be entertained, to appreciate a writer's craft, to be informed, to take action, and to discover models to use in his or her own writing

(B) read in such varied sources as diaries, journals, textbooks, maps, newspapers, letters, speeches, memoranda, electronic texts, and other media

(C) read world literature, including classic and contemporary works

(D) interpret the possible influences of the historical context on a literary work.

Reading/culture. The student reads widely, including world literature, to increase knowledge of his or her own culture, the culture of others, and the common elements across cultures. The student is expected to:

(A) recognize distinctive and shared characteristics of cultures through reading

(B) compare text events with his or her own and other readers' experiences.

Reading/literary response. The student expresses and supports responses to various types of texts. The student is expected to:

(A) respond to informational and aesthetic elements in texts such as discussions, journals, oral interpretations, and dramatizations

(B) use elements of text to defend his or her own responses and interpretations

(C) compare reviews of literature, film, and performance with his or her own responses.

Reading/literary concepts. The student analyzes literary elements for their contributions to meaning in literary texts. The student is expected to:

(A) recognize the theme (general observation about life or human nature) within a text

(B) analyze the relevance of setting and time frame to the text's meaning

(C) analyze characters and identify fictional time and point of view

(D) identify basic conflicts

(E) analyze the development of plot in narrative text

(F) recognize and interpret important symbols

(G) recognize and interpret poetic elements like metaphor, simile, personification, and the effect of sound on meaning

(H) understand literary forms and terms such as author, drama, biography, autobiography, myth, tall tale, dialogue, tragedy and comedy, structure in poetry, epic, ballad, protagonist, antagonist, paradox, analogy, dialect, and comic relief as appropriate to the selections being read.

Reading/analysis/evaluation. The student reads critically to evaluate texts. The student is expected to:

(A) analyze characteristics of the text, including its structure, word choices, and intended audience

(B) evaluate the credibility of information sources and determine the writer's motives

(C) analyze text to evaluate the logical argument and to determine the mode of reasoning used such as induction and deduction

(D) analyze editorials, documentaries, and advertisements for bias and use of common persuasive techniques.

Reading/inquiry/research. The student reads in order to research self-selected and assigned topics. The student is expected to:

(A) generate relevant, interesting, and researchable questions

(B) locate appropriate print and non-print information using texts and technical resources, periodicals and book indices, including databases and the Internet

(C) organize and convert information into different forms such as charts, graphs, and drawings

(D) adapt researched material for presentation to different audiences and for different purposes, and cite sources completely

(E) draw conclusions the information gathered.

Listening/speaking/critical listening. The student listens attentively for a variety of purposes. The student is expected to:

(A) focus attention on the speaker's message;

(B) use knowledge of language and develop vocabulary to interpret accurately the speaker's message

(C) monitor speaker's message for clarity and understanding such as asking relevant questions to clarify understanding

(D) formulate and provide effective verbal and nonverbal feedback.

Listening/speaking/evaluation. The student listens to analyze, appreciate, and evaluate oral performances and presentations. The student is expected to:

(A) listen and respond appropriately to presentations and performances of peers or published works such as original essays or narratives, interpretations of poetry, or individual or group performances of scripts

(B) identify and analyze the effect of artistic elements within literary texts such as character development, rhyme, imagery, and language

(C) evaluate informative and persuasive presentations of peers, public figures, and media presentations

(D) evaluate artistic performances of peers, public presenters, and media presentations

(E) use audience feedback to evaluate his or her own effectiveness and set goals for future presentations.

Listening/speaking/purposes. The student speaks clearly and effectively for a variety of purposes and audiences. The student is expected to:

(A) use the conventions of oral language effectively

(B) use informal, standard, and technical language effectively to meet the needs of purpose, audience, occasion, and task

(C) prepare, organize, and present a variety of informative messages effectively

(D) use effective verbal and nonverbal strategies in presenting oral messages

(E) ask clear questions for a variety of purposes and respond appropriately to the questions of others

(F) make relevant contributions in conversations and discussions.

Listening/speaking/presentations. The student prepares, organizes, and presents informative and persuasive oral messages. The student is expected to:

(A) present and advance a clear thesis and support the major thesis with logical points or arguments

(B) choose valid evidence, proofs, or examples to support claims

(C) use appropriate and effective appeals to support points or claims

(D) use effective verbal and nonverbal strategies such as pitch and tone of voice, posture, and eye contact.

Listening/speaking/literary interpretation. The student prepares, organizes, and presents literary interpretations. The student is expected to:

(A) make valid interpretations of literary texts such as telling stories, interpreting poems, stories, or essays

(B) analyze purpose, audience, and occasion to choose effective verbal and nonverbal strategies such as pitch and tone of voice, posture, and eye contact.

Viewing/representing/interpretation. The student understands and interprets visual representations. The student is expected to:

(A) describe how meanings are communicated through elements of design, including shape, line, color, and texture

(B) analyze relationships, ideas, and cultures as represented in various media

(C) distinguish the purposes of various media forms such as informative texts, entertaining texts, and advertisements.

Viewing/representing/analysis. The student analyzes and critiques the significance of visual representations. The student is expected to:

(A) investigate the source of a media presentation or production such as who made it and why it was made

(B) deconstruct media to get the main idea of a message ;

(C) evaluate and critique the persuasive techniques of media messages such as glittering generalities, logical fallacies, and symbols

(D) recognize how visual and sound techniques or design convey messages in media such as special effects, editing, camera angles, reaction shots, sequencing, and music

(E) recognize genres such as nightly news, news magazines, and documentaries and identify the unique properties of each

(F) compare, contrast, and critique various media coverage of the same event such as in newspapers, television, and on the Internet.

Viewing/representing/production. The student produces visual representations that communicate with others. The student is expected to:

(A) examine the effect of media in influencing his or her own perception of reality

(B) use a variety of forms and technologies such as videos, photographs, and web pages to communicate specific messages

(C) use a range of techniques to plan and create a media text and then reflect critically on the work produced

(D) create media products to include a billboard, cereal box, short editorial, and a three-minute documentary or print ad to engage specific audiences

(E) create, present, test, and revise a project and analyze a response, using data-gathering techniques such as questionnaires, group discussions, and feedback forms.

B. **Understands the importance of integrating the language arts to improve students' language and literacy**

Instruction in the English classroom has changed greatly over the last 20 years. Gone are the days when literature is taught on Monday, grammar is taught on Wednesday, and Friday is devoted to assigned writing. Instead, reading, writing, speaking, listening, and viewing are integrated to allow students to make connections among all aspects of language development during each class.

Suggestions for Integrating Language Arts

- Use prereading activities such as discussion, writing, research, and journals. Use writing to tap into prior knowledge before students read. Engage students in class discussions about themes, issues, and ideas explored in journals, predicting the outcome and exploring related information.

- Use prewriting activities such as reading model essays, researching, interviewing others, and combining sentences. Remember that developing language proficiency is a recursive process that involves practice in reading, writing, thinking, speaking, listening, and viewing.

- Create writing activities that are relevant to students by having them write and share with real audiences.

- Connect correctness—including skills of conventional usage, spelling, grammar, and punctuation—to the revising and editing stage of writing. Review of mechanics and punctuation can be done with mini-lessons that use sentences from student papers, sentence-combining strategies, and model passages from skilled writers.

- Connect reading, writing, listening, speaking, and viewing by using literature as a springboard for a variety of activities.

C. **Understands the interrelationship between the language arts and other areas of the curriculum and uses this knowledge to facilitate students' learning across the curriculum**

Ideas for Interdisciplinary Classroom Activities

- Have students produce a newspaper that incorporates many different subject areas (sports, weather, crossword puzzles, books reviews, pictures, poetry, advertisements, and so on).

- Connect each student with an "adoptive grandparent" at a nearby nursing home. Have students write their grandparent letters and stories, make timelines of their grandparents' lives, and learn about life during the time period in which their grandparents grew up.

- Have students create a PowerPoint presentation on a career they are interested in pursuing. Research pros and cons, salary information, skills necessary for the job, and so on.

- Using a book the entire class is reading, have students pick out any words with which they are unfamiliar. Have students research the origin of those words and their definitions, and then have them write a creative story using each word.

D. **Understands relationships among reading, writing, speaking, listening, and complex thinking and uses instruction to make connections among them in order to improve performance in each area**

Gone are the days when students engaged in skill practice using grammar worksheets. Grammar needs to be taught in the context of the students' own work. Listed below is a series of classroom practices that encourage meaningful context-based grammar instruction, combined with occasional mini-lessons and other language strategies that can be used on a daily basis.

- Connect grammar with the students' own writing while emphasizing grammar as a significant aspect of effective writing.

- Make editing and proofreading an essential part of classroom activities.

- Provide students with an opportunity to practice editing and proofreading cooperatively.

- Give instruction in the form of 15–20 minute mini-lessons.

- Emphasize the sound of punctuation by connecting it to pitch, stress, and pause.

- Involve students in all facets of language learning including reading, writing, listening, speaking, and thinking. Good use of language comes from exploring all forms of it on a regular basis.

There are a number of approaches that involve grammar instruction in the context of writing:

- Sentence combining: Try to use the students' own writing as much as possible. The theory behind combining ideas and the correct punctuation should be emphasized.

- Sentence and paragraph modeling: Provide students with the opportunity to practice imitating the style and syntax of professional writers.

- Sentence transforming: Give students an opportunity to change sentences from one form to another (for example, changing them from passive to active voice, inverting the sentence order, and changing forms of words).

- Daily language practice: Introduce or clarify common errors using daily language activities. Use actual student examples whenever possible. Correct and discuss the problems with grammar and usage.

E. **Understands and teaches how the expressive uses of language and the receptive uses of language influence one another**

See Competencies 1.B and 10.D.

COMPETENCY 002   THE TEACHER IS AWARE OF THE DIVERSITY OF THE STUDENT POPULATION AND PROVIDES INSTRUCTION THAT IS APPROPRIATE FOR ALL STUDENTS

A.   Knows how individual differences may affect students' language skills

Language, though an innate human ability, must be learned. Thus, the acquisition and use of language is subject to many influences on the learner. Linguists agree that language is first a vocal system of word symbols that enables a human to communicate his or her feelings, thoughts, and desires to other humans. Language was instrumental in the development of all cultures and is influenced by the changes in these societies.

Influences on Developing Language Skills
Historical influences

English is an Indo-European language that evolved through several periods.

The origin of English dates to the settlement of the British Isles in the fifth and sixth centuries CE by Germanic tribes called the Angles, Saxons, and Jutes. The original Britons spoke a Celtic tongue; the Angles spoke a Germanic dialect. Modern English derives from the speech of the Anglo-Saxons, who imposed not only their language but also their social customs and laws on their new land. From the fifth to the tenth century, Britain's language was the tongue we now refer to as Old English. During the next four centuries, the many French attempts at English conquest introduced many French words into English. However, the grammar and syntax of the language remained Germanic.

Middle English, most evident in the writings of Geoffrey Chaucer, dates from approximately 1066 to 1509. William Caxton brought the printing press to England in 1474, which increased literacy. Old English words required numerous inflections to indicate noun cases and plurals as well as verb conjugations. Middle English continued the use of many inflections and pronunciations that treated these inflections as separately pronounced syllables. *English* in 1300 would have been written *Olde Anglishe* with the *e*'s at the ends of the words pronounced as our short *a* vowel. Even adjectives had plural inflections: *long dai* became *longe daies*, pronounced "long-a day-as." Spelling was phonetic, so every vowel had multiple pronunciations, a fact that continues to affect the language.

Modern English dates from what linguists call the Great Vowel Shift because it created guidelines for spelling and pronunciation. Before the printing press, books were copied laboriously by hand and the language was subject to the individual interpretation of the scribes. Printers—and later, lexicographers like Samuel Johnson and Noah Webster—influenced the guidelines. As reading matter was mass produced, the reading public was forced to adopt the speech and writing habits developed by those who wrote and printed books.

Despite many students' insistence to the contrary, Shakespeare's writings are in Modern English. It is important to stress to students that language, like customs, morals, and other social factors, is constantly subject to change. Immigration, inventions, and cataclysmic events change language as much as they change any other facet of life. The domination of one race or nation over others can change a language significantly. Beginning with the colonization of the New World, English and Spanish became dominant languages in the Western Hemisphere. American English today is somewhat different in pronunciation and sometimes vocabulary from British English. The British call a truck a *lorry*; call a baby carriage a *pram*, short for *perambulator*; and call an elevator a *lift*. There are very few syntactical differences, and even the tonal qualities that were once so clearly different are converging.

Though Modern English is less complex than Middle English, having lost many unnecessary inflections, it is still considered difficult to learn because of its many exceptions to the rules.

English has, however, become the world's dominant language by reason of the great political, military, and social power of England from the fifteenth to the nineteenth century and of America in the twentieth century. Modern inventions—the telephone, phonograph, radio, television, and motion pictures—have especially affected English pronunciation. Regional dialects, once a hindrance to clear understanding, have fewer distinct characteristics. The speakers from different parts of the United States can be identified by their accents, but less so as educators and media personalities stress uniform pronunciation and proper grammar.

The English language has a more extensive vocabulary than any other language. English is a language of synonyms, words borrowed from other languages, and coined words—many of them introduced by the rapid expansion of technology. It is important for students to understand that language is in constant flux.

Emphasis should be placed on learning and using language for specific purposes and audiences. Negative feedback about a student's errors in word choice or sentence structure will inhibit creativity. Positive feedback that suggests ways to enhance communication skills will encourage exploration.

Geographical influences

Dialect differences occur primarily in pronunciation. Bostonians say "pahty" for "party," and Southerners blend words like "you all" into "y'all." In addition to the dialect differences already mentioned, the biggest geographical differences in American English stem from minor word choice variances. Depending on the region where you live, when you order a carbonated, syrupy beverage most generically called a *soft drink*, you might ask for a *soda* in the South, or a *pop* in the Midwest. If you order a soda in New York, then you will get a scoop of ice cream in your soft drink, while in other areas you would have to ask for a *float*.

Social influences

Social influences come mainly from family, peer groups, and mass media. The economic and educational level of a family determines the properness of that family's language use. Exposure to adults who encourage and assist children to speak well enhances readiness for other areas of learning and contributes to a child's ability to communicate his or her needs. Historically, children learned language, speech patterns, and grammar from members of the extended family, just like they learned the rules of conduct within their family unit and community. More recently, the mother in a nuclear family became the dominant force in influencing the child's development. With increasing social changes, many children are not receiving the proper guidance in all areas of development, especially language.

Those who are fortunate to be in educational day care programs like Head Start or in certified preschools generally develop better language skills than those whose care is entrusted to untrained care providers. Once a child enters elementary school, he or she is also greatly influenced by peer language. This peer influence becomes significant in adolescence as the use of jargon gives teenagers a sense of identity within their chosen group(s) and independence from the influence of adults. In some lower socioeconomic groups, children use standard English in school and street language outside school. Some children of immigrant families become bilingual by necessity if no English is spoken in the home.

Research has shown a strong correlation between socioeconomic characteristics and all areas of intellectual development. Traditional assessment instruments rely on verbal ability to establish intelligence. Research findings and test scores reflect that children reared in nuclear families who provide cultural experiences and individual attention become more language proficient than those who do not have that security and stimulation.

Personal influences

The rate of physical development and identifiable language disabilities also influence language development. Nutritional deficiencies, poor eyesight, and conditions such as stuttering or dyslexia can inhibit a child's ability to master language. Unless diagnosed early, such conditions can hamper communication into adulthood. These conditions also stymie the development of self-confidence and, therefore, the willingness to learn or to overcome the handicap. Children should receive proper diagnosis and positive corrective instruction.

In adolescence, the child's choice of role models and his or her decision about his or her future determine the growth of identity. Rapid physical and emotional changes and the stress of coping with the pressure of sexual awareness make concentration on any educational pursuits difficult. The easier the transition from childhood to adulthood, the better the child's competence will be in all learning areas.

Middle school and junior high school teachers are confronted by a student body ranging from fifth graders who are still childish to eighth or ninth graders who—at least in their minds—are young adults. Teachers must approach language instruction as a social development tool with emphasis on vocabulary acquisition, reading improvement, and speaking/writing skills. High school teachers can provide more formalized instruction in grammar, usage, and literature for older adolescents whose social development allows them to pay more attention to studies that will improve their chances for a better adult life.

As a tool, language must have relevance to the students' real environment. Many high schools have developed practical English classes for business/vocational students whose specific needs are determined by their desire to enter the workforce upon graduation. In these classes, emphasis is placed upon accuracy of mechanics and understanding verbal and written directions because these are skills desired by employers. Writing résumés, completing forms, reading policy and operations manuals, and generating reports are some of the desired skills. Emphasis is placed on higher-level thinking skills, including inferential thinking and literary interpretation, in literature classes for college-bound students.

Approaches to Teaching Language Skills
Learning approach

Early theories of language development were formulated from learning theory research. The assumption was that language development evolved from learning the rules of language structures and applying them through imitation and reinforcement. This approach also assumed that language, cognitive, and social developments were independent of one another. Thus, children were expected to learn language from patterning after adults who spoke and wrote standard English. No allowance was made for communication through child jargon, for idiomatic expressions, or for grammatical and mechanical errors resulting from too strictly adhering to the rules of inflection (*childs* instead of *children*) or conjugation (*runned* instead of *ran*). No association was made between physical and operational development and language mastery.

Linguistic approach

Studies spearheaded by Noam Chomsky in the 1950s formulated the theory that language ability is innate and develops through natural human maturation as environmental stimuli trigger acquisition of syntactical structures appropriate to each exposure level. The assumption of a hierarchy of syntax downplayed the significance of semantics. Because of the complexity of syntax and the relative speed with which children acquire language, linguists attributed language development to biological rather than cognitive or social influences.

Cognitive approach

Researchers in the 1970s proposed that language knowledge derives from both syntactic and semantic structures. Drawing on the studies of Piaget and other cognitive learning theorists, supporters of the cognitive approach maintained that children acquire knowledge of linguistic structures after they have acquired the cognitive structures necessary to process language. For example, joining words for specific meaning necessitates sensory motor intelligence. The child must be able to coordinate movement and recognize objects before he or she can identify words to name the objects or word groups to describe the actions performed with those objects.

Adolescents must have developed the mental abilities for organizing concepts and concrete operations, predicting outcomes, and theorizing before they can assimilate and verbalize complex sentence structures, choose vocabulary for particular nuances of meaning, and examine semantic structures for tone and manipulative effect.

Sociocognitive approach

Other theorists in the 1970s proposed that language development results from sociolinguistic competence. Language, cognitive, and social knowledge are interactive elements of total human development. Emphasis on verbal communication as the medium for language expression resulted in the inclusion of speech activities in most language arts curricula.

Unlike previous approaches, the sociocognitive approach posited that determining the appropriateness of language in given situations for specific listeners is as important as understanding semantic and syntactic structures. By engaging in conversation, children at all stages of development have opportunities to test their language skills, receive feedback, and make modifications. As a social activity, conversation is as structured by social order as grammar is structured by the rules of syntax. Conversation satisfies the learner's need to be heard and understood and to influence others. Thus, the learner's choices of vocabulary, tone, and content are dictated by his or her ability to assess the language capacities of his listeners. The learner is constantly applying his or her cognitive skills to using language in a social interaction. If the capacity to acquire language is inborn, without an environment in which to practice language, a child would not pass beyond grunts and gestures, as did primitive humans.

Of course, the varying degrees of environmental stimuli to which children are exposed at all age levels create a slower or faster development of language. Some children are prepared to articulate concepts and recognize symbolism by the time they enter fifth grade because they have been exposed to challenging reading and conversations with well-spoken adults at home or in their social groups. Others are still trying to master the sight recognition skills and are not yet ready to combine words in complex patterns.

Concerns for the Teacher

Because teachers must—by virtue of tradition and the dictates of the curriculum—teach grammar, usage, and writing in addition to reading and, later, literature, the problem becomes when to teach what to whom. The profusion of approaches to teaching grammar alone is mind-boggling. In college and graduate school, teachers learn about transformational grammar, stratificational grammar, sectoral grammar, and so on. But in practice, most teachers, supported by presentations in textbooks and by the methods they learned themselves, keep coming back to the traditional prescriptive approach (read and imitate) or structural approach (learn the parts of speech, the parts of a sentence, punctuation rules, and sentence patterns). Some educators opt to not teach grammar at all, which is the worst solution to this challenge.

The same problems occur in teaching usage. To what extent can teachers demand or expect that students communicate in only standard English? Different schools of thought suggest that a study of dialect and idiom and recognition of various jargons is a vital part of language development. Social pressures—especially on students in middle and junior high schools—to be accepted within their peer groups and to speak the non-standard language spoken outside the school make adolescents resistant to the corrective, remedial approach. In many communities that have large immigrant populations, new words are entering English from other languages while words and expressions that were common a generation ago are becoming obsolete.

Regardless of differences of opinion concerning language development, it is safe to say that a language arts teacher will be most effective using the styles and approaches with which he or she is most comfortable. If a teacher subscribes to a student-centered approach, he or she may find that the students have a lot to teach him or her and one another. Moffett and Wagner, in the fourth edition of *Student-centered Language Arts, K–12*, stress the three I's: individualization, interaction, and integration. Essentially, they are supporting the sociocognitive approach to language development. By providing an opportunity for students to select their own activities and resources, the teacher individualizes students' instruction. By encouraging students to teach one another, the teacher makes the lessons interactive. Finally, by allowing students to synthesize a variety of knowledge structures, the teacher integrates different approaches to learning. In this approach, the teacher becomes a facilitator.

Benefits of the sociocognitive approach

The sociocognitive approach has tended to guide the whole language movement, which is currently very popular. Most basal readers utilize an integrated, cross-curricular approach to successful grammar, language, and usage, which is reinforced across subjects. Language incorporates diction and terminology across the curriculum. Standard usage is encouraged and supported by the core classroom textbooks and current software and technology. Teachers need to acquaint themselves with the technology available in their school district and at their individual school and with programs that would serve their students' needs. Students respond enthusiastically to technology and several highly effective programs are available in various formats to assist students with initial instruction or remediation. Grammar texts, such as the Warriner's series, employ various methods to reach individual learning styles. The school library media center should become a focal point for individual exploration.

B. Designs learning experiences and selects materials that respond to and show respect for student diversity

Research is beginning to document the ways in which parents from different cultures interact with their children to support their learning. Many of these ways differ from traditional, mainstream approaches, and are therefore not necessary recognized by educators or school personnel. Building a body of knowledge about the specific practices of various cultural groups can support the validation of those practices and may support the sharing of effective practices across cultural groups.

Teachers have a critical role to play in encouraging multicultural experiences. They have an opportunity to incorporate activities that reflect our nation's increasing diversity and allow students to share their similarities, develop a positive cultural identity, and appreciate the unique contributions of all cultures. The best way to incorporate multicultural literature depicting African American, Asian, Middle Eastern, Native American, and Hispanic heritage is to integrate it into the established reading program rather than presenting it as a separate or distinct area of study.

Homework activities

Interactive homework assignments

Homework activities that are explicitly designed to encourage interaction between parents and children have shown positive results for increasing achievement in several subject areas, including science and language arts. Well-designed interactive assignments can have a number of positive outcomes: they can help students practice study skills, prepare for class, participate in learning activities, and develop personal responsibility for homework. They can also promote parent-child relations, develop parent-teacher communication, and fulfill policy directives from administrators.

School support of parental homework help

Although parents express positive feelings about homework, they also have concerns about their personal limitations in subject-matter knowledge, and effective helping strategies. More research is needed on how school personnel can effectively support parental homework help.

Reading workshops

In reading workshops, students select from a variety of reading materials such as fiction books, nonfiction books (for example, biographies), encyclopedias, and magazines.

Students share their responses to the material they have chosen by writing or talking with teachers and classmates, which allows them to take ownership of their reading. Teachers need to have a large supply of multicultural literature from which students can choose that is sensitive to and reflective of students' diverse cultural backgrounds. By reading these materials, students can learn that most people have similar emotions, needs, and dreams.

During reading workshops, students usually engage in reading, responding, sharing, and reading aloud.

Reading. Students usually spend an hour independently reading books and other written materials that include diverse cultures.

Responding. After students read a multicultural text, teachers should direct the students to reflect on the meaning of the text in their own lives. In this process, students interpret meanings and draw inferences based upon their own cultural perspectives and experiences. Students might keep journals in which they write their initial responses to the materials they are reading. They might also talk with the teacher about their texts. Teachers should help students move beyond simply writing summaries and toward reflecting and making connections between literature and their own lives.

Sharing. Sharing differences among diverse families heightens students' sensitivity to issues involving prejudice, racism, and intolerance toward students of different cultures. Exposing students to culturally diverse literature provides them with a means to become global citizens who can perform more effectively in a culturally diverse society.

Reading aloud. Teachers read aloud when they wish to present literature that students might not be able to read themselves, such as classics to which they feel every student should be exposed. Students should participate in a class discussion about the book, share the reading experience, and respond to the story together as a community of learners, not as individuals.

Writing workshops

In a writing workshop, teachers can encourage students to write a story depicting the lives of persons around the world, imagining a setting and characters in a culture different from their own. Then students can make a box containing cultural items—such as ornaments, clothing, pictures, or music recordings—associated with the country and the story they create.

Another way of integrating multicultural activities into a writing workshop is to involve students in a multicultural pen-pal project. Students can compose group letters to partner classes in other nations about their school, their lives, or a favorite part of the books they have read about the partner's country. Internet resources such as epals.com are available for whole classrooms to connect virtually through email. Classroom teachers display their needs and wants on the site, naming a language and country they wish to connect with, and may send a request to partner with an appropriate classroom internationally through the site's global partnership,

Hard copies of correspondence, books, thank you notes, etc., from partner classes also can be displayed on bulletin boards in the classroom. This activity teaches students that there are interesting books to read and kids to talk to via the written word from different countries all around the world. As students engage in these writing activities, they expand their views about other cultures by sharing language, beliefs, religion, heritage, and their school and home lives.

Teachers can also invite guest speakers available in their local area by contacting a cultural community center. A guest speaker could be a director of an international program at a local university or a community leader. It is useful for the students to prepare questions in advance. Students should write the invitation and a follow-up letter of appreciation to the speaker.

C. **Knows strategies for providing reading, writing, and oral language instruction for all students, including English Language Learners and students with reading, writing, or oral language difficulties and/or disabilities**

The more information a speaker has about an audience, the more likely he or she is to communicate effectively with that audience. Several factors figure into the speaker/audience equation: age, ethnic background, educational level, knowledge of the subject, and interest in the subject.

Speaking about computers to senior citizens who have, at best, rudimentary knowledge about the way computers work must take that into account. Perhaps handing out a glossary would be useful for this audience. Speaking to first-graders about computers presents its own challenges. In contrast, the average high school student has more experience with computers than most adults, and that should be taken into account. In considering the age of the audience, it's best not to make assumptions. The gathering of senior citizens might include retired systems engineers or people who have made their livings using computers, so research about the audience is important. Speaking to a room full of computer systems engineers requires a rather thorough understanding of the jargon related to the field. It might not be wise to assume that high school students have a certain level of understanding, either.

With an audience that is primarily Hispanic with varying levels of competence in English, the speaker is obligated to adjust the presentation to fit that audience. The same would be true when the audience is composed of people who may have been in the country for a long time but who speak their first language at home. Speaking to an audience of college graduates will require different skills than speaking to an audience of people who have never attended college. However, it's unwise to talk down to any audience; your listeners will almost certainly be insulted.

Finally, consider why the audience has gathered. Have people come to hear you speak because of an interest in the topic or because they have been influenced or forced? If the audience comes with an interest in the subject, efforts to motivate or draw them into the discussion might not be needed. In contrast, if you know that audience members do not have a high level of interest in the topic, it would be wise to use devices to draw them into it and to motivate them to listen.

D. **Understands basic processes of first- and second-language acquisition and their impact on learning in the English language arts classroom**

Students who are raised in homes in which English is not the first language or in which standard English is not spoken may have difficulty with hearing the difference between similar-sounding words like *send* and *sent*. Any student who is not in an environment in which English phonology operates may have difficulty perceiving and demonstrating the differences among English language phonemes. If students cannot hear the difference between words that sound the same, like *grow* and *glow*, they will be confused when these words appear in a print context, and this confusion will impact their comprehension.

Considerations for teaching English Language Learners include recognizing that what works for English-speaking students from English-speaking families does not necessarily work for students whose first language is not English.

Research recommends that ELL students initially learn to read in their first language. It has been found that a priority for ELL instruction should be learning to speak English before being taught to read English. Research supports oral language development because it lays the foundation for phonological awareness.

E. **Understands how a first language or dialect differences may affect students' use of English and knows strategies for promoting all students' ability to use standard English**

Academic literacy, which encompasses ways of knowing particular content and refers to strategies for understanding, discussing, organizing, and producing texts, is key to success in school. To be literate in an academic sense, one should be able to understand and to articulate conceptual relationships within, between, and among disciplines. Academic literacy also encompasses critical literacy, that is, the ability to evaluate the credibility and validity of informational sources.

In a practical sense, when a student is academically literate, he or she should be able to read and understand interdisciplinary texts, to articulate comprehension through expository written pieces, and to further his or her knowledge through sustained and focused research.

Developing academic literacy is especially difficult for ELL students who are struggling to acquire and improve their language and critical thinking skills. The needs of these ELL students may be met through the creation of a functional language learning environment that engages them in meaningful and authentic language processing through planned, purposeful, and academically based activities. One strategy would be to pair ELL students with a partner or embed them within small groups of native English speakers and writers. The activities of reading and discussing the native English speakers' and writers' written works is invaluable in helping ELL students to understand the nuances and conventions of standard English.

Sustained content area study is more effectively carried out when an extensive body of instructional and informational resources, such as is found on the Internet, is available. Through its extensive collection of reading materials and numerous contexts for meaningful written communication and analysis of issues, the Internet creates a highly motivating learning environment that encourages ELL students to interact with language in new and varied ways. Used as a resource for focus discipline research, the Internet is highly effective in helping these students develop and refine the academic literacy necessary for a successful educational experience.

Academic research skills are often underdeveloped in the ELL student population, making research reports especially daunting and enormously challenging. The research skills students need to complete focus discipline projects are the same skills they need to succeed in classes. Instruction that targets the development of research skills teaches ELL students the rhetorical conventions of term papers, which subsequently leads to better writing and hence improved performance in class. Moreover, the research skills acquired through sustained content study and focus discipline research enable students to manage information more effectively, which serves them throughout their academic years and into the workforce.

F. **Promotes students' understanding of the situational nature of language use and the value of knowing and using standard English while fostering pride in their own language background and respect for the language backgrounds of other people.**

See Competencies 2.B, 3.F, 10.B, and 10.E.

COMPETENCY 003   **THE TEACHER UNDERSTANDS THE STRUCTURE AND DEVELOPMENT OF THE ENGLISH LANGUAGE AND PROVIDES STUDENTS WITH OPPORTUNITIES TO DEVELOP RELATED KNOWLEDGE AND SKILLS IN MEANINGFUL CONTEXTS**

A.   **Demonstrates knowledge of major historical, regional, and cultural influences on the ongoing development of the English language**

See Competency 2.A.

The most basic principle about changes and variations in language is simple: language inevitably changes over time. If a community that speaks a homogeneous language and dialect is for some reason split, and there is no contact between the two resulting communities, after a few generations the communities will be speaking different dialects and eventually will have difficulty understanding each other.

Language changes in all its manifestations. At the phonetic level, the sounds of a language change, as does its orthography. The vocabulary level often manifests the greatest changes. Changes in syntax are slower and less likely to occur. For example, English has changed in response to the influences of many other languages and cultures and as a result of internal cultural changes such as the development of the railroad and the computer. However, its syntax still relies on word order—it has not shifted to an inflected system even though many of the cultures that have influenced it do have an inflected language, such as Spanish.

The most significant changes in a language are a result of the blending of cultures. The Norman Conquest that brought the English speakers in the British Isles under the rule of French speakers impacted the language, but it's significant that English speakers did not adopt the language of the ruling class—they did not become speakers of French. Even so, many vocabulary items entered the English language during that period.

The Great Vowel Shift that occurred between the fourteenth and sixteenth centuries is somewhat of a mystery, although it's generally attributed to the migration to southeast England following the Black Death. The Great Vowel Shift largely accounts for the discrepancy between orthography and speech—the difficult spelling system in Modern English.

Colonization of other countries has also brought new vocabulary items into the English language. Indian English has its own easily recognizable attributes, as do Australian and North American English. The fact that English is the most widely spoken and understood language around the world in the twenty-first century implies that it is constantly changing as it is adopted by diverse cultures.

Other influences also impact language. The introduction of television, particularly television programs from the United States, has greatly influence the English that is spoken and understood all over the world. The same is true of the spread of computer technology (Tom Friedman called it "flattening" in his book *The World Is Flat: A Brief History of the Twenty-First Century*). New terms have been added, old terms have changed meaning (*mouse*, for instance), and nouns have been turned into verbs.

B. **Understands and teaches how to research word origins and analyze word formation as an aid to understanding meanings, derivations, and spellings**

In the past, the Oxford English Dictionary was the most reliable source for etymologies. *Merriam-Webster's Collegiate Dictionary, Eleventh Edition,* is also useful in tracing the sources of words in American English.

Now, there are many up-to-date sources for keeping up with and keeping track of changes in the English language that have occurred recently and are occurring constantly. Google *etymology*, for instance, or any other word about which you're uncertain, and you will find a multitude of sources. Don't trust any single source; validate the information by checking at least three sources. Wikipedia is useful, but it can be changed by anyone who chooses, so verify any information you find on Wikipedia by checking other sources. If you go to http://www.etymonline.com/sources.php, you will find a long list of resources on etymology.

Spelling in English is complicated by the fact that it is not phonetic—that is, it is not based on the one sound/one letter formula used by many other languages. The English alphabet is based on the Latin one, which originally had 20 letters, consisting of the present English alphabet minus J, K, V, W, Y, and Z. The Romans added K to be used in abbreviations and Y and Z in words that came from the Greek. This 23-letter alphabet was adopted by the English, who developed W as a ligatured doubling of U and later J and V as consonantal variants of I and U. The result was the present-day English alphabet of 26 letters with uppercase (capital) and lowercase forms.

Spelling is based primarily on fifteenth-century English. However, pronunciation has changed drastically since then, especially long vowels and diphthongs. This Great Vowel Shift affected the seven long vowels. For a long time, spelling was erratic—there were no standards. As long as the meaning was clear, spelling was not considered very important. Samuel Johnson tackled this problem, and his *Dictionary of the English Language* (1755) brought standards to spelling, which was particularly important when the printing press was invented. There have been changes through the years, but spelling is still not strictly phonetic. There have been many attempts to nudge spelling into a more phonetic representation of the sounds, but for the most part, they have failed.

A good example is *The American Spelling Book* by Noah Webster (1783), which was a precursor to the first edition of his *American Dictionary of the English Language* (1828). Although there are rules for spelling and it's important that students learn the rules, there are many exceptions; memorizing exceptions and giving plenty of opportunities for practicing them seems the only solution for the teacher of English.

ENGLISH LANG. ARTS & READING

C. **Understands and teaches relationships among words and issues related to word choice**

Students frequently encounter problems with homonyms—words that are spelled and pronounced the same but that have different meanings, such as *mean*, a verb, "to intend"; *mean*, an adjective, "unkind"; and *mean*, a noun or adjective, "average." These words are actually both homographs and homophones (they are both written and pronounced the same way).

A similar phenomenon that causes trouble is heteronyms (also sometimes called heterophones), words that are spelled the same but have different pronunciations and meanings (in other words, they are homographs that differ in pronunciation or, technically, homographs that are not homophones). For example, the homographs *desert* (abandon) and *desert* (arid region) are heteronyms (pronounced differently); but *mean* (intend) and *mean* (average) are not (they are pronounced the same, so they are homonyms).

Another similar occurrence in English is the capitonym, a word that is spelled the same but has different meanings and may or may not have different pronunciations when it is capitalized. An example is *polish* (to make shiny) and *Polish* (from Poland).

Some of the most troubling homonyms are those that are spelled differently but sound the same. Examples: *its* (third-person singular neuter pronoun) and *it's* ("it is"); *there*, *their* (third-person plural pronoun), and *they're* ("they are"); and *to*, *too*, and *two*.

Some homonyms/homographs are particularly complicated. *Fluke*, for instance is a fish, a flatworm, the end parts of an anchor, the fins on a whale's tail, and a stroke of luck.

Common Homonyms/Homographs

The following homonyms/homographs are often troubling to student writers:

accept: tolerate; *except*: everything but

add: put together with; *ad*: short for *advertisement*

allowed: permitted; *aloud*: audibly

allot: to distribute, allocate; *a lot* (often *alot*): much, many (a lot of)

allusion: indirect reference; *illusion*: a distortion of sensory perception

bare: naked, exposed, or very little (bare necessities); *bear*: as a noun, a large mammal, and as a verb, to carry *boy*: a male adolescent or child; *buoy*: (noun) a floating marker in the sea

bridal: pertaining to a bride (bridal gown, bridal suite); *bridle*: (noun) part of a horse's tack

capital: punishable by death; in initial uppercase: principal town or city, wealth and money; *Capitol*: the home of the Congress of the United States and some other legislatures

chord: group of musical notes; *cord*: rope, long electrical line

compliment: a praising or flattering remark; *complement*: something that completes

discreet: tactful or diplomatic; *discrete*: separate or distinct

dyeing: artificially coloring; *dying*: passing away

effect: outcome; *affect*: to have an effect on

gorilla: the largest of the great apes; *guerrilla*: a small combat group

hair: an outgrowth of the epidermis in mammals; *hare*: a rabbit

hoard: to accumulate and store up; *horde*: a large group of warriors, mob

lam: U.S. slang, *on the lam* means "on the run"; *lamb*: a young sheep

lead: pronounced to rhyme with *seed*, to guide or serve as the head of; *lead*: pronounced to rhyme with *head*, a heavy metal; *led*: the past tense of *lead*

medal: an award to be strung around the neck; *meddle*: to stick one's nose into others' affairs; *metal*: a shiny, malleable element or alloy like silver or gold; *mettle*: toughness, guts

morning: the time between midnight and midday; *mourning*: a period of grieving after a death

past: time before now (past, present, and future); *passed*: past tense of *to pass*

piece: a portion; *peace*: opposite of war

peak: tip, height, to reach its highest point; *peek*: to take a brief look; *pique*: a fit of anger; to incite (pique one's interest)

Strategies to help students conquer these tricky spellings include the following:

- Practice using them in sentences, because context is useful in understanding the differences.
- Drill students on words and spellings with which they have particular difficulty; this is necessary to overcome the misuses.

Denotative and Connotative Meanings

To effectively teach language, it is necessary to understand that, as human beings acquire language, they realize that words have denotative and connotative meanings. Generally, denotative meanings point to things, and connotative meanings deal with mental suggestions that the words convey. The word *skunk* has a denotative meaning when the speaker points to the actual animal as he or she speaks the word and intends the word to identify the animal. *Skunk* can have connotative meanings, too, depending upon the tone of delivery, the audience's attitudes about the animal, and the speaker's personal feelings about the animal.

Informative connotations

Informative connotations are definitions agreed upon by the society in which the learner operates. A *skunk* is "a black and white mammal of the weasel family with a pair of perineal glands which secrete a pungent odor." The *Merriam-Webster Collegiate Dictionary* adds ". . . and offensive" odor. The color, species, and glandular characteristics are informative. The interpretation of the odor as *offensive* is affective.

Affective connotations

Affective connotations are the personal feelings a word arouses. A child who has no personal experience with a skunk and its odor will feel differently about the word *skunk* than a child who has smelled the spray or been conditioned vicariously to associate offensiveness with the animal denoted *skunk*. The fact that our society views a skunk as an animal to be avoided will affect the child's interpretation of the word. In fact, it is not necessary for one to have actually seen a skunk (that is, have a denotative understanding) to use the word in either connotative expression. For example, one child might call another child a skunk, connoting an unpleasant reaction (affective use) or, seeing another small black and white animal, call it a skunk based on the definition (informative use).

Using connotations

In everyday language, we attach affective meanings to words unconsciously; we exercise more conscious control of informative connotations. In the process of language development, the leaner not only must come to grasp the definitions of words but also must become more conscious of the affective connotations and how his or her listeners process these connotations. Gaining this conscious control over language makes it possible to use language appropriately in various situations and to evaluate its uses in literature and other forms of communication.

The manipulation of language for a variety of purposes is the goal of language instruction. Advertisers and satirists are especially conscious of the effect word choice has on their audiences. By evoking the proper responses from readers/listeners, we can prompt them to take action.

The medium through which the message is delivered to the receiver is a significant factor in controlling language. Spoken language relies as much on the gestures, facial expression, and tone of voice of the speaker as on the words he or she speaks. Slapstick comics can evoke laughter without speaking a word. Young children use body language overtly and older children use it more subtly to convey messages. This refining of body language is paralleled by an ability to recognize and apply the nuances of spoken language.

D. **Knows and teaches rules of grammar, usage, sentence structure, punctuation, and capitalization in standard English and is able to identify and edit nonstandard usage in his or her own discourse and the discourse of others**

Sentence Completeness

Avoid fragments and run-on sentences. Recognition of sentence elements necessary to make a complete thought, proper use of independent and dependent clauses, and proper punctuation will correct such errors.

Sentence Structure

Recognize simple, compound, complex, and compound-complex sentences. Use dependent (subordinate) and independent clauses correctly to create these sentence structures.

Simple	Joyce wrote a letter.
Compound	Joyce wrote a letter and Dot drew a picture.
Complex	While Joyce wrote a letter, Dot drew a picture.
Compound/complex	When Mother asked the girls to demonstrate their newfound skills, Joyce wrote a letter and Dot drew a picture.

Note: Do *not* confuse compound sentence elements with compound sentences.

Simple sentence with compound subject:
Joyce and Dot wrote letters.
The girl in row three and the boy next to her were passing notes across the aisle.

Simple sentence with compound predicate:
Joyce wrote letters and drew pictures.
The captain of the high school debate team graduated with honors and studied broadcast journalism in college.

Simple sentence with compound object of preposition:
Coleen graded the students' essays for style and mechanical accuracy.

Parallelism

Recognize parallel structures using phrases (prepositional, gerund, participial, and infinitive) and omissions from sentences that create the lack of parallelism.

Prepositional phrase/single modifier:
Incorrect: Coleen ate the ice cream with enthusiasm and hurriedly.
Correct: Coleen ate the ice cream with enthusiasm and in a hurry.
Correct: Coleen ate the ice cream enthusiastically and hurriedly.

Participial phrase/infinitive phrase:
Incorrect: After hiking for hours and to sweat profusely, Joe sat down to rest and drinking water.
Correct: After hiking for hours and sweating profusely, Joe sat down to rest and drink water.

Recognition of Dangling Modifiers

Dangling phrases are attached to sentence parts in such a way that they create ambiguity and incorrectness of meaning.

Participial phrase:
Incorrect: Hanging from her skirt, Dot tugged at a loose thread.
Correct: Dot tugged at a loose thread hanging from her skirt.

Incorrect: Relaxing in the bathtub, the telephone rang.
Correct: While I was relaxing in the bathtub, the telephone rang.

Infinitive phrase:
Incorrect: To improve his behavior, the dean warned Fred.
Correct: The dean warned Fred to improve his behavior.

Prepositional phrase:
Incorrect: On the floor, Father saw the dog eating table scraps.
Correct: Father saw the dog eating table scraps on the floor.

Recognition of Syntactical Redundancy or Omission

These errors occur when superfluous words have been added to a sentence or key words have been omitted from a sentence.

Redundancy

Incorrect:	Joyce made sure that when her plane arrived that she retrieved all of her luggage.
Correct:	Joyce made sure that when her plane arrived she retrieved all of her luggage.
Incorrect:	He was a mere skeleton of his former self.
Correct:	He was a skeleton of his former self.

Omission

Incorrect:	Dot opened her book, recited her textbook, and answered the teacher's subsequent question.
Correct:	Dot opened her book, recited from the textbook, and answered the teacher's subsequent question.

Avoidance of Double Negatives

This error occurs from positioning two negatives that cancel each other out (create a positive statement).

Incorrect:	Dot didn't have no double negatives in her paper.
Correct:	Dot didn't have any double negatives in her paper.

Types of Clauses

Clauses are connected word groups that are composed of *at least* one subject and one verb. (A subject is the doer of an action or the element that is being joined. A verb conveys either the action or the link.)

<u>Students</u> <u>are waiting</u> for the start of the assembly.
 subject   verb

At the end of the play, <u>students</u> <u>waited</u> for the curtain to come down.
                         subject verb

Clauses can be independent or dependent.

Independent clauses can stand alone or can be joined to other clauses, either independent or dependent. Words that can be used to join clauses include the following:

- for
- and
- nor
- but
- or
- yet
- so

Dependent clauses, by definition, contain at least one subject and one verb. However, they cannot stand alone as a complete sentence. They are structurally dependent on an independent clause (the main clause of the sentence).

There are two types of dependent clauses: (1) those with a subordinating conjunction and (2) those with a relative pronoun

Coordinating conjunctions include the following:

- although
- when
- if
- unless
- because

Example: Unless a cure is discovered, many more people will die of the disease. (dependent clause with coordinating conjunction [unless] + independent clause)

Relative pronouns include the following:

- who
- whom
- which
- that

Example: The White House has an official website, <u>which</u> contains press releases, news updates, and biographies of the president and vice president.
(independent clause + relative pronoun [which] + relative dependent clause)

Misplaced and Dangling Modifiers

Particular phrases that are not placed near the word they modify often result in misplaced modifiers. Particular phrases that do not relate to the subject being modified result in dangling modifiers.

Error: Weighing the options carefully, a decision was made regarding the punishment of the convicted murderer.
Problem: Who is weighing the options? No one capable of weighing is named in the sentence; thus, the participle phrase *weighing the options carefully* dangles. This problem can be corrected by adding a subject of the sentence who is capable of doing the action.
Correction: Weighing the options carefully, the judge made a decision regarding the punishment of the convicted murderer.

Error: Returning to my favorite watering hole brought back many fond memories.
Problem: The person who returned is never indicated, and the participle phrase dangles. This problem can be corrected by creating a dependent clause from the modifying phrase.
Correction: When I returned to my favorite watering hole, many fond memories came back to me.

Error: One damaged house stood only to remind townspeople of the hurricane.
Problem: The placement of the modifier *only* suggests that the sole reason the house remained was to serve as a reminder. The faulty modifier creates ambiguity.
Correction: Only one damaged house stood, reminding townspeople of the hurricane.

Spelling

This section will concentrate on spelling plurals.

Because spelling rules based on phonics, rules of letter doubling, and exceptions to rules are so complex, even adults who have a good command of written English benefit from using a dictionary. Because spelling mastery is also difficult for adolescents, they will also benefit from learning how to use a dictionary and thesaurus.

Most plurals of nouns that end in hard consonants or hard consonant sounds followed by a silent *e* are made by adding *s*. Some nouns ending in vowels only add *s*.

    fingers, numerals, banks, bugs, riots, homes, gates, radios, bananas

Nouns that end in the soft consonant sounds *s, j, x, z, ch,* and *sh* add *es*. Some nouns ending in *o* add *es*.

> dresses, waxes, churches, brushes, tomatoes, potatoes

Nouns ending in *y* preceded by a vowel just add *s*.

> boys, alleys

Nouns ending in *y* preceded by a consonant change the *y* to *i* and add *es*.

> babies, corollaries, frugalities, poppies

Some noun plurals are formed irregularly or are the same as the singular.

> sheep, deer, children, leaves, oxen

Some nouns derived from foreign words, especially Latin, may make their plurals in two different ways, one of them anglicized. Sometimes, the meanings are the same; other times, the two plurals are used in slightly different contexts. It is always wise to consult the dictionary.

> appendices, appendixes
> criterion, criteria
> indexes, indices
> crisis, crises

Make the plurals of closed (solid) compound words in the usual way except for words ending in *ful*, which make their plurals on the root word.

> timelines, hairpins, cupsful

Make the plurals of open or hyphenated compounds by adding the change in inflection to the word that changes in number.

> fathers-in-law, courts-martial, masters of art, doctors of medicine

Make the plurals of letters, numbers, and abbreviations by adding *s*.

> fives and tens, IBMs, 1990s, *p*s and *q*s (Note that letters are italicized.)

Capitalization

Capitalize all proper names of persons (including specific organizations or agencies of government); places (countries, states, cities, parks, and specific geographical areas); things (political parties, structures, historical and cultural terms, and calendar and time designations); and religious terms (any deity, revered person or group, or sacred writing).

> Percy Bysshe Shelley, Argentina, Mount Rainier National Park, Grand Canyon, League of Nations, the Sears Tower, Birmingham, Lyric Theater, Americans, Midwesterners, Democrats, Renaissance, Boy Scouts of America, Easter, God, Bible, Dead Sea Scrolls, Koran

Capitalize proper adjectives and titles used with proper names.

> California Gold Rush, President John Adams, Senator John Glenn

Note: Some words that represent titles and offices are not capitalized unless used with a proper name.

Capitalized	Not Capitalized
Congressman McKay	the congressman from Florida
Commander Alger	commander of the Pacific Fleet
Queen Elizabeth	the queen of England
President George Washington	the president

Capitalize all main words in titles of works of literature, art, and music.

Punctuation

Using terminal punctuation in relation to quotation marks

In a quoted statement that is either declarative or imperative, place the period inside the closing quotation marks.

> "The airplane crashed on the runway during takeoff."

If the quotation is followed by other words in the sentence, place a comma inside the closing quotations marks and a period at the end of the sentence.

> "The airplane crashed on the runway during takeoff," said the announcer.

In most instances in which a quoted title or expression occurs at the end of a sentence, the period is placed before either the single or double quotation marks.

"The middle school readers were unprepared to understand Bryant's poem 'Thanatopsis.'"

Early book-length adventure stories like *Don Quixote* and *The Three Musketeers* were known as "picaresque novels."

There is an instance in which the final quotation mark would precede the period: if the content of the sentence were about a speech or quote so that the understanding of the meaning would be confused by the placement of the period.

The first thing out of his mouth was "Hi, I'm home."
but
The first line of his speech began "I arrived home to an empty house".

In sentences that are interrogatory or exclamatory, the question mark or exclamation point should be positioned outside the closing quotation marks if the quote itself is a statement, a command, or a cited title.

Who decided to lead us in the recitation of the "Pledge of Allegiance"?

Why was Tillie shaking as she began her recitation, "Once upon a midnight dreary . . ."?

I was embarrassed when Mrs. White said, "Your slip is showing"!

In sentences that are declarative but in which the quotation is a question or an exclamation, place the question mark or exclamation point inside the quotation marks.

The hall monitor yelled, "Fire! Fire!"

The hall monitor asked, "Where's the fire?"

Cory shrieked, "Is there a mouse in the room?" (In this instance, the question supersedes the exclamation.)

Using periods with parentheses or brackets

Place the period inside the parentheses or brackets if they enclose a complete sentence independent of the other sentences around it.

Stephen Crane was a confirmed alcohol and drug addict. (He admitted as much to other journalists in Cuba.)

ENGLISH LANG. ARTS & READING

If the parenthetical expression is a statement inserted within another statement, the period in the enclosure is omitted.

>Mark Twain used the character Indian Joe (he also appeared in *The Adventures of Tom Sawyer*) as a foil for Jim in *The Adventures of Huckleberry Finn*.

When enclosed matter comes at the end of a sentence requiring quotation marks, place the period outside the parentheses or brackets.

>"The secretary of state consulted with the ambassador [Albright]."

Using commas

Separate two or more coordinate adjectives modifying the same word and three or more nouns, phrases, or clauses in a list.

>Maggie's hair was dull, dirty, and lice-ridden.

>Dickens portrayed the Artful Dodger as skillful pickpocket, loyal follower of Fagin, and defender of Oliver Twist.

>Ellen daydreamed about getting out of the rain, taking a shower, and eating a hot dinner.

>In Elizabethan England, Ben Johnson wrote comedy, Christopher Marlowe wrote tragedies, and William Shakespeare composed both.

Use commas to separate antithetical or complimentary expressions from the rest of the sentence.

>The veterinarian, not his assistant, would perform the delicate surgery.

>The more he knew about her, the less he wished he had known.

>Randy hopes to, and probably will, get an appointment to the United States Naval Academy.

>His thorough, though esoteric, scientific research could not be easily understood by high school students.

Using double quotation marks with other punctuation

Quotations—whether words, phrases, or clauses—should be punctuated according to the rules of the grammatical function they serve in the sentence.

The works of Shakespeare, "the bard of Avon," have been contested as originating with other authors.

"You'll get my money," the old man warned, "when hell freezes over."

Sheila cited the passage that began "Four score and seven years ago . . . ." (Note the ellipsis followed by an enclosed period.)

"Old Ironsides" inspired the preservation of the U.S.S. *Constitution*.

Use quotation marks to enclose the titles of shorter works: songs, short poems, short stories, essays, and chapters of books. (For title of longer works, see "Using italics," below.)

"The Tell-Tale Heart"   "Casey at the Bat"   "America the Beautiful"

Using semicolons

Use semicolons to separate independent clauses when the second clause is introduced by a transitional adverb. (These clauses may also be written as separate sentences, preferably by placing the adverb within the second sentence.)

The Elizabethans modified the rhyme scheme of the sonnet; thus, it was called the English sonnet.
or
The Elizabethans modified the rhyme scheme of the sonnet. It thus was called the English sonnet.

Use semicolons to separate items in a series that are long and complex or have internal punctuation.

The Italian Renaissance produced masters in the fine arts: Dante Alighieri, author of the *Divine Comedy*; Leonardo da Vinci, painter of *The Last Supper*; and Donatello, sculptor of the *Quattro Santi Coronati*, the Four Crowned Saints.

The leading scorers in the WNBA were Haizhou Zheng, averaging 23.9 points per game; Lisa Leslie, 22; and Cynthia Cooper, 19.5.

Using colons

Place a colon at the beginning of a list of items. (Note its use in the sentence about Renaissance Italians under "Using semicolons," above.)

The teacher directed us to compare Faulkner's three symbolic novels: *Absalom, Absalom!*; *As I Lay Dying*; and *Light in August*.

Do *not* use a comma if the list is preceded by a verb.

> Three of Faulkner's symbolic novels are *Absalom, Absalom!*; *As I Lay Dying*, and *Light in August*.

Using dashes

Place en dashes to denote sudden breaks in thought.

> Some periods in literature - the Romantic Age, for example - spanned different time periods in different countries.

Use em dashes instead of commas if commas are used elsewhere in the sentence for amplification or explanation.

> The Fireside Poets included three Brahmans—James Russell Lowell, Henry Wadsworth Longfellow, Oliver Wendell Holmes—and John Greenleaf Whittier.

Using italics

Use italics to style the titles of long works of literature, names of periodical publications, musical scores, works of art, movies, and television and radio programs. (When unable to write in italics, students should be instructed to underline in their own writing where italics would be appropriate.)

> *Idylls of the King* *Hiawatha* *The Sound and the Fury*
> *Mary Poppins* *Newsweek* *Nutcracker Suite*

E.   Knows how to provide explicit and contextual instruction that enhances students' knowledge of and ability to use standard English

See Competencies 3.D and 8.C.

F.   Knows and teaches how purpose, audience, and register affect discourse

Slang comes about for many reasons: amelioration is an important one that often results in euphemisms. Examples are *passed away* for dying and *senior citizens* for old people. Some euphemisms have become so embedded in the language that their sources are long forgotten. For example, *fame* originally meant "rumor." Some words that were originally intended as euphemisms, such as *mentally retarded*, have themselves become pejorative.

Slang is lower in prestige than standard English; tends to first appear in the language of groups with low status; is often taboo and unlikely to be used by people of high status; and tends to displace conventional terms, either as shorthand or as a defense against perceptions associated with the conventional term.

Register or Informal and formal language is a distinction made on the basis of the occasion and the audience. The formality or informality of the language used is considered the register of a piece. At a formal occasion, such as a meeting of executives or of government officials, even conversational exchanges are likely to be formal. Other occasions for formal English would be speeches delivered to executives, college professors, government officials, and so on. In written English, a formal register would be used for scholarly works, research papers, literary criticisms, professional conference presentations, and other serious works. When the register is formal, longer sentences, more complex and exact syntax are used, as is more complex vocabulary. Slang is eschewed, as are common expressions or colloquialisms and contractions. Informal works or occasions call for more informal use of language; for example, a cocktail party or golf game is a situation where language is likely to be informal. Speeches made to fellow employees, for example, are likely to be informal. In informal discourse, vocabulary is more casual; slang, colloquialisms, and contractions are used freely. Syntax is more relaxed; sentences are shorter in informal discourse. Informal written communications would include newspaper and magazine articles, popular books, and everyday conversations.

Jargon is a specialized vocabulary. It may be the vocabulary peculiar to a particular industry such as computers or of a field such as religion. It may also be the vocabulary of a social group. The jargon of bloggers comprises a whole vocabulary that has even developed its own dictionaries. The speaker must be knowledgeable about and sensitive to the jargon peculiar to the particular audience. That may require some research and some vocabulary development on the speaker's part.

Technical language is a form of jargon. It is usually specific to an industry, profession, or field of study. Sensitivity to the language familiar to the particular audience is important.

Regionalisms are those usages that are peculiar to a particular part of the country. A good example is the second-person plural pronoun *you*. Because the plural is the same as the singular, speakers in various parts of the country have developed their own solutions to be sure that they are understood when they are speaking to more than one "you." In the South, "you-all" or "y'all" is common. In the Northeast, one often hears "youse." In some areas of the Midwest, "you'ns" can be heard.

See also Competency 2.A.

In the past, teachers have assigned reports, paragraphs, and essays that focused on the teacher as the audience with the purpose of explaining information.

However, for students to be meaningfully engaged in their writing, they must write for a variety of reasons. Writing for different audiences and aims allows students to be more involved in their writing. If they write for only one audience and purpose, they will see writing as just another assignment. Listed below are suggestions that give students an opportunity to write in more creative and critical ways.

- Write stories that would be read aloud to a group (such as the class, another group of students, or a group of elementary school students) or published in a literary magazine or class anthology.

- Write letters to the editor, to a college, to a friend, or to another student, and then send the letters to the intended recipient.

- Write plays that are then performed.

- Have students discuss the parallels between different speech styles and writing styles for different readers or audiences.

- Allow students to write a few versions a particular piece for different audiences.

- Make sure students consider the following when analyzing the needs of their audience:

    o Why is the audience reading my writing? Do they expect to be informed, amused, or persuaded?
    o What does my audience already know about my topic?
    o What does the audience want or need to know? What will interest them?
    o What type of language suits my audience?

- As part of prewriting, have students identify the audience.

- Expose students to writing that is on the same topic but is written for a different audience, and then have them identify the variations in sentence structure and style.

- Remind your students that it is not necessary to identify all the specifics of the audience in the initial stage of the writing process but that at some point they must make some determinations about audience.

G. **Demonstrates an understanding of informal and formal procedures for monitoring and assessing students' ability to use the English language effectively**

Language Skills to Evaluate

- The ability to talk at length with few pauses and fill time with speech
- The ability to call up appropriate things to say in a wide range of contexts
- The size and range of a student's vocabulary and the student's syntax skills
- The coherence of the student's sentences and the ability to speak in reasoned and semantically dense sentences

- Knowledge of the various forms of interaction and conversation for various situations
- Knowledge of the standard rules of conversation
- The student's ability to be creative and imaginative with language and express him- or herself in original ways
- The ability to invent and entertain and take risks in linguistic expression

Methods of Evaluation

- Commercially designed language assessment products
- Instructor observation using a rating scale from 1 to 5 (where 1 = limited proficiency and 5 = native speaker equivalency)
- Informal observation of students' behaviors

Uses of Language Assessment

- Diagnosis of language strengths and weaknesses
- Detection of patterns of systematic errors
- Appropriate bilingual/ELL program placement if necessary

Common Language Errors

- Application of rules that apply in a student's first language but not in the second
- Using pronunciation that applies to a student's first language but not to the second
- Applying a general rule to all cases even when there are exceptions
- Trying to cut corners by using an incorrect word or syntactic form
- Avoiding use of precise vocabulary or idiomatic expressions
- Using incorrect verb tense

H. **Uses assessment results to plan and adapt instruction that addresses students' strengths, needs, and interests and that builds on students' current skills to increase proficiency in using the English language effectively**

See Competencies 1.D and 2.B.

TEACHER CERTIFICATION STUDY GUIDE

DOMAIN II. LITERATURE, READING PROCESSES, AND SKILLS FOR READING LITERARY AND NONLITERARY TEXTS

COMPETENCY 004 THE TEACHER UNDERSTANDS READING PROCESSES AND TEACHES STUDENTS TO APPLY THESE PROCESSES

A. **Understands and promotes reading as an active process of constructing meaning**

Children become curious about printed symbols once they recognize that print, like speech, conveys meaningful messages that direct, inform, or entertain people. By school age, many children are eager to continue their exploration of print.

One goal is to develop fluent and proficient readers who are knowledgeable about the reading process. Effective reading instruction should enable students to eventually become self-directed readers who can

- construct meaning from various types of print material
- recognize that there are different kinds of reading materials and different purposes for reading
- select strategies appropriate for different reading activities
- develop a lifelong interest and enjoyment in reading a variety of material for different purposes

To achieve these goals, teachers should make use of the wide variety of fiction and nonfiction resources available, including

- environmental signs and labels
- rhymes, chants, songs
- poetry
- wordless picture books
- predictable books
- cumulative stories
- maps and charts
- novels
- print resources from all subject areas
- notes, messages, letters
- folktales
- myths and legends
- writing by students and teachers
- newspapers, magazines, pamphlets
- mysteries

These resources should stimulate students' imaginations and kindle their curiosity. Familiarization with narrative and expository materials and frequent opportunities to write in all subject areas facilitate the reading process. By becoming authors themselves, students increase their awareness of the organization and structures of printed language.

To read for meaning, students must simultaneously utilize clues from all cueing systems. Readers bring knowledge and past experiences to the reading task to construct interpretations and to determine if the print makes sense to them. It is easier for readers to understand print when the content is relevant to their personal experiences. Familiar content and topics convey meaning or clues through the semantic cueing system. When students are comfortable and familiar with the content of a passage, they can predict upcoming text and take greater risks in reading. Research has repeatedly shown that fluent readers risk more guesses when interacting with unfamiliar print than poorer readers do. They derive more meaning from passages than readers who frequently stop to sound or decode words by individual phonemes or letters.

Knowledge of word order and the rules of grammar that structure oral language guide readers' predictions for printed language. Such language-pattern clues comprise the syntactic cueing system. Readers should constantly question the text to ensure that what they are reading makes sense and sounds like language.

Reading experiences that focus on relevant and familiar content, vocabulary, and language patterns increase students' chances of constructing meaning and being successful readers. At the middle school level, successful reading experiences reaffirm students' confidence as language users and learners.

The holistic approach to the reading process stresses the importance of presenting students with whole and meaningful reading passages. This approach is based on the principle that the readers' understanding of an entire sentence, passage, or story facilitates the reading and comprehension of individual words within those passages.

B. **Understands reader response and promotes students' responses to various types of text**

Reading literature involves a reciprocal interaction between the reader and the text.

Types of Responses

Emotional

The reader can identify with the characters and situations to project him- or herself into the story. The reader feels a sense of satisfaction by associating aspects of his or her own life with the people, places, and events in the literature. Emotional responses are observed in a reader's verbal and nonverbal reactions—laughter, comments, and retelling or dramatizing the action.

Interpretive

Interpretive responses include inferences about character development, setting, or plot; analysis of style elements, such as metaphor, simile, allusion, rhythm, and tone; outcomes derivable from information provided in the narrative; and assessment of the author's intent. Interpretive responses can be made verbally or in writing.

Critical

Critical responses involve making value judgments about the quality of a piece of literature. Reactions to the effectiveness of the writer's style and language use are observed through discussion and written reactions.

Evaluative

Some reading response theory researchers add an evaluative response, which is the reader's considerations of such factors as how well the piece of literature represents its genre, how well it reflects the social/ethical mores of society, and how well the author has approached the subject.

Middle school readers will exhibit both emotional and interpretive responses. Naturally, making interpretive responses depends on the degree of knowledge the student has of literary elements. Being able to say why a particular book was boring or why a particular poem made him or her sad is evidence of the student's critical reactions on a fundamental level.

Adolescents in ninth and tenth grades should begin to make critical responses by addressing the specific language and genre characteristics of literature. Evaluative responses are harder to detect and typically are made by only a few advanced high school students. However, if the teacher knows what to listen for, he or she can recognize evaluative responses and incorporate them into discussions.

For example, if a student says, "I don't understand why that character is doing that," he or she is making an interpretive response to character motivation. However, if the student goes on to say, "What good is that action?" he or she is giving an evaluative response that should be explored by posing a question such as, "What good should it do and why isn't that positive action happening?"

On an emotional level, the student says, "I almost broke into a sweat when he was describing the heat in the burning house." An interpretive response says, "The author used descriptive adjectives to bring the setting to life." Critically, the student adds, "The author's use of descriptive language contributes to the success of the narrative and maintains reader interest through the whole story." If the student goes on to wonder why the author allowed the grandmother in the story to die in the fire, he or she is making an evaluative response.

ENGLISH LANG. ARTS & READING

Levels of Response

The levels of reader response will depend largely on the reader's level of social, psychological, and intellectual development. Most middle school students have progressed beyond merely involving themselves in the story enough to be able to retell the events in some logical sequence or describe the feeling that the story evoked. They are aware to some degree that the feeling evoked was the result of a careful manipulation of good elements of fiction writing. They may not explain that awareness as successfully as a high school student, but they are beginning to grasp the concepts and not just the personal reactions. They are beginning to differentiate between responding to the story itself and responding to a literary creation.

Fostering self-esteem and empathy

A particularly important use of literature is as bibliotherapy, which allows the reader to identify with others and become aware of alternatives without feeling directly betrayed or threatened. For the high school student, the ability to empathize is an evaluative response, a much-desired outcome of literature studies.

Cautions

The teacher should always be cautious when reading materials of a sensitive or controversial nature. He or she must be cognizant of what is happening in the school and the community. A child who has experienced a recent death in his family or circle of friends may need to distance himself from classroom discussion. Whenever open discussion of a topic brings pain or embarrassment, the child should be excused from the conversation. The teacher must be able to gauge the level of emotional development of his or her students when selecting subject matter and the strategies for studying it.

Some students or their parents may consider some material objectionable. Should a student choose not to read assigned material, it is the teacher's responsibility to allow the student to select an alternate title. It is always advisable to notify parents if a particularly sensitive piece is to be studied.

C. **Knows how text characteristics and purposes for reading determine the selection of reading strategies and teaches students to apply skills and strategies for reading various types of texts for a variety of purposes**

The first question to be asked when approaching a reading task is: What is my objective? What do I want to achieve from this reading? How will I use the information I gain from this reading? Do I only need to grasp the gist of the piece? Do I need to know the line of reasoning—not only the thesis but also the subpoints? Will I be reporting important and significant details orally or in a written document?

A written document can be expected to have a thesis—either expressed or derived. To discover the thesis, the reader needs to ask what point the writer intended to make. The writing can also be expected to be organized in some logical way and to have subpoints that support or establish that the thesis is valid. It is also reasonable to expect that there will be details or examples that will support the subpoints. Knowing this, the reader can make a decision about reading techniques required to achieve the objective that has already been established.

If the reader only needs to know the gist of a written document, speed-reading skimming techniques may be sufficient: using the forefinger, moving the eyes down the page, picking up the important statements in each paragraph, and deducing the basic content and message of the document. If the reader needs a better grasp of how the writer achieved his or her purpose in the document, a quick and cursory glance—a skimming—of each paragraph will yield the subpoints, the topic sentences of the paragraphs, and how the thesis is developed, resulting in a greater understanding of the author's purpose and method of development.

In-depth reading requires the reader to scrutinize each phrase and sentence, looking first for the thesis and then for the topic sentences in the paragraphs that develop the thesis, and, at the same time, looking for connections such as transitional devices that provide clues to the direction the reasoning is taking.

Sometimes it is necessary to reread a document to create an oral or written report on it. If the purpose of reading the document is to create a report, the first reading should provide a map for the rereading. The second reading should follow this map, and the reader should focus carefully on the points that he or she will use in the report or analysis. Some new understandings may occur in this rereading, and it may become apparent that the map that was derived from the first reading will need to be adjusted. During the rereading, highlighting or note-taking can help identify the material to be used in the report.

D. **Knows how to use and teaches students to use word analysis skills, word structure, word order, and context for word identification and to confirm word meaning**

Identification of Common Morphemes, Prefixes, and Suffixes

This aspect of vocabulary development helps students look for structural elements within words that they can use independently to help them determine meaning.

The terms listed below are generally recognized as the key structural analysis components.

Root words: A root word is a word from which another word is developed. The second word can be said to have its "root" in the first. This structural component lends itself to an illustration of a tree and its roots, which can concretize the meaning for students.

Base words: A base word is a stand-alone linguistic unit that cannot be deconstructed or broken down into smaller words. For example, in the word *retell*, the base word is *tell*.

Contractions: Contractions are shortened forms of two words from which a letter or letters have been deleted. These deleted letters have been replaced by an apostrophe.

Prefixes: Prefixes are beginning units of meaning that can be added (affixed) to the beginning of a base word or root word. They cannot stand alone. They are also known as *bound morphemes*, meaning that they cannot stand alone as words.

Suffixes: Suffixes are ending units of meaning that can be affixed to the end of a base word or root word. Suffixes transform the original meanings of base and root words. Like prefixes, they are also known as *bound morphemes*, because they cannot stand alone as words.

Compound words: Compound words occur when two or more base words are connected to form a new word. The meaning of the new word is in some way connected to the meanings of the base words.

Inflectional endings: Inflectional endings are types of suffixes that impart a new meaning to the base word or root word. These endings change the gender, number, tense, or form of the base or root word. Just like other suffixes, these are *bound morphemes*.

E. **Demonstrates an understanding of the role of reading fluency in reading comprehension and knows how to select and use instructional strategies and materials to enhance students' reading fluency**

See Competency 2.E

Reading is a reader-active process of constructing meaning. As was mentioned in Competency 2.E, this may mean that students from different backgrounds (ELL students in particular) may construct meaning very differently, and teachers must account for this. To construct meaning, students need to have word analysis skills and be able to discern and confirm meaning through word structure and also through context. To attain reading fluency, students attach new information to prior knowledge. Prior knowledge is a most important prerequisite to understanding new information. As noted, students have different prior knowledge and previously acquired understanding; what is more, many modern students do not have an extensive prior knowledge base. Teachers enhance reading comprehension and reading fluency by providing real world experiences designed to increase students' prior knowledge.

Reading fluency is also increased by using reading materials of high interest, Young Adult novels often engage students and appeal to their experiences and prior knowledge; re-reading treasured books or dynamic passages; acting out stories of their own composition; reading aloud as groups or as individuals to fellow students or to family members and friends also enhance reading fluency.

F. **Knows and applies strategies for enhancing students' comprehension through vocabulary study**

A planned, effective vocabulary program is not an extra—it is an across-the-curriculum necessity. There are four steps in an effective vocabulary program:

1. Evaluate to determine what the students know.

2. Devise a plan to teach the students what they must learn as part of a continuum.

3. Determine if students have heard the words to be studied and in what context.

4. Teach vocabulary for *mastery*.

To reach mastery, clear-cut objectives and pacing are important since some students will need more practice than others. Building in time for practice, review, and testing is an integral component of a successful program.

Reteaching words missed on tests or misused in writing is essential until mastery is achieved. Learning vocabulary through visual, auditory, kinesthetic, and tactical experiences in a systematic order will enhance the learning process.

Methods of presentation for a well-balanced program at all levels include

- recognizing and using words in context
- giving attention to varying definitions of the same word
- studying word families (synonyms, antonyms, and homonyms)
- locating etymologies (word origins)
- analyzing word parts (roots, prefixes, suffixes)
- locating phonetic spellings and identifying correct pronunciation
- spelling words properly
- using words semantically

Countless enrichment materials are available, including computer programs and games, board games, flashcards, and puzzles. The more varied the experience, the more easily and quickly students will commit the words to memory and achieve mastery.

The Shostak Vocabulary Series that spans middle school through grade 13, including SAT/ACT preparation, is recommended for use in grades 9–12.

The literature series includes vocabulary lists and practices. Classroom teachers should also review content area texts to add technical and specialized words to the weekly vocabulary study.

G. **Understands and teaches students comprehension strategies to use before reading, during reading, and after reading**

Reading Emphasis in Middle School

Reading for comprehension of factual material—content-area textbooks, reference books, and newspapers—is closely related to study strategies in middle school/junior high. Organized study models such as the SQ3R method (Survey, Question, Read, Recite, and Review), a technique that makes it possible to learn the content of even large amounts of text, teach students to locate main ideas and supporting details, to recognize sequential order, to distinguish fact from opinion, and to determine cause/effect relationships.

Strategies

- Teacher-guided activities that require students to organize and to summarize information based on the author's explicit intent are pertinent strategies in middle grades. Evaluation techniques include oral and written responses to standardized or teacher-made worksheets.

- Reading fiction introduces and reinforces the skills of inferring meaning from narration and description. Teacher-guided activities such as reading for meaning should be followed by cooperative planning of the skills to be studied and of the selection of reading resources. Many printed reading for comprehension instruments and individualized computer software programs exist to monitor progress in acquiring comprehension skills.

- Older middle school students should be given more student-centered activities, such as individual and collaborative selection of reading choices based on student interest, small-group discussions of selected works, and greater written expression. Evaluation techniques include teacher monitoring and observation of discussions and written work samples.

- Certain students may begin fundamental critical interpretation—for example, recognizing fallacious reasoning in news media, examining the accuracy of news reports and advertising, or explaining their reasons for preferring one author's writing to another's. Development of these skills may require a more learning-centered approach in which the teacher identifies a number of objectives and suggests resources from which the student may choose his or her course of study. The teacher should stress self-evaluation in a reading diary. Teacher and peer evaluation of creative projects resulting from such study is encouraged.

- Reading aloud before the entire class as a formal means of teacher evaluation should be phased out in favor of one-to-one tutoring or peer-assisted reading. Occasional sharing of favored selections by both teacher and willing students is good for basic interpretation.

Reading Emphasis in High School

Students in high school literature classes should focus on interpretive and critical reading. Teachers should guide the study of the elements of inferential (interpretive) reading such as drawing conclusions, predicting outcomes, recognizing examples of specific genre characteristics, and reading critically to judge the quality of the writer's work against recognized standards. At this level, students should understand the skills of language and reading that they are expected to master and should be able to evaluate their own progress.

Strategies

- The teacher becomes more facilitator than instructor, helping students diagnose their own strengths and weaknesses, keep a record of progress, and interact with other students and the teacher to practice skills.

- Despite the requisites and prerequisites of most literature courses, students should be encouraged to pursue independent study and enrichment reading.

- Ample opportunities should be provided for oral interpretation of literature, special projects in creative dramatics, writing for publication in school literary magazines or newspapers, and speech/debate activities. A student portfolio provides for teacher and peer evaluation.

H. Understands the role of visualization, metacognition, self-monitoring, and social interaction for reading comprehension and promotes students' use of these processes

Metacognition refers to the ability of students to be aware of and monitor their learning processes. In other words, it is the process of "thinking about thinking."

Provide students with a mental checklist of factors to keep in mind while reading so they can self-monitor their reading comprehension:

- Am I engaged with what I am reading?
- Do I understand what I am reading?
- Am I reading words by sounding them out?
- Am I paying attention to what I read?
- Am I reading fast enough to keep up?
- Does what I'm reading make sense?
- Am I constructing the meaning of words I don't know?
- What can I do to understand this reading better?

Understanding is gleaned through activating previous or prior knowledge, so any activities that build prior knowledge will help students grow in reading comprehension. Social interaction that includes class discussions, small group work, and partnering all aid in building prior knowledge and also making the connections that link to comprehension. The social interactions of students chiming in, adding to, or leading the class into further and deeper thinking during class discussions or in small group or partner discussions are all beneficial, as studies have shown that students learn through interactions with their peers and with adults. Retelling a story to the class or small group is a social interaction that helps increase comprehension

The mental exercise of having the students visualize what the characters of a book look like, what the setting of a book looks like, and visualizing possible alternative plot twists or endings is an important tool for building reading comprehension.

I. **Understands levels of reading comprehension and strategies for teaching literal, inferential, creative, and critical comprehension skills**

There are three basic levels of reading comprehension: Literal, inferential, and applied. In literal comprehension the student is able to comprehend the obvious, face-value, or factual aspects of a work. In inferential comprehension, the student is able to interpret the material and ascertain broader truths from it, extrapolating from the specific to the general, as in inductive reasoning. In other words, the student can draw certain conclusions, make associations and connections with the material in order to enhance comprehension and see the larger picture. In applied comprehension, the student is able to extrapolate even further; that is, the student is able to expand outward from the material into the realms of creative and critical thinking about it. In applied comprehension, the material may inspire new material, deeper questions, or questions that call the materials' validity into doubt or which test or lay conditions upon its validity in various settings; applied comprehension may also creatively apply the material to wholly different situations, resulting in something entirely new.

To develop the higher order thinking skills to enhance reading comprehension, teachers should ask students to find similarities and differences between texts in regard to explanations, points of view, and themes; ask students to identify explicit and implicit meanings of texts, i.e., explore both the literal and the deeper meanings; make sure students support any inferences, conclusions, generalizations, or predictions they make with evidence from the text or from their own experience or from other texts they have read, and lead the students in exercises that help them to understand the difference between facts and opinions.

See also Competency 6.H

J. **Knows how to intervene in students' reading process to promote their comprehension and enhance their reading experience**

If students take turns reading aloud in your classroom, those who read word to word and haltingly have probably not developed reading fluency and could use some special help to improve their reading skills. Readers who are not fluent must intentionally decode a majority of the words they encounter in a text. Fluent readers are able to read texts with expression or *prosody*, the combination that makes oral reading sound like spoken language.

If students don't read aloud in your classroom but have reading assignments that call for written reports, those reports also will have clues to reading ability. If sentences are poorly structured, if words are left out, or if the student uses a vocabulary over which he or she does not have control, these are signs that the student's reading level is below par.

There are a number of reliable reading tests that can be administered to provide empirical data about where your students' reading skills lie. Your school or your district can probably recommend one. Some of these can be given at the beginning of the school year and at the end to give you information about the impact of your teaching.

For struggling readers, a special section with activities designed to improve reading may be in order, but make certain that it isn't seen as criticism or judgment. Some of the activities that might be useful for that separate section include the following:

- Repeated readings: Using short passages, the group will read several times, trying to improve with each reading.
- Echo reading: The teacher reads a sentence and students read after her. Once a story has been completed, repeat the exercise, using the same text.
- Wide reading: The teacher reads a sentence and students read after her, but they move on to a new reading once the first one is finished.
- Choose a story that the students like and have each student read a page, going around the group, until the story is completed. Discuss what the story is about and then give an exam on the content of the story. When the focus of an assignment is on meaning, students tend to make greater gains in comprehension than when the focus is on word analysis and accurate reading.
- Sometimes watching a dramatization of a story in a TV program or movie will encourage an interest in reading that story and will provide variety and an opportunity to think about language in both spoken and written form.

Among the causes that make reading a struggle for some students are auditory trauma and ear infections that affect the student's ability to hear. Such a student will need one-on-one support with articulation and perception of different sounds. It might be necessary to consult with a speech therapist or audiologist. As a teacher, you need to take time to identify those children who may be struggling because of a hearing difficulty. Some students may have vision problems that call for treatment. Inquiring about a vision examination is in order if you suspect that a child is not reading well because of a vision impairment.

Students who are using English as a second language may need special consideration. If they are not able to comprehend at a passing level in your class, they should be referred to an ELL class.

If you conclude that a student is not prepared to participate successfully in your classroom, then referral may be the best choice. Guidance counselors, speech pathologists, and school psychologists are available in most schools.

K. **Knows how to provide students with reading experiences that enhance their understanding of and respect for diversity and guides students to increase knowledge of cultures through reading**

Children tend to rely heavily on an either "that is me" or "that is not me" mentality when evaluating literature. A modern, diverse classroom has the potential to break down those barriers and open students' minds to redefine "what COULD be me" or "what I'd LIKE to learn more about." Differences should be seen as valuable assets to the classroom.

The teacher should be careful when selecting material that emphasizes diversity to avoid works that perpetuate stereotypes.

Holidays are a great way to explore diversity. They provide a fun and interesting context to learn about other cultures. Choose books that explore Kwanza, Chinese New Year, Cinco de Mayo, or Ramadan. Focusing on how other cultures have fun is likely to foster future interest in them.

L. **Knows how to use technology to enhance reading instruction**

A 2010 survey by the U.S. Department of Education (SETDA 2010) found that nearly all U.S. public schools have at least one instructional computer with access to the Internet. Almost 100% of schools have one or more computers in the classroom, and more than half have laptops available for student use. A majority of schools have other education technology devices for use in instruction as well, such as LCD and DLP projectors, digital cameras, and interactive whiteboards. The U.S. Department of Education is investing large amount of money in education technology in both elementary and secondary schools.

A John Hopkins University study said that research on the effectiveness of education technology for improving learning outcomes is abundant. The study, reported in The Best Evidence Encyclopedia, created by the Johns Hopkins University School of Education's Center for Data-Driven Reform in Education, funded by the Institute of Education Sciences, the U.S. Department of Education, evaluated all types of technology used for educational purposes, including computers, multimedia, interactive whiteboards (which are extremely popular with teachers and students) and various other technologies. The study evaluated technology-assisted reading programs for students K-12.

The findings, which were consistent with previous similar studies, showed that education technology produce a small but positive effect compared to traditional methods.

READ 180 and Voyager Passport, which are widely used in secondary reading instruction, combine computer and non-computer instruction with the support of extensive professional development. Reading strategies, comprehension, word study, and vocabulary are included in these resources. A comprehensive approach, that includes computer- and non-computer-assisted instruction and professional development training are most effective in enhancing reading instruction.

M.   Demonstrates an understanding of informal and formal procedures for monitoring and assessing students' reading, such as using reading-response journals

Competencies to Evaluate

- Ability to use syntactic cues when encountering an unknown word. A good reader will expect the word to fit the syntax with which he or she is familiar. A poor reader may substitute a word that does not fit the syntax and will not correct him- or herself.
- Ability to use semantic cues to determine the meaning of an unknown word. A good reader will consider the meanings of all the known words in the sentence. A poor reader may read one word at a time with no regard for the other words.
- Ability to use schematic cues to connect words read with prior knowledge. A good reader will incorporate what he or she knows with what the text says or implies. A poor reader may think only of the word he or she is reading without associating it with prior knowledge.
- Ability to use phonics cues to improve the ease and efficiency of reading. A good reader will apply letter and sound associations almost subconsciously. A poor reader may have one of two kinds of problems. He or she may have underdeveloped phonics skills and use only an initial clue without analyzing vowel patterns before quickly guessing the word. Or he or she may use phonics skills in isolation, becoming so absorbed in the word "noises" that he or she ignores or forgets the message of the text.
- Ability to process information from text. A student should be able to get information from the text and store, retrieve, and integrate that information for later use.
- Ability to use interpretive thinking to make logical predictions and inferences.
- Ability to use critical thinking to make decisions and insights about the text.
- Ability to use appreciative thinking to respond to the text, whether emotionally, mentally, ideologically, and so on.

Methods of Evaluation

- Assess students at the beginning of each year to determine grouping for instruction.
- Judge whether a student recognizes when a word does not make sense.

- Monitor whether the student corrects him- or herself and if the student knows when to ignore and read on or when to reread a sentence.
- Look for skills such as recognizing cause and effect, finding main ideas, and using comparison and contrast techniques.
- Use oral reading to assess reading skills. Pay attention to word recognition skills rather than the reader's ability to communicate the author's message. Strong oral reading sounds like natural speech, utilizes phrasing and pace that match the meaning of the text, and uses pitch and tone to interpret the text.
- Keep dated records to follow individual progress. Focus on a few students each day. Grade them on a scale of 1 to 5 according to how well they demonstrate certain reading abilities (for example, *logically predicts coming events*). Also include informal observations, such as "Ed was able to determine the meaning of the word *immigrant* by examining the other words in the sentence."
- Remember that evaluation is important, but enjoyment of reading is the most important thing to emphasize. Keep reading as a pressure-free, fun activity so students do not become intimidated by reading. Even if students are not meeting expected standards, if they continue wanting to read each day, that is a success!
- Reading-response journals are useful tools to engage students in reading. Reading-response journals require that students record their emotional responses and their thoughts as to what was read. The fact that reading-response journals are personal and that they are not assessed in terms of right or wrong responses liberates students to engage with texts in an individual and meaningful way, spurring deeper thought, connections to the students' specific prior knowledge and previously acquired understanding. Reading-response journals also furnish a forum for and encourage opinions, judgments, and critical thinking.

Although there are no right and wrong answers in a reading-response journal, the journals lend themselves to formal assessment as to students' reading and writing skills.

N. **Uses assessment results to plan and adapt instruction that addresses students' strengths, needs, and interests and that builds on students' current skills to increase their reading proficiency**

See Competency 4.M.

COMPETENCY 005 THE TEACHER UNDERSTANDS READING SKILLS AND STRATEGIES FOR VARIOUS TYPES OF NONLITERARY TEXTS AND TEACHES STUDENTS TO APPLY THESE SKILLS AND STRATEGIES TO ENHANCE THEIR LIFELONG LEARNING

A. Demonstrates knowledge of types of nonliterary texts and their characteristics

Informational Books and Articles

Magazines began to be popular in the nineteenth century in this country, and while many of the contributors to those publications intended to influence the political/social/religious convictions of their readers, many simply intended to pass on information. A book or article whose purpose is to impart is called *exposition* (adjectival form: *expository*). An example of an expository book is the *MLA Style Manual*. The writers do not intend to persuade their readers to use the recommended stylistic features in their writing; they are simply making them available in case a reader needs such a guide. Articles in magazines such as *Time* may be persuasive in purpose, but for the most part they are expository, giving information that television coverage of a news story might not have time to include.

News Accounts of Events

News that reports events is usually expository. An event might be a school board meeting, an automobile accident that sent several people to a hospital, or the election of the mayor. These reports are not intended to be persuasive, although the bias of a reporter or of an editor must be considered. A news organization's editorial stance is often openly declared, and it may be reflected in such things as news reports. Reporters are expected to be unbiased in their coverage, and most of them will defend their disinterest fiercely, but what a writer *sees* in an event is inevitably shaped to some extent by the writer's beliefs and experiences. Newspaper editorials, which do project opinions, are another type of nonliterary text.

Other types of nonliterary texts include reports, history books, biographies, science books, and other informational, nonfiction works. Such works will include characteristics such as a dignified cover, a source or reference list at the back, glossaries, indices, tables, charts, and diagrams to enhance their authority and fact-delivering mission. Biographies would include photographs of the subject and his or her environment, facsimiles of handwritten letters, photographs of progenitors or important friends, associates, and influencers, etc. Brochures and advertisements are also types of nonliterary text, and they would include the characteristics of information about a product or service, testimonials or recommendations, glowing language, a glossy format, photographs of the product or people using the product, results of using the product or service, illustrations, or other graphics with carefully orchestrated use of colors, fonts, and language to convey a persuasive message about the desirability of the product or service.

B. Understands purposes for reading nonliterary texts, reading strategies associated with different purposes, and ways to teach students to apply appropriate reading strategies for different purposes

The purpose for reading nonliterary texts varies with the kind of information the nonliterary text contains or conveys. If the text is information about culture and/or history, the purpose in reading it is to gain information and learning through understanding culture and/or history. If the text is persuasive in nature, the reader will be presented with an opinion backed by some research and will need to employ the strategies of sifting through the strengths of the sources and arguments and possibly assessing them in relationship to works of a different opinion or conclusion. If the purpose of the nonliterary text is procedural, the student is to learn a process or set of applicable skills. There may be other purposes behind nonliterary texts as well.

The strategy of the SQ3R method (Survey, Question, Read, Recite, and Review) will help a reader comprehend nonliterary texts for purpose. After surveying or scanning the book as a whole to catch title, major headings, subheadings, and graphics, the students may then formulate questions, including the question of purpose, and read the books to discern it. Reciting the answer, reviewing the main ideas and significant information, and further reflecting upon it will help students ascertain the purpose of the text.

Many nonliterary texts follow the classic pattern of being divided into three parts: an introduction, a body, and a conclusion. These three main sections should be discerned first, and then read in more detail while asking such questions as:

Introduction
- Is it made clear what the text is going to be about?
- Are author credentials for writing the text included that establish the author's credibility, not excluding personal experience?
- Are the sections and/or chapters summarized or sketched concisely?
- Does the Introduction make clear what the purpose of the text is?

Body
- Is an argument or viewpoint being put forth? How is it developed?
- Are other viewpoints or argument given appropriate "air time" in the text?
- Is the information well-organized?
- Is there a logical progression of ideas or information presented?
- What are the main ideas?
- What are the supporting details?
- What purpose does the information given point to?

Conclusion
- Does the conclusion cogently summarize or wrap up all that has gone before in the text?
- Does the conclusion seem valid and well-supported by the body of the text?

- Is the reader persuaded?
- Has the author achieved his or her purpose?
- Is the reader satisfied?

The reader will also work to understand the purpose of a nonliterary text by asking such questions as: What was the author's intention? Why did he or she write this book? Was the book written to inform people? Was it written to call people to action for a certain cause? Was it written to laud or memorialize a pivotal person or an event? Was it written to refute another book or opinion? Was it written to teach a process or application?

C. **Knows strategies for monitoring one's own understanding of nonliterary texts and for addressing comprehension difficulties that arise and knows how to teach students to use these strategies**

See Competency 5.B. The strategies for comprehending a nonliterary text listed in Competency 5.B will help the teacher as well as the student. Further strategies include analyzing:

Structure:
Where does the thesis—the point—of the document or speech occur?
>At the beginning
>In the middle
>At the end
>Unstated

Is the reasoning deductive (general to specific) or inductive (specific to general)?

Is the outline chronological or spatial?

What figures of speech are used?
>Metaphor?
>Allegory?
>Simile?

Content:
Thesis—the *point* the document or speech makes.
Support—the points or examples the writer/speaker uses to establish the thesis.
Purpose—persuasive, descriptive, expository, or narrative.
Detecting Fallacies:
Ad hominem
>Slippery slope
>False dilemma
>Begging the question
Post hoc ergo propter hoc (false cause)
>Red herring
>Hasty conclusion

ENGLISH LANG. ARTS & READING

Coherence—the supporting points move in a logical sequence from first to last and have transitions that establish the relationship to the preceding point.
Bias—does the background or belief system of the speaker/writer affect the position taken?
Value—is the information useful or relevant?
Ethics—Respect for sensitivities of diverse audience/readership. Honesty, transparency.

Considering the points above will aid the teacher in self-monitoring his or her own understanding of nonliterary texts and reinforce such strategies for student instruction.

D. **Demonstrates knowledge of skills for comprehending nonliterary texts and knows how to provide students with opportunities to apply and refine these skills**

The skills needed for reading/comprehension of informational, nonliterary texts are that students are able to analyze, make inferences, and draw conclusions about the author's purpose in appropriate contexts and provide evidence from the texts in support. Students are able to explain the overarching, main ideas, as well as discern less important details, all of which adhere to the author's purpose in writing an expository text.

See Competency 5.B.

In persuasive informational nonliterary texts, students are expected further to be able to summarize text and be able to distinguish between an objective summary and one that takes a position and expresses an opinion. Any opinions in a persuasive, informational, nonliterary text should be recognized by the student as being supported or unsupported by the text. Students should be able to synthesize, analyze, and connect logically the main ideas and supporting details in several texts representing different viewpoints on the same topic and be able to point to the texts for support. Students should be able to discern evidence given in support of an argument and whether it is credible, relevant, and of high quality. When analyzing speeches, students should recognize rhetorical devices used to persuade and convince. In procedural texts, students should be able to discern order and clarity and also analyze any technical data provided.

E. **Understands types of text organizers and their use in locating and categorizing information**

Text organizers help to locate and categorize information by serving the reader "at a glance". Overviews, often marked as such or appearing within shaded or colored borders within a text give the "aerial" view of the material or the overarching and broad themes and categories the information will cover. A Table of Contents is a text organizer that is extremely helpful in locating information according to categories. Headings and subheadings, usually in large and diminishing sized font point sizes, catch the eye and the attention and point to categories and subcategories of subjects being covered in the text underneath them. Indices are important text organizers, showing in alphabetical order the pages where specific topics appear in the text.

Graphic features also help categorize information in a succinct way. Graphic text organizers include charts, tables, figures, diagrams and other visuals that present significant amounts of information, or which compare and contrast information in a condensed, visual way.

F. **Demonstrates knowledge of types of text structure and strategies for promoting students' ability to use text structure to facilitate comprehension of nonliterary texts**

Organizational Structures

Authors use a particular organization to best present the concepts that they write about. Teaching students to recognize organizational structures helps them understand authors' literary intentions and decide which structure to use in their own writing.

Cause and effect: When authors write about *why* things happen in addition to *what* happens, they commonly use the cause and effect structure. For example, when writing about how he became successful, a CEO might talk about how he excelled in math in high school, moved to New York after college, and stuck to his goals even after multiple failures. These are all *causes* that lead to the *effect*, or result, of him becoming a wealthy and powerful businessman.

Compare and contrast: The examination of the merits of multiple concepts or products requires that they be compared and contrasted. For example, a person writing about foreign policy in different countries will evaluate those policies against one another to point out differences and similarities, focusing on the elements the author wishes to emphasize.

Problem and solution: This structure is often used in handbooks and manuals. Anything organized around procedure-oriented tasks, such as a computer repair manual, gravitates toward a problem and solution format, in which text is organized clearly and sequentially.

G. **Knows strategies for helping students increase their knowledge of specialized vocabulary in nonliterary texts and for facilitating reading comprehension**

As school progresses students are required to learn more and more specialized words in order to understand the increasingly complex texts and concepts they are encountering. Word walls are useful strategies for helping students increase their knowledge of specialized vocabulary in nonliterary texts and facilitate reading comprehension. A word wall may be a literal wall with cardboard cards taped to it, an electronic whiteboard, a chalkboard, bulletin or other display that lists key new words (in alphabetical order) that students will need to master in their studies. This gives students visual cues that will aid them in recognizing the words and having some sense of the words' meanings when the words appear in the nonliterary text. Word walls will aid in spelling accuracy and reinforce comprehension as they are referred to again and again. Word wall entries can include the words themselves and brief definitions.

Students may also discern the meaning of new words from context. Teachers can write the target word on the board and ask students to find the target word in the text. Using surrounding sentences and the paragraph, students may be asked to make connections between words, phrases, and concepts that they already understand and the new word. The teacher asks the students to make suggestions as to what the word might mean and confirms close or exact meanings.

H. **Knows how to locate, retrieve, and retain information from a range of texts, including interpreting information presented in various formats, and uses effective instructional strategies to teach students these skills**

In spite of the prevalence of the Internet, it is important not to neglect the local library as a tremendous source of information. Not only does it have numerous books, videos, CDs, and periodicals to use for references, the librarian is always a valuable resource for information of where to get that information.

> *"Those who declared librarians obsolete when the Internet rage first appeared are now red-faced. We need them more than ever. The Internet is full of 'stuff' but its value and readability is often questionable. 'Stuff' doesn't give you a competitive edge, high-quality related information does."*
>
> -Patricia Schroeder, President of the Association of American Publishers

Of course, modern libraries are well-equipped with computers and Internet access. Whether using the library's or one's own computer, there is no question that the Internet is a multifaceted goldmine of information, but one must be careful to discriminate between reliable and unreliable sources. Teachers should instruct students to stick to sites that are associated with an academic or governmental institution, such as a university, scholarly organizations, or offices of state or federal government.

Students should be reminded to keep **content** and **context** in mind when researching. It is easy to get so wrapped up in a project as to how to apply the resource to a project that the author's main purpose or message is lost. The whole work should be considered, rather than picking and choosing parts of it that may appear to support one's own thesis or purpose for the project.

Students should be reminded that there are multiple ways to get information. Encyclopedia articles are a good place for students to start when researching a topic in order to get a general overview, and then they can focus in from there. Some encyclopedias include links to other sources or references the students can then follow up on. Students should note important names of people associated with the subject, time periods, and geographic areas. They can make a list of key words and their synonyms to use while searching for information.

Articles in magazines and newspapers, or even personal interviews with experts related to the field of interest are also viable sources of information.

I. **Knows how to evaluate the credibility and accuracy of information in nonliterary texts, including electronic texts, and knows how to teach students to apply these critical-reading skills**

Students should be instructed that before they accept without question anything that is printed in a newspaper or advertising or presented on radio, television, or the Internet, it is wise to consider the source. Even though news reporters and editors claim to be unbiased in the presentation of news, they usually take an editorial point of view. A newspaper may avow a political position and may even make recommendations at election time, but it will still claim to present the news without bias. Sometimes this is true and sometimes it is not.

Advertising, whether in print or electronic media, is always biased. Will using certain toothpaste improve a person's love life? Is satellite TV better than cable? The best recourse a reader/viewer has is to do his or her own research, perhaps by speaking to people who have used the product or by reading online consumer reviews and reports, which are readily available.

Preparation to read a text by giving background knowledge on the subject is important in starting the critical-reading process. Integrating reading and writing activities also help students make connections that stimulate higher order thinking skills such as critical thinking. Providing instruction in vocabulary development also gives students the fluency to engage in higher order thinking skills such as critical reading.

In the age of hypermedia, critical thinking is more important than ever, as sources on the Internet are not always reliable, as noted. It is important to include textbooks as part of information that may be used as tools of learning rather than as dispensers of received knowledge. The teacher's role also should be increasingly less as a repository of knowledge and more as a facilitator of the students' own quest for knowledge. Using a mixture of learning tools: textbooks, magazines, Internet sources, other media sources, student-generated texts and classroom and small group discussions—helps students develop critical thinking skills to apply to all forms of transmission of knowledge.

J. **Demonstrates an understanding of the characteristics and uses of various types of research tools and information sources and promotes students' understanding of and ability to use these resources**

See Competency 5.H, 5.I, and 5.K

K. **Understands steps and procedures for engaging in inquiry and research and provides students with learning experiences that promote their knowledge and skills in this area**

An easy and effective way of organizing information to be used in a work of nonfiction is to ask specific questions that are geared toward a particular mode of presentation. This method keeps you from getting lost or off-track when looking for information, because you focus on finding the answers to the questions you have posed when you do your research.

After you have written your statement of purpose and have a focused topic to ask questions about, begin research.

First, make two lists of questions. Label one *factual questions* and one *interpretive questions*. The answers to factual questions will give your readers the basic background information they need to understand your topic. The answers to interpretive questions will show your creative thinking in your project and can become the basis for your thesis statement.

Factual Questions

Assume your readers know nothing about your subject. Make an effort to tell them everything they need to know to understand what you will say in your presentation. **Make a list of specific questions that ask *who*, *what*, *when*, and *where***

Example: For a report about President Abraham Lincoln's attitude and policies toward slavery, people will have to know the following: Who was Abraham Lincoln? Where and when was he born? What political party did he belong to? When was he elected president? What were the attitudes and laws about slavery during his lifetime? How did his actions affect slavery?

Interpretive Questions

These kinds of questions are the result of your own original thinking. They can be based on the preliminary research you have done on your chosen topic. Select one or two questions to answer in your presentation. They can be the basis of your thesis statement. The following are some types of interpretive questions.

Hypothetical: How would things be different today if something in the past had been different?

- **Example:** How would our lives be different today if the Confederate (southern) states had won the U.S. Civil War? How would the course of World War II have changed if the United States had not dropped atomic bombs on Hiroshima and Nagasaki?

Prediction: How will something look or be in the future, based on the way it is now?

- **Example:** What will happen to sea levels if global warming due to ozone layer depletion continues and the polar caps melt significantly? If the population of China continues to grow at the current rate for the next 50 years, how will that impact its role in world politics?

Solution: What solutions can be offered to a problem that exists today?

- **Example:** How could global warming be stopped? What can be done to stop the spread of sexually transmitted diseases among teenagers?

Comparison or analogy: What are the similarities and differences between your main subject and a similar subject or another subject from the same time period or place?

- **Example:** In what ways was the civil war in the former Yugoslavia similar to (or different from) the U.S. Civil War? What is the difference in performance between a Porsche and a Lamborghini?

Judgment: Based on the information you find, what is your informed opinion about the subject?

- **Example:** How does tobacco advertising affect teen cigarette smoking? What are the major causes of eating disorders among young women? How does teen parenthood affect the future lives of young women and men?

L. **Demonstrates an understanding of informal and formal procedures for monitoring and assessing students' reading of nonliterary texts**

To evaluate students' comprehension of nonliterary texts, it may be helpful to consult the following checklist.

Is the student

- reading and considering the title?
- finding the author's name and any other information about the author?
- identifying the source (that is, the original publication and date) of the text?
- reading the introduction or opening paragraphs carefully, checking these against the title?
- skimming through the text and reading all boldface subheadings, pulling out quotes, and reading sidebar information?
- skimming through the text and reading the first sentence of each paragraph; then, if this sentence is clearly not the topic sentence, locating and reading the topic sentence?
- examining any other typographical features such as italicized words?

- examining any graphic content (such as maps, illustrations, or images)?
- reading the last paragraph carefully?
- studying any questions or additional information provided at the end of the text?
- reading the entire text, keeping in mind what he or she has gained from prereading, and checking his or her new understanding against his or her initial understanding, revising as needed?

Students should be formally assessed as to their ability to determine the central idea or main thrust of a nonliterary work; how successful they have been at evaluating the premises or assumptions upon which the nonliterary text is built; whether they successfully corroborated evidence from the nonliterary text's assertions by consulting other primary and secondary sources; whether they recognized where assertions in the text could be challenged; whether they were able to extrapolate questions, further areas for study, or solve problems suggested by the reading whether they successfully are able to understand, explain and justify or critique the hierarchy of the nonliterary text's structure (including the use of headings and subheadings) and determining through dictionary use, memorization, or in confirming meaning derived through context, the meaning of key terms.

M. **Uses assessment results to plan and adapt instruction that addresses students' strengths, needs, and interests and that builds on students' current skills to increase their proficiency in reading nonliterary texts**

If a student is not following the guidelines for reading nonliterary texts discussed in Competency 5.L, he or she most likely will have a skewed outlook on expository reading. The student may find it boring and complex, with none of the imagination and stimulation that reading fictional stories provides. However, in the information age in which we find ourselves, reading nonliterary texts has never been more important.

Try to implement texts that use illustrations and photographs to satisfy students' need for engagement. Also, stress the benefits of understanding nonliterary texts for researching, solving problems, and so on. If students see nonliterary texts as a way to pursue their curiosities, they will be more open-minded about reading them, and in turn, more successful in understanding them.

COMPETENCY 006 THE TEACHER UNDERSTANDS LITERARY ELEMENTS, GENRES, AND MOVEMENTS AND DEMONSTRATES KNOWLEDGE OF A SUBSTANTIAL BODY OF LITERATURE

A. Demonstrates knowledge of genres and their characteristics through analysis of literary texts

The major literary genres include allegory, ballad, drama, epic, epistle, essay, fable, novel, poem, romance, and short story.

Allegory: A story in verse or prose with characters representing virtues and vices. An allegory has two meanings: symbolic and literal. John Bunyan's *The Pilgrim's Progress* is the most renowned of this genre.

Ballad: An *in medias res* story told or sung, usually in verse, and accompanied by music. Literary devices found in ballads include the refrain, or repeated section, and incremental repetition, or anaphora, for effect. Earliest forms were anonymous folk ballads. Later forms include Coleridge's masterpiece, *The Rime of the Ancient Mariner*.

Drama: Plays—sometimes comedy or tragedy—typically in five acts. Traditionalists and neoclassicists adhere to Aristotle's unities of time, place, and action. Plot development is advanced via dialogue. Literary devices include asides, soliloquies, and the chorus, representing public opinion. Greatest of all dramatists/playwrights is William Shakespeare. Other dramaturges include Ibsen, Williams, Miller, Shaw, Stoppard, Racine, Molière, Sophocles, Aeschylus, Euripides, and Aristophanes.

Epic: A long poem (usually book length) reflecting values inherent in the generative society. Epic devices include an invocation to a muse for inspiration, universal setting, protagonist and antagonist who possess supernatural strength and acumen, and interventions of a god or the gods. Understandably, there are very few epics: Homer's *Iliad* and *Odyssey*, Virgil's *Aeneid*, Milton's *Paradise Lost*, Spenser's *The Faerie Queene*, Barrett Browning's *Aurora Leigh*, and Pope's mock-epic, *The Rape of the Lock*.

Epistle: A letter that was not always intended for public distribution, but due to the fame of the sender and/or recipient, becomes widely known. Paul wrote epistles that were later placed in the Bible.

Essay: Typically a relatively short prose work focusing on a topic, propounding a definite point of view and using an authoritative tone. Great essayists include Carlyle, Lamb, DeQuincy, Emerson, and Montaigne, who is credited with defining this genre.

Fable: A terse tale offering a moral or exemplum. Chaucer's "The Nun's Priest's Tale" is a fine example of a *bete fabliau*, or beast fable, in which animals speak and act characteristically human, illustrating human foibles.

Legend: A traditional narrative or collection of related narratives, popularly regarded as historically factual but actually a mixture of fact and fiction.

Myth: Stories that are more or less universally shared within a culture to explain its history and traditions.

Novel: The longest form of fictional prose containing a variety of characters, settings, local color, and regionalism. Most have complex plots, expanded description, and attention to detail. Some of the great novelists include Austen, the Brontës, Twain, Tolstoy, Hugo, Hardy, Dickens, Hawthorne, Forster, and Flaubert.

Poem: The only element that defines this genre is rhythm. Subgenres include fixed types of poetry such as the sonnet, elegy, ode, pastoral, and villanelle. Unfixed types of literature include blank verse and dramatic monologue.

Romance: A highly imaginative tale set in a fantastical realm dealing with the conflicts between heroes, villains, and/or monsters. "The Knight's Tale" from Chaucer's *Canterbury Tales*, *Sir Gawain and the Green Knight*, and Keats' "The Eve of St. Agnes" are representatives.

Short story: Typically a terse narrative, with less development and background about characters; may include description, author's point of view, and tone. Poe emphasized that a successful short story should create one focused impact. Some great short story writers are Hemingway, Faulkner, Twain, Joyce, Shirley Jackson, Flannery O'Connor, de Maupassant, Saki, Edgar Allen Poe, and Pushkin.

Dramatic Genres

Comedy: The comedic form of dramatic literature is meant to amuse and often ends happily. It uses techniques such as satire or parody, and can take many forms, from farce to burlesque. Examples include Dante Alighieri's *The Divine Comedy,* Noel Coward's *Private Lives,* some of Geoffrey Chaucer's *Canterbury Tales*, and William Shakespeare's plays.

Tragedy: Tragedy is comedy's other half. It is defined as a work of drama written in either prose or poetry, telling the story of a brave, noble hero who, because of some tragic character flaw, brings ruin upon him or herself. It is characterized by serious, poetic language that evokes pity and fear. In modern times, dramatists have tried to update this form by drawing their main characters from the middle class and showing their nobility through their nature instead of their standing. The classic example of tragedy is Sophocles' *Oedipus Rex*. Henrik Ibsen and Arthur Miller epitomize modern tragedy.

Drama: In its most general sense, a drama is any work that is designed to be performed by actors onstage. It can also refer to the broad literary genre that includes comedy and tragedy. In contemporary usage, however, *drama* is a work that treats serious subjects and themes but does not aim for the same grandeur as tragedy. Drama usually deals with characters of a less stately nature than tragedy. A classical example is Aeschylus's *The Persians*, and Eugene O'Neill's *The Iceman Cometh* represents modern drama.

Features of dramatic genres

Dramatic monologue: A dramatic monologue is a speech given by an actor, usually giving voice to the actor's internal thoughts, but with the intended audience in mind. It reveals key aspects of the character's psyche and sheds light on the situation at hand. The audience takes the part of the silent listener, passing judgment and giving sympathy at the same time. This form was invented and used predominantly by Victorian poet Robert Browning.

Tempo: Interpretation of dialogue must be connected to motivation and detail, which requires variations in tempo. If the overall pace is too slow, then the action becomes dull and dragging. If the overall pace is too fast, then the audience will not be able to understand what is going on because they are being hit with too much information to process.

Dramatic arc

Good drama is built on conflict of some kind—an opposition of forces or desires that must be resolved by the end of the story.

The conflict can be internal, involving emotional and psychological pressures, or it can be external, drawing the characters into tumultuous events. These themes are presented to the audience in a narrative arc that looks roughly like this:

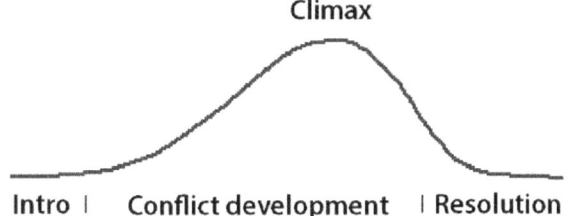

Following the arc

Although any performance may have a series of rising and falling levels of intensity, in general the opening should set in motion the events that will generate an emotional high toward the middle or end of the story. Then, regardless of whether the ending is happy, sad, bittersweet, or despairing, the resolution eases the audience down from those heights and establishes some sense of closure. Reaching the climax too soon undermines the dramatic impact of the remaining portion of the performance, whereas reaching it too late rushes the ending and creates a jarringly abrupt end to events.

B. Demonstrates knowledge of literary elements and devices, including ways in which they contribute to meaning and style, through analysis of literary texts

The following list is essential terminology and literary devices germane to literary analysis at a high school level.

Antithesis: Conflicting or directly opposite ideas expressed near one another, often within the same sentence, such as, "The antithesis of love is not hate but indifference"; "Fear is not the antithesis of courage; courage is acting bravely in spite of fear."

Aphorism: A focused, succinct expression about life from a sagacious viewpoint. Writings by Ben Franklin, Sir Francis Bacon, and Alexander Pope contain many aphorisms. "Whatever is begun in anger ends in shame" is an aphorism.

Apostrophe: An address to an absent or dead person, an abstract idea, or an inanimate object. Sonneteers, such as Sir Thomas Wyatt, John Keats, and William Wordsworth, address the moon, the stars, and the dead. For example, in William Shakespeare's *Julius Caesar*, Mark Antony addresses the corpse of Caesar in the speech that begins: "O, pardon me, thou bleeding piece of earth, That I am meek and gentle with these butchers! Thou art the ruins of the noblest man that ever lived in the tide of times. Woe to the hand that shed this costly blood!"

Blank verse: Poetry written in iambic pentameter but unrhymed. Works by Shakespeare and Milton are epitomes of blank verse. For example, in *Paradise Lost*, Milton writes: "Illumine, what is low raise and support/That to the height of this great argument I may assert Eternal Providence/ And justify the ways of God to men."

Caesura: A pause, usually signaled by punctuation, in a line of poetry. The earliest usage occurs in *Beowulf*, the first English epic dating from the Anglo-Saxon era.

Conceit: A comparison, usually in verse, between seemingly disparate objects or concepts. John Donne's metaphysical poetry contains many clever conceits. Donne's "The Flea" (1633) compares a flea bite to the act of love, and "A Valediction: Forbidding Mourning" (1633) compares separated lovers to the legs of a compass, the leg drawing the circle eventually returning home to "the fixed foot."

Connotation: The emotional effects stemming from the implications and associations of a given word, distinct from the denotative or literal meaning. For example, "Good night, sweet prince, and flights of angels sing thee to thy rest," a line from Shakespeare's *Hamlet*, literally refers to death; connotatively, it renders the harsh reality of death in gentle terms such as those used in putting a child to sleep.

Consonance: The repeated usage of similar consonant sounds, most often used in poetry. "Sally sat sifting seashells by the seashore" is a familiar example.

Couplet: Two rhyming lines of poetry. Shakespeare's sonnets end in heroic couplets written in iambic pentameter. Pope is also a master of the couplet. His *Rape of the Lock* is written entirely in heroic couplets.

Denotation: What a word literally means, as opposed to its connotative meaning.

Diction: The right word in the right spot for the right purpose. The hallmark of a great writer is precise, unusual, and memorable diction.

Epiphany: The moment when a profound insight and comprehension occurs.

Exposition: Background information about characters meant to clarify and add to the narrative or the initial plot element that precedes the buildup of conflict.

Figurative language: Language intended to be interpreted through symbolism. Figurative language includes such literary devices as hyperbole, metonymy, synecdoche, and oxymoron. A synecdoche is a figure of speech in which the word for part of something is used to mean the whole; for example, *the church* for the congregation.

Free verse: Poetry that does not have any predictable meter or patterning. Margaret Atwood, e. e. cummings, and Ted Hughes write in this form. Some free verse poets in the early twentieth century (c. 1910-1918) advocated the use of precise visual images based upon detailed observation of concrete things with minimal use of words to produce suggested, metaphorical understanding. Ezra Pound was an advocate of Imagism.

Hyperbole: Exaggeration for a specific effect. For example, "I'm so hungry that I could eat a horse."

Iambic pentameter: The two elements in a set five-foot line of poetry. An iamb is two syllables, unaccented and accented, per foot or measure. Pentameter means five feet of these iambs per line, or 10 syllables.

Inversion: An atypical sentence order to create a given effect or interest. Bacon's and Milton's work use inversion successfully. Emily Dickinson was fond of arranging words differently from their familiar order. For example, in "Chartless," she writes: "Yet know I how the heather looks" and "Yet certain am I of the spot." She reverses the usual order of the words ("yet I know" and "yet I am certain") to shift the emphasis to the more important words.

Irony: An unexpected disparity between what is written or stated and what is really meant or implied by the author. Verbal, situational, and dramatic are the three literary ironies. Verbal irony is when an author or character says one thing and means something else. Dramatic irony is when an audience perceives something that a character in the play does not. Situational irony is a discrepancy between the expected result and actual results. Shakespeare's plays contain numerous instances of irony. O. Henry's short stories have ironic endings.

Kenning: Another way to describe a person, place, or thing so as to avoid prosaic repetition. The earliest examples can be found in Anglo-Saxon literature such as *Beowulf* and "The Seafarer." In *Beowulf*, instead of writing *King Hrothgar*, the anonymous author wrote *great Ring-Giver* or *Father of his people*. A lake becomes *the swans' way*, and the ocean or sea becomes *the great whale's way*. In ancient Greek literature, this device was called an *epithet*.

Metaphysical poetry: Verse characterized by ingenious wit, unparalleled imagery, and clever conceits. The greatest metaphysical poet is John Donne. Henry Vaughn and other seventeenth-century British poets contributed to this movement. An example from "The World" by Vaughn is: "I saw eternity the other night, like a great ring of pure and endless light."

Metonymy: Use of an object or idea closely identified with another object or idea to represent the second. *Hit the books* means "go study." *Washington, D.C.*, means the U.S. government, and *the White House* means the U.S. president.

Motif: A key, often-repeated phrase, name, or idea in a literary work. Dorset/Wessex in Hardy's novels and the moors and the harsh weather in the Brontë sisters' novels are motifs. Shakespeare's *Romeo and Juliet* represents the ill-fated young lovers' motif.

Onomatopoeia: A word used to evoke the sound in its meaning. The early Batman series used *pow, zap, whop, zonk,* and *eek* in an onomatopoetic way.

Octava rima: A specific eight-line stanza of poetry whose rhyme scheme is abababcc. Lord Byron's mock epic poem, *Don Juan*, is written in octava rima.

Oxymoron: A contradictory form of speech, such as *jumbo shrimp, unkindly kind*, or singer John Mellencamp's song "Hurts So Good."

Paradox: A seeming contradiction that is nevertheless true. John Donne's sonnet "Death Be Not Proud" postulates that death shall die and humans will triumph over death, at first thought not true, but ultimately explained and "proven" in this sonnet.

Parallelism: A type of close repetition of clauses or phrases that emphasize key topics or ideas in writing. The psalms in the Bible contain many examples.

Personification: Giving human characteristics to inanimate objects or concepts. Great writers, with few exceptions, are masters of this literary device.

Quatrain: A poetic stanza composed of four lines. A Shakespearean or Elizabethan sonnet is made up of three quatrains and ends with a heroic couplet.

Scansion: The two-part analysis of a poetic line. Count the number of syllables per line and determine where the accents fall. Divide the line into metric feet. Name the meter by the type and number of feet. Much is written about scanning poetry. Try not to inundate your students with this jargon; instead, allow them to feel the power of the poet's words, ideas, and images.

Soliloquy: A highlighted speech in drama, usually delivered by a major character expounding on the author's philosophy or expressing, at times, universal truths. This is done with the character alone on the stage.

Spenserian stanza: Invented by Sir Edmund Spenser for usage in *The Faerie Queene*, his epic poem honoring Queen Elizabeth I. Each stanza consists of nine lines, eight in iambic parameter. The ninth line, called an alexandrine, has two extra syllables or one additional foot.

Sprung rhythm: Invented and used extensively by the poet Gerard Manley Hopkins. It consists of variable meter, which combines stressed and unstressed syllables fashioned by the author. Hopkins's poems "Pied Beauty" and "God's Grandeur" use sprung rhythm.

Stream of consciousness: A style of writing that reflects the loose, often irrational, mental processes of the characters expressing, at times, jumbled memories, feelings, and dreams. Well-known writers who use this type of expression are James Joyce, Virginia Woolf, and William Faulkner.

Terza rima: A series of poetic stanzas utilizing the recurrent rhyme scheme of aba, bcb, cdc, ded, and so forth. The second-generation Romantic poets—Keats, Byron, Shelley, and, to a lesser degree, Yeats—used this Italian verse form, especially in their odes. Dante used this stanza in the *Divine Comedy*.

Tone: The discernible attitude inherent in an author's work regarding the subject, readership, or characters. Swift's or Pope's tone is satirical. Boswell's tone toward Johnson is admiring.

Wit: Writing of genius, keenness, and sagacity expressed through clever use of language. Alexander Pope and the Augustans wrote about and were themselves said to possess wit.

C. **Demonstrates knowledge of major literary movements in American, British, and world literature, including their characteristics, the historical contexts from which they emerged, major authors and their impact on literature, and representative works and their themes**

American Literature

The Colonial Period

William Bradford's excerpts from *The Mayflower Compact* relate vividly the hardships of crossing the Atlantic in a tiny vessel, the misery and suffering of the first winter, the approaches of the Native Americans, the decimation of their ranks, and the establishment of the Bay Colony of Massachusetts.

Anne Bradstreet's poetry relates much concerning colonial New England life. From her journals, modern readers learn of the everyday life of the early settlers, the hardships of travel, and the responsibilities of different groups and individuals in the community. Colonial American literature also reveals the commercial and political adventures of the Cavaliers who came to the New World with King George's blessing.

William Byrd's journal, *The History of the Dividing Line,* concerning his trek into the dismal swamp separating the Carolinian territories from Virginia and Maryland makes quite lively reading. A privileged insider to the English royal court, Byrd, like other southern Cavaliers, was given grants to pursue business ventures.

The Revolutionary Period

The Revolutionary Period brought great orations such as Patrick Henry's *Speech to the Virginia House of Burgesses* (the "Give me liberty or give me death" speech) and George Washington's *Farewell to the Army of the Potomac.* The Declaration of Independence, the brainchild predominantly of Thomas Jefferson, with some prudent editing by Ben Franklin, is a prime example of neoclassical writing—balanced, well crafted, and focused.

Epistles include the exquisitely written, moving correspondence between John Adams and Abigail Adams. The poignancy of their separation—she in Boston, he in Philadelphia—is palpable and real.

The Romantic Period

Nathaniel Hawthorne and Herman Melville are the preeminent early American novelists, writing on subjects definitely regional, specific, and American, yet sharing insights about human foibles, fears, loves, doubts, and triumphs. Hawthorne's writings range from children's stories, like the Cricket on the Hearth series, to adult fare of dark, brooding short stories such as "Dr. Heidegger's Experiment," "The Devil and Tom Walker," and "Rappaccini's Daughter."

Hawthorne's masterpiece, *The Scarlet Letter*, takes on the society of hypocritical Puritan New Englanders, who left England to establish religious freedom, but who have been entrenched in judgmental finger wagging. They ostracize Hester and condemn her child, Pearl, as a child of Satan. Great love, sacrifice, loyalty, suffering, and related epiphanies add universality to this tale. *The House of the Seven Gables* also deals with kept secrets, loneliness, social pariahs, and love ultimately triumphing over horrible wrong.

Herman Melville's great opus, *Moby–Dick*, follows a crazed Captain Ahab on his Homeric odyssey to conquer the great white whale that has outwitted him and his whaling crews time and again. The whale has taken Arab's leg and, according to Ahab, wants all of him. Melville recreates in painstaking detail and with insider knowledge the harsh life of a whaler out of New Bedford, by way of Nantucket.

Melville's novella *Billy Budd* is the succinct tale of the sailor Billy Budd and his Christ-like sacrifice to the black-and-white maritime laws on the high seas. An accident results in the death of one of the ship's officers, a slug of a fellow, who had taken a dislike to the young, affable, and shy Billy. Captain Vere must hang Billy for the death of Claggert, but knows that this is not right. However, an example must be given to the rest of the crew so that discipline can be maintained.

Edgar Allan Poe creates a distinctly American version of romanticism with his 16-syllable line in "The Raven," the classical "To Helen," and his gothic "Annabelle Lee." The horror short story can be said to originate from Poe's pen. "The Tell-Tale Heart," "The Cask of Amontillado," "The Fall of the House of Usher," and "The Masque of the Red Death" are exemplary short stories. The new genre of detective story also emerged with Poe's "Murders in the Rue Morgue."

American Romanticism has its own offshoot in the Transcendentalism of Ralph Waldo Emerson and Henry David Thoreau. Emerson wrote about transcending the complexities of life; Thoreau, who wanted to get to the "marrow of life," pitted himself against nature at Walden Pond and wrote an inspiring autobiographical account of his sojourn, *On Walden Pond*. He also wrote passionately on his objections to the interference of government in the life of the individual in "On the Duty of Civil Disobedience."

Emerson's elegantly crafted essays and war poetry still give validation to several important universal truths. Probably most remembered for his address to Thoreau's Harvard graduating class, "The American Scholar," he defined the qualities of hard work and intellectual spirit required of Americans in their growing nation.

The Transition from Romanticism to Realism

The Civil War period ushered in the poignant poetry of Walt Whitman and his homage to all who suffer from the ripple effects of war and presidential assassination. His "Come up from the Fields, Father" about a Civil War soldier's death and his family's reaction and "When Lilacs Last in the Dooryard Bloom'd" about the effects of Abraham Lincoln's assassination on the poet and the nation, should be required reading in any American Literature course. Further, his *Leaves of Grass* gave America its first poetry truly unique in form, structure, and subject matter.

Emily Dickinson, like Walt Whitman, wrote a vast array of poems, only three of which were published in her lifetime. Her themes of introspection and attention to nature's details and wonders are, by any measurement, world-class works. Her posthumous recognition reveals the timeliness of her work. American writing had most certainly arrived.

Mark Twain also left giant footprints with his unique blend of tall tale and fable. "The Celebrated Jumping Frog of Calaveras County" and "The Man who Stole Hadleyburg" are epitomes of American short story writing.

Mark Twain again stands head and shoulders above others by his bold, still disputed, often-banned novel *The Adventures of Huckleberry Finn*, which examines such taboo subjects as a white person's love of a slave, leaving children with abusive parents, and the outcomes of family feuds. Written partly in dialect and southern vernacular, *The Adventures of Huckleberry Finn* is touted by some as the greatest American novel.

Contemporary American Literature
America drama

The greatest and most prolific of American playwrights include:

Eugene O'Neill—*Long Day's Journey into Night, Mourning Becomes Electra,* and *Desire Under the Elms*

Arthur Miller—*The Crucible, All My Sons,* and *Death of a Salesman*

Tennessee Williams—*Cat on a Hot Tin Roof, The Glass Menagerie*, and *A Street Car Named Desire*

Edward Albee—*Who's Afraid of Virginia Woolf?, Three Tall Women,* and *A Delicate Balance*

American fiction

The renowned American novelists of this century include:

John Updike—*Rabbit Run* and *Rabbit Redux*

Sinclair Lewis—*Babbit* and *Elmer Gantry*

F. Scott Fitzgerald—*The Great Gatsby* and *Tender Is the Night*

Ernest Hemingway—*A Farewell to Arms* and *For Whom the Bell Tolls*

William Faulkner—*The Sound and the Fury* and *Absalom, Absalom!*

Bernard Malamud—*The Fixer* and *The Natural*

American poetry

The poetry of the twentieth century is multifaceted, as represented by Edna St. Vincent Millay, Marianne Moore, Richard Wilbur, Langston Hughes, Maya Angelou, and Rita Dove.

The many-layered poems of Robert Frost are distinctly American. His New England motifs of snowy evenings, birches, apple picking, stone wall mending, hired hands, and detailed nature studies relate universal truths in exquisitely simple diction, polysyllabic words, and allusions to mythology and the Bible.

British Literature
Anglo-Saxon

The Anglo-Saxon period spans six centuries but produced only a smattering of literature. The first British epic is *Beowulf,* anonymously written by Christian monks many years after the events in the narrative supposedly occurred.

This Teutonic saga relates the triumph three times over monsters by the hero, Beowulf. "The Seafarer" (a shorter poem), some history, and some riddles are the rest of the Anglo-Saxon canon.

Medieval

The medieval period introduces Geoffrey Chaucer, the father of English literature, whose *Canterbury Tales* are written in the vernacular, or street language, of England, rather than in Latin. Thus, the tales are said to be the first work of British literature. Next, Thomas Malory's *Le Morte d'Arthur* calls together the extant tales from Europe as well as England concerning the legendary King Arthur, Merlin, Guenevere, and the Knights of the Round Table. This is the generative work that gave rise to the many Arthurian legends that stir the chivalric imagination.

Renaissance and Elizabethan

The Renaissance, the most important period of British literature because it is synonymous with William Shakespeare, began with importing the idea of the Petrarchan or Italian sonnet into England. Sir Thomas Wyatt and Sir Philip Sydney wrote English versions. Next, Sir Edmund Spenser invented a variation on this Italian sonnet form, aptly called the Spenserian sonnet. His masterpiece is the epic *The Faerie Queene*, honoring Queen Elizabeth I's reign. He also wrote books on the Red Cross Knight, St.

George and the Dragon, and a series of Arthurian adventures. Spencer was dubbed the Poet's Poet. He created a nine-line stanza, eight lines of iambic pentameter and an extra-footed ninth line, an alexandrine, known as the Spenserian stanza.

William Shakespeare, the Bard of Avon, wrote 154 sonnets, 39 plays, and two long narrative poems. The sonnets are justifiably called the greatest sonnet sequence in all literature. Shakespeare dispensed with the octave/sestet format of the Italian sonnet and invented his three quatrains, one heroic couplet format. His plays are divided into comedies, history plays, and tragedies. Great lines from these plays are more often quoted than from any other author. Four of Shakespeare's tragedies, *Hamlet*, *Macbeth*, *Othello*, and *King Lear*, are acknowledged to be the most brilliant examples of this genre.

Seventeenth Century

John Milton's devout Puritanism was the wellspring of his creative genius that closes the remarkable productivity of the English Renaissance. His social commentary in such works as *Areopagitica*, *Samson Agonistes*, and his elegant sonnets would be enough to solidify his stature as a great writer. It is his masterpiece *Paradise Lost*, based in part on the biblical book of Genesis that places Milton among a handful of the most renowned of all writers.

Paradise Lost, written in balanced, elegant neoclassic form, truly does justify the ways of God to man. It is the greatest allegory about man's journey to the Celestial City (Heaven). John Bunyan's *The Pilgrim's Progress*, which describes virtues and vices personified, was also written during this period. This work is, or was for a long time, second only to the Bible in numbers of copies printed and sold.

The Jacobean Age gave us the marvelously witty and cleverly constructed conceits of John Donne's metaphysical sonnets, as well as his insightful meditations and his version of sermons or homilies. "Ask not for whom the bell tolls" and "No man is an island unto himself" are famous epigrams from Donne's *Meditations*. His most famous conceit compares lovers to a footed compass, the arms of which seem to travel separately but are always leaning toward each other and conjoined in "A Valediction Forbidding Mourning."

Eighteenth Century

Ben Johnson, author of the wickedly droll play *Volpone,* and the Cavalier *carpe diem* poets Robert Herrick, Sir John Suckling, and Richard Lovelace also wrote during King James I's reign.

The Restoration and Enlightenment reflect the political turmoil of the regicide of Charles I, the interregnum Puritan government of Oliver Cromwell, and the restoring of the monarchy to England by the coronation of Charles II, who had been given refuge by the French King Louis. Neoclassicism became the preferred writing style, especially for

Alexander Pope. New styles, such as seen in *The Diary of Samuel Pepys*, the novels of Daniel Defoe, the periodical essays and editorials of Joseph Addison and Richard Steele, and Alexander Pope's mock epic *The Rape of the Lock*, demonstrate the diversity of expression during this time.

Writers who followed were contemporaries of Dr. Samuel Johnson, the lexicographer of *The Dictionary of the English Language*. This period has been called the Age of Johnson, which encompasses James Boswell's biography of Dr. Johnson.

Robert Burns' Scottish dialect and regionalism in his evocative poetry and the mystical pre-Romantic poetry of William Blake usher in the Romantic Age and its revolution against neoclassicism.

Romantic Period

The Romantic Age encompasses the writers known as the First Generation Romantics, William Wordsworth and Samuel Taylor Coleridge, who collaborated on *Lyrical Ballads*, which defines and exemplifies the tenets of this style of writing. The Second Generation includes George Gordon, Lord Byron, Percy Bysshe Shelley, and John Keats. These poets wrote sonnets, odes, epics, and narrative poems, most dealing with homage to nature.

Wordsworth's most famous other works are "Intimations of Immortality" and "The Prelude." Byron's satirical epic, *Don Juan*, and his autobiographical *Childe Harold's Pilgrimage* are irreverent, witty, self-deprecating and, in part, cuttingly critical of other writers and critics. Shelley's odes and sonnets are remarkable for their sensory imagery. Keats's sonnets, odes, and longer narrative poem, *The Eve of St. Agnes*, are remarkable for their introspection and the tender age of the poet, who died when he was only 25. In fact, all of the Second Generation died before their times. Wordsworth, who lived to be 80, outlived them all, as well as his friend and collaborator, Coleridge. Others who wrote during the Romantic Age are the essayist Charles Lamb and the novelist Jane Austin. The Brontë sisters, Charlotte and Emily, wrote one novel each, which are noted as two of the finest ever written, *Jane Eyre* and *Wuthering Heights*. Marianne Evans, also known as George Eliot, wrote several important novels; her masterpiece, *Middlemarch*, and *Silas Marner*, *Adam Bede*, and *The Mill on the Floss*.

Nineteenth Century

The Victorian Period is remarkable for the diversity and proliferation of work in three major areas. Poets who are typified as Victorians include Alfred Lord Tennyson, who wrote *Idylls of the King*, twelve narrative poems about the Arthurian legend, and Robert Browning, who wrote chilling, dramatic monologues, such as "My Last Duchess," as well as long poetic narratives such as *The Pied Piper of Hamlin*. Browning's wife Elizabeth wrote two major works, the epic feminist poem *Aurora Leigh* and her deeply moving and provocative *Sonnets from the Portuguese*, in which she details her deep love for Robert and his startling, to her, reciprocation.

Gerard Manley Hopkins, a Catholic priest, wrote poetry with sprung rhythm. A. E. Housman, Matthew Arnold, and the Pre-Raphaelites, especially the brother and sister duo Dante Gabriel Rosetti and Christina Rosetti, contributed much to round out the Victorian Era poetic scene. The Pre-Raphaelites, a group of nineteenth-century English painters, poets, and critics, reacted against Victorian materialism and the neoclassical conventions of academic art by producing earnest, quasi-religious works. Medieval and early Renaissance painters up to the time of the Italian painter Raphael inspired the group.

Robert Louis Stevenson, the great Scottish novelist, wrote his adventure/history books for young adults. Victorian prose ranges from the incomparable, keenly woven plot structures of Charles Dickens to the deeply moving Dorset/Wessex novels of Thomas Hardy, in which women are repressed and life is more struggle than euphoria. Rudyard Kipling wrote about colonialism in India in works like *Kim* and *The Jungle Book* that create exotic locales and a distinct main point concerning the Raj, the British Colonial government during Queen Victoria's reign. Victorian drama is a product mainly of Oscar Wilde, whose satirical masterpiece, *The Importance of Being Earnest*, farcically details and lampoons Victorian social mores.

Twentieth Century

The early twentieth century is represented mainly by the towering achievement of George Bernard Shaw's dramas: *St. Joan*, *Man and Superman*, *Major Barbara*, and *Arms and the Man,* to name a few. Novelists are too numerous to list, but Joseph Conrad, E. M. Forster, Virginia Woolf, James Joyce, Graham Greene, George Orwell, and D. H. Lawrence comprise some of the century's very best.

Twentieth-century poets of renown and merit include W. H. Auden, Robert Graves, T. S. Eliot, Edith Sitwell, Stephen Spender, Dylan Thomas, Philip Larkin, Ted Hughes, and Hugh MacDarmid (this list is by no means complete).

World Literature

Germany

German poet and playwright Friedrich von Schiller is best known for his history plays, *William Tell* and *The Maid of Orleans*. He is a leading literary figure in the "golden age" of German literature. Also from Germany, Rainer Maria Rilke, the great lyric poet, is one of the poets of the unconscious or stream of consciousness. Germany also has given the world Herman Hesse (*Siddhartha*), Gunter Grass (*The Tin Drum*), and the greatest of all German writers, Goethe.

Scandinavia

Scandinavian literature includes the work of Hans Christian Andersen in Denmark, who advanced the fairy tale genre with such wistful tales as "The Little Mermaid" and "Thumbelina." The social commentary of Henrik Ibsen in Norway startled the world of drama with such issues as feminism (*A Doll's House* and *Hedda Gabler*) and the effects of sexually transmitted diseases (*The Wild Duck* and *Ghosts*). Sweden's Selma Lagerlof is the first woman to ever win the Nobel Prize for literature. Her novels include *Gosta Berling's Saga* and the world-renowned *The Wonderful Adventures of Nils*, a children's work.

Russia

Russian literature is vast and monumental. Who has not heard of Fyodor Dostoyevsky's *Crime and Punishment* or *The Brothers Karamazov*, or Count Leo Tolstoy's *War and Peace*? These are examples of psychological realism. Dostoyevsky's influence on modern writers cannot be overstated. Tolstoy's *War and Peace* is the sweeping account of the invasion of Russia and Napoleon's taking of Moscow, which was abandoned by the Russians. This novel is called the national novel of Russia. Further advancing Tolstoy's greatness is his ability to create believable, unforgettable female characters, especially Natasha in *War and Peace* and the heroine of *Anna Karenina*. Pushkin is famous for great short stories; Anton Chekhov for drama (*Uncle Vanya*, *The Three Sisters*, *The Cherry Orchard*); and Yevtushenko for poetry (*Babi Yar*).

Boris Pasternak won the Nobel Prize (*Dr. Zhivago*). Aleksandr Solzhenitsyn (*The Gulag Archipelago*) was exiled from Russia for his writings on the gulag system. Ilya Varshavsky, who creates dystopian fictional societies, represents the genre of science fiction.

France

France has a multifaceted canon of great literature that is universal in scope, almost always championing some social cause: the poignant short stories of Guy de Maupassant; the fantastic poetry of Charles Baudelaire (*Fleurs du Mal*); and the groundbreaking lyrical poetry of Rimbaud and Verlaine. Drama in France is best represented by Rostand's *Cyrano de Bergerac* and the neoclassical dramas of Racine and Corneille (*Le Cid*). The great French novelists include Andre Gide, Honoré de Balzac (*Cousin Bette*), Stendhal (*The Red and the Black*), and the father/son duo of Alexandre Dumas (*The Three Musketeers* and *The Man in the Iron Mask*). Victor Hugo is the Charles Dickens of French literature, having penned the masterpieces *The Hunchback of Notre Dame* and the French national novel *Les Misérables*. The stream of consciousness of Proust's *Remembrance of Things Past* and the absurdist theatre of Samuel Beckett and Eugene Ionesco (*Rhinoceros*) attest to the groundbreaking genius of the French writers.

French literature of the twentieth century is defined by the existentialism of Jean-Paul Sartre (*No Exit*, *The Flies*, *Nausea*), Andre Malraux (*The Fall*), and Albert Camus (*The Stranger*, *The Plague*), the recipient of the 1957 Nobel Prize for literature. Feminist writings include those of Sidonie-Gabrielle Colette, known for her short stories and novels, as well as Simone de Beauvoir.

Spain

Spain's great writers include Miguel de Cervantes (*Don Quixote*) and Juan Ramon Jimenez. The anonymous national epic *El Cid* has been translated into many languages.

Italy

Italy's greatest writers include Virgil, who wrote the great epic *The Aeneid*; Giovanni Boccaccio (*The Decameron*); and Dante Alighieri (the *Divine Comedy*).

Ancient Greece

Greece will always be foremost in literary assessments because of Homer's epics, *The Iliad* and *The Odyssey*. No one except Shakespeare is more often cited. Add to these the works of Plato and Aristotle for philosophy, the dramatists Aeschylus, Euripides, and Sophocles for tragedy, and Aristophanes for comedy and it is clear that Greece is the cradle not only of democracy but also of literature.

Far East

The classical Age of Japanese literary achievement includes the father Kiyotsugu Kanami and the son Motokkiyo Zeami who developed the theatrical experience known as Noh drama to its highest aesthetic degree. The son is said to have authored over 200 plays, of which 100 still are extant.

Katai Tayama (*The Quilt*) is touted as the father of the genre known as the Japanese confessional novel. His work is considered naturalism, and is definitely not for the squeamish.

The "slice of life" psychological writings of Ryunosuke Akutagawa gained him acclaim in the Western world. His short stories, especially "Rashamon" and "In a Grove," are greatly praised for style as well as content.

China, too, has given to the literary world. Li Po, the T'ang dynasty poet from the Chinese Golden Age, revealed his interest in folklore by preserving the folk songs and mythology of China. Po further allows his reader to enter into the Chinese philosophy of Taoism and to know this feeling against expansionism during the T'ang dynastic rule. During the T'ang dynasty, which was one of great diversity in the arts, the Chinese version of the short story was created with the help of Jiang Fang. His themes often express love between a man and a woman.

Asia has many modern writers whose works are being translated for Western readers. India's Krishan Chandar has authored more than 300 stories. Rabindranath Tagore won the Nobel Prize for literature in 1913 (*Song Offerings*). Narayan, India's most famous writer (*The Guide*) is highly interested in mythology and legends of India. Santha Rama

Rau's work, *Gifts of Passage*, is her true story of life in a British school where she tries to preserve her Indian culture and traditional home.

Revered as Japan's most famous female author, Fumiko Hayashi (*Drifting Clouds*) had written more than 270 literary works at the time of her death.

In 1968 the Nobel Prize for literature was awarded to Yasunari Kawabata (*The Sound of the Mountain*, *The Snow Country*, considered to be his masterpieces). His *Palm-of-the-Hand Stories* take the essentials of Haiku poetry and transform them into the short story genre.

Modern feminist and political concerns are written eloquently by Ting Ling, who used the pseudonym Chiang Ping-Chih. Her stories reflect her concerns about social injustice and her commitment to the women's movement.

North America

Literature from the United States is discussed at length at the beginning of this skill.

North American literature is divided among the United States, Canada, and Mexico. Canadian writers of note include feminist Margaret Atwood (*The Handmaid's Tale*); Alice Munro, a remarkable short story writer; and W. P. Kinsella, another short story writer whose two major subjects are Native Americans and baseball. Mexican writers include 1990 Nobel Prize winning poet Octavio Paz (*The Labyrinth of Solitude*) and feminist Rosarian Castellanos (*The Nine Guardians*).

Africa

African literary greats include South Africans Nadine Gordimer (winner of the Nobel Prize for literature) and Peter Abrahams (*Tell Freedom: Memories of Africa*, an autobiography of life in Johannesburg). Chinua Achebe (*Things Fall Apart*) and the poet Wole Soyinka hail from Nigeria. Mark Mathabane's autobiography *Kaffir Boy* is about growing up in South Africa. Egyptian writer Naguib Mahfouz and British writer Doris Lessing, who lived in Zimbabwe, write about race relations in their respective countries. Because of her radical politics, Lessing was banned from her homeland and South Africa, as was Alan Paton, whose seemingly simple story, *Cry, the Beloved Country*, brought the plight of black South Africans under apartheid to the rest of the world.

Central America/Caribbean

The Caribbean and Central America encompass a vast area and cultures that reflect oppression and colonialism by England, Spain, Portugal, France, and the Netherlands. Caribbean writers include Samuel Selvon of Trinidad and Armado Valladres of Cuba. Central American authors include dramatist Carlos Solorzano from Guatemala, whose plays include *Dona Beatriz, The Hapless, The Magician,* and *The Hands of God*.

South America

Chilean Gabriela Mistral was the first Latin American writer to win the Nobel Prize for literature. She is best known for her collections of poetry, including *Desolation*. Chile was also home to Pablo Neruda, who in 1971 also won the Nobel Prize for literature for his poetry. His 29 volumes of poetry have been translated into more than 60 languages, attesting to his universal appeal. *Twenty Love Poems* and *Song of Despair* are justly famous. Isabel Allende is carrying on the Chilean literary standards with her acclaimed novel *The House of the Spirits*. Argentinian Jorge Luis Borges is considered by many literary critics to be the most important writer of his century from South America. His collection of short stories, *Ficciones*, brought him universal recognition.

Also from Argentina, Silvina Ocampo, a collaborator with Borges on a collection of poetry, is famed for her poetry and short story collections, which include *The Fury* and *The Days of the Night*.

Noncontinental Europe

Horacio Quiroga represents Uruguay, and Brazil has Joao Guimaraes Rosa, whose novel, *The Devil to Pay*, is considered first-rate world literature.

Slavic nations

Austrian writer Franz Kafka (*The Metamorphosis, The Trial,* and *The Castle*) is considered by many to be the literary voice of the first half of the twentieth century. Representing the Czech Republic is the poet Vaclav Havel. Slovakia has dramatist Karel Capek (*R.U.R.*), and Romania is represented by Elie Wiesel (*Night*), a Nobel Prize winner.

Genres of World Literature

World folk epics are poems (or sometimes prose works) that are an integral part of the worldview of a people. In many cases, they were originally oral texts that were eventually written by a single author or several.

Some examples of world folk epics:

- *Soundiata,* an African epic
- *Tunkashila,* a Native American epic
- *Gilgamesh,* the oldest known epic, from Mesopotamia
- *Aeneid,* a Roman epic
- *Moby–Dick,* which some consider an American folk epic.

A **national myth** is an inspiring narrative or anecdote about a nation's past. These often overdramatize true events, omit important historical details, or add details for which there is no evidence. It can be a fictional story that no one takes to be true, such as

Paul Bunyan, which was created by French Canadians during the Papineau Rebellion of 1837, when they revolted against the young English Queen. In older nations, national myths may be spiritual and refer to the nation's founding by God or gods or other supernatural beings.

Some national myths:

- The legend of King Arthur in Great Britain
- Sir Francis Drake in England
- The Pilgrims and the Mayflower in the United States
- Pocahontas, who is said to have saved the life of John Smith from her savage father, Powhatan
- The legendary ride of Paul Revere
- The last words of Nathan Hale
- The person of George Washington and apocryphal tales about him, such as his cutting down a cherry tree with a hatchet and then facing up to the truth: "I cannot tell a lie."

D. **Demonstrates knowledge of a substantial body of classic and contemporary American literature**

See also Competency 6.C

Native American Literature

The foundation of Native American writing is found in storytelling, oratory, autobiographical and historical accounts of tribal village life, reverence for the environment, and the postulation that the Earth with all of its beauty was given in trust, to be cared for and passed on to future generations.

Early Native American literature

Barland, Hal. *When the Legends Die*
Barrett, S. M., ed. *Geronimo: His Own Story* (Apache)
Eastman, C. & Eastman E. *Wigwam Evenings: Sioux Folktales Retold*
Riggs, L. *Cherokee Night* (drama)

Twentieth-century Native American literature

Deloria, V. *Custer Died for your Sins* (Sioux)
Dorris, M. *The Broken Cord: A Family's Ongoing Struggle with Fetal Alcohol Syndrome*
Hogan, L. *Mean Spirited* (Chickasaw)
Taylor, C. F. *Native American Myths and Legends*

African American Literature

Pre–Civil War African American literature

Stowe, Harriet Beecher. *Uncle Tom's Cabin*
Wheatley, Phyllis. *Memoirs and Poems*

Post-Civil War and Reconstruction African American literature

Armstrong, William. *Sounder*
Gaines, Ernest. *The Autobiography of Miss Jane Pittman*

Twentieth-century African American literature

Angelou, Maya. *I Know Why the Caged Bird Sings*
Baldwin, James. *Go Tell It on the Mountain*
Bonham, Frank. *Durango Street*
Childress, Alice. *A Hero Ain't Nothin' But a Sandwich*
Fast, Howard. *Freedom Ride*
Haley, Alex. *Roots*
Hansberry, Lorraine. *A Raisin in the Sun*
Haskins, James. *Black Music in America: A History Through Its People*
Hughes, Langston. "I, Too, Sing America"
Wright, Richard. *White Man Listen!* and *Native Son*

Latino Literature

Latino literature is a growing body of American literature. Latino authors celebrate their cultural heritage, share their people's struggle for recognition, independence, and survival, and express their hopes for the future.

Latino/Latina writers include the following:

De Cervantes, Lora (Chicana). *Starfish*
Cisneros, Sandra (Hispanic). *House on Mango Street* and other short story collections
Marquez, Gabriel Garcia (Colombian). *A Hundred Years of Solitude*
Nunoz, A. Lopez (Spanish). *Programas Para Dias Especiales*
Neruda, Pablo (Chile). Nobel Prize winner for his collections of poetry
Silko, Leslie Marmon (Mexican). *The Time We Climbed Snake Mountain*
Soto, Gary (Mexican). *The Tales of Sunlight*

Female Writers and Feminist Literature

Edith Wharton's *Ethan Frome* is a heartbreaking tale of lack of communication, lack of funds, the unrelenting cold of the Massachusetts winter, and a toboggan ride that gnarls Ethan and Mattie just like the old tree which they smash into. The *Age of Innocence*, in contrast to *Ethan Frome*, is set in the upper echelons of fin-de-siècle New York and explores marriage without stifling social protocols.

Willa Cather's work moves the reader to the prairies of Nebraska and the harsh eking out of existence by the immigrant families who chose to stay there and farm. Her most acclaimed works include *My Antonia* and *Death Comes for the Archbishop*.

Kate Chopin's regionalism and local color takes her readers to the upper-crust Creole society of New Orleans and resort isles off the Louisiana coast. "The Story of an Hour" is lauded as one of the greatest of all short stories. Her feminist liberation novel, *The Awakening*, is still hotly debated.

Eudora Welty's regionalism and dialect shine in her short stories of rural Mississippi, especially in "The Worn Path."

Twentieth-century African American female writers who explore the world of feminist/gender issues as well as class prohibitions are Alice Walker (*The Color Purple*), Zora Neale Hurston (*Their Eyes Were Watching God*), and Toni Morrison (*Beloved*, *Jazz*, and *Song of Solomon*).

Well-known examples of female writers and feminist literature include the following:

    Alcott, Louisa May. *Little Women*
    Friedan, Betty. *The Feminine Mystique*
    Bronte, Charlotte. *Jane Eyre*
    Chopin, Kate. *The Awakening*
    Hurston, Zora Neale. *Their Eyes Were Watching God*
    Janeway, Elizabeth. *Woman's World, Woman's Place: A Study in Social Mythology*
    Rich, Adrienne. *Motherhood as Experience* and *Diving into the Wreck* (poetry)
    Woolf, Virginia. *A Room of One's Own*

Periods of American Literature

See also Competency 6.C

Native American works from various tribes

These were originally part of a vast oral tradition that spanned most of continental America from as far back as before the fifteenth century.

Characteristics of Native American literature include:
- Reverence for and awe of nature
- The interconnectedness of the elements in the life cycle

Themes of Native American literature include:
- The hardiness of the body and soul
- Remorse for the destruction of their way of life
- The genocide of many tribes by the encroaching settlement and Manifest Destiny policies of the U.S. government

The Colonial Period in New England and the South

Stylistically, early colonists' writings were neoclassical, emphasizing order, balance, clarity, and reason. Schooled in England, their writing and speaking was still decidedly British even as their thinking became entirely American.

Early American literature reveals the lives and experiences of the New England expatriates who left England to find religious freedom.

The Revolutionary Period contains nonfiction genres: essay, pamphlet, speech, famous document, and epistle.

Thomas Paine's pamphlet, *Common Sense*, even though written by a recently transplanted Englishman, spoke to the American patriots dealing with the issues in the cause of freedom.

Other influential writings from this period are Benjamin Franklin's essays from *Poor Richard's Almanac* and his satires such as "How to Reduce a Great Empire to a Small One" and "A Letter to Madame Gout."

The Romantic Period

Early American folktales and the emergence of a distinctly American writing, in contrast to English forms, appear during the Romantic Period of American literature.

Washington Irving's characters, such as Ichabod Crane and Rip Van Winkle, created a uniquely American folklore devoid of English influences. The characters are indelibly marked as American by their environment and the superstitions of New Englanders. The early American writings of James Fenimore Cooper, such as his Leatherstocking Tales with their stirring accounts of the French and Indian Wars, the futile British defense of Fort William Henry, and the brutalities of this time allow readers a window into the uniquely American world. Natty Bumppo, Chingachgook, Uncas, and Magua are unforgettable characters that reflect the American spirit in thought and action.

The poetry of Fireside Poets—James Russell Lowell, Oliver Wendell Holmes, Henry Wadsworth Longfellow, and John Greenleaf Whittier—was recited by American families and read in the long New England winters. In "The Courtin'," Lowell used Yankee dialect to tell a narrative. Spellbinding epics by Longfellow such as *Hiawatha*, *The Courtship of Miles Standish*, and *Evangeline* told of adversity, sorrow, and ultimate happiness in a uniquely American character. "Snowbound" by Whittier relates the story of a captive family isolated by a blizzard, stressing family closeness. Holmes' "The Chambered Nautilus" and other poems put American poetry on a firm footing with British literature of the time.

The transition between Romanticism and Realism

During this period such legendary figures as Paul Bunyan and Pecos Bill rose from the oral tradition. Anonymous storytellers around campfires told tales of a huge lumberman and his giant blue ox, Babe, whose adventures were explanations of natural phenomena (such as footprints filled with rainwater becoming the Great Lakes). Similarly, the whirling-dervish speed of Pecos Bill explained the tornadoes of the Southwest. Like earlier peoples finding reasons for the happenings in their lives, these American pioneer storytellers created a mythology appropriate to the vast reaches of the unsettled frontier.

The Realistic Period

The late nineteenth century saw a reaction against the tendency of romantic writers to look at the world through rose-colored glasses. Writers like Frank Norris (*The Pit*) and Upton Sinclair (*The Jungle*) used their novels to decry conditions for workers in slaughterhouses and wheat mills. In *The Red Badge of Courage*, Stephen Crane wrote of the daily sufferings of the common soldier in the Civil War. Realistic writers wrote of common, ordinary people and events using detail that revealed the harsh realities of life. They broached taboos by creating protagonists whose environments often destroyed them, in contrast to Romantic writers, whose protagonists' indomitable wills helped them rise above adversity. Crane's *Maggie: A Girl of the Streets* deals with a young woman forced into prostitution to survive. In "The Occurrence at Owl Creek Bridge," Ambrose Bierce relates the hanging of a Confederate soldier.

Short stories, like Bret Harte's "The Outcasts of Poker Flat" and Jack London's "To Build a Fire," deal with unfortunate people whose luck in life has run out. Many writers, sub classified as naturalists, believed that people are subject to a fate over which they have no control.

The Modern Era

Twentieth-century American writing can be classified into three basic genres:

- Drama
- Fiction
- Poetry

Prominent American Fiction Writers

Herman Melville was born in 1819 and grew up in upper-class New York neighborhoods. His mother was a strict Calvinist Presbyterian and had strong views regarding proper behavior. Melville tended to be a rebellious sort and to some extent his conflicts regarding his mother's viewpoints were never resolved.

When Melville was 11 years old, his father's business failed, and he died shortly afterward. Melville tried working in business for a while but soon decided he wanted to go to sea.

Working on ships and traveling, he began to write nonfiction pieces about his experiences. In July 1851, he wrote his most famous work, *Moby–Dick*. Before he died, he wrote poems and another well-known novella, *Billy Budd*, which was not published until 1924. Just as he began to write *Moby–Dick*, he became friends with Nathaniel Hawthorne, who happened to be his neighbor. Hawthorne's works and friendship became an important influence on Melville's writing.

In *Moby–Dick*, the style is indicative of the reportorial writing of the earlier period; however, it is far more than that. It is seen as a great American epic, even though it is not poetry. It was not successful while Melville was alive. Its success came much later.

Some themes in Melville's writing:

- Man in conflict with the natural world
- Religion and God's role in the universe
- Good and evil
- Cause and effect
- Duty
- Conscience

Richard Wright was the grandson of slaves and grew up in a time when the lives of African Americans tended to be grim. The experience of life lived so close to those who had recently risen from bondage permeates his writing.

His writing went through many changes just as his response to the reality of life as an African American in a white-dominated world went through many changes. Therefore, to understand his work, it's critical to know the date of the writing. He was influenced early by Maxim Gorky, some of whose life experiences were similar to those of Wright. Later, Wright was heavily influenced by Dostoevsky, and that writer's themes can be identified in his work from this period.

Survival for many African Americans and African American communities required conformity to whatever white people demanded, and Wright rejected that. He felt profoundly alienated. He became a proletarian revolutionary artist in the earliest years of his career. The American Communist Party considered him its most illustrious recruit because he wrote to the newly established literary standards of proletarian realism. He rejected the "conspicuous ornamentation" of institutions imposed by segregation such as the Harlem Renaissance. At the same time, he felt that consciousness must draw its strength from the lore of a great people, his own.

Wright sought, in the early years of the twentieth century, to integrate the progressive aspects of the folk culture of African Americans into a collective myth that would promote a revolutionary approach to reality.

Wright left the Communist Party in 1944, largely as a result of his own evolution. *Black Boy*, an autobiographical account of his childhood and young manhood, appeared in 1945. He settled in Paris as a permanent expatriate shortly after its publication. His first stories—*Uncle Tom's Children*—are a reconception of African American spirituals and Christianity, in which the hero chooses to risk martyrdom in progressively elevated stages of class consciousness.

Some themes in Wright's writing:

- Environment of the South as too small to nourish human beings, especially African Americans
- Rejection of black militancy
- Violent, battered childhood and victorious adulthood
- Suffocation of instinct and stifling of potential
- Mature reminiscences of a battered childhood
- African American mother's protective nature and the trauma of an absent or impotent father
- Each is responsible for everyone and everything (in his later works)

Wright's technique and style are not as important as the impact his ideas and attitudes have had on American life. He set out to portray African Americans to readers in such a way that the myth of the uncomplaining, comic, obsequious African American might be replaced.

Willa Cather grew up on the western plains in Nebraska, and much of her best fiction focuses on the pioneering period in that part of the country. She was born in Virginia in 1873 on her family's farm, but in 1884 the family moved to Nebraska where other relatives had settled. Much of the lore that is the basis of her stories came from her visits with immigrant farm women around Red Cloud, where the family eventually made its home.

When she was 16, she enrolled at the University of Nebraska in Lincoln, where she received praise for an essay in her English class and began to support herself as a journalist. She moved to Pittsburgh and was working as a writer and editor when she decided that she wanted to teach school and develop her writing career. On a trip back to Nebraska, she witnessed a wheat harvest, which triggered her motive for writing about the pioneer period of American history.

Some themes in Cather's writing:

- The American Dream
- Prejudice
- Coming of age
- Nostalgia

Maxine Hong Kingston's parents were Chinese immigrants who lived in Stockton, California. Her fiction is highly autobiographical, and she weaves Chinese myths and fictionalized history with the aim of exploring the conflicts between cultures faced by Chinese Americans. Her writing exposes the ordeals of the Chinese immigrants who were exploited by American companies, particularly railroad and agriculture industries. She also explores relationships within Chinese families, particularly between parents who were born in China and children who were born in America. In a 1980 *New York Times Book Review* interview, she said, "What I am doing in this new book [*China Men*] is churning America."

Some themes in Kingston's writing:

- Discovery
- The American Dream
- Male/female roles
- Metamorphosis
- Enforced muteness
- Vocal expression
- Family

Prominent American Poets

Walt Whitman's poetry was more often than not inspired by the Civil War. He is America's greatest romantic poet, and many of his poems are related to and come directly from the conflict between the northern and southern states. This is not to say that the war was his only influence; he wrote many poems on topics that are not directly related to it. His major work, *Leaves of Grass,* was revised nine times, the last in 1892 shortly before he died. He used sophisticated linguistic devices much ahead of his time. Even though he dealt with a vast, panoramic vision, his style has a personal and immediate effect on the reader.

When Whitman was born in 1819 on Long Island in New York, it was a time of great patriotism for the new nation; however, he experienced the conflict that presented a serious threat to its survival—the Civil War—and it's no wonder that this conflict became the subject matter for most of his creative output. His father was a carpenter and then a farmer. Whitman was the second-born of eight, the first son. He had six years of public education before he went to work for Brooklyn lawyers and began to educate himself in the library.

Whitman began his writing career with newspaper articles and eventually wrote short stories that were published in newspapers. His unconventional techniques were his own creation. In *Leaves of Grass* he intended to speak for all Americans.

Whitman worked as a volunteer in hospitals to help care for soldiers, and he was deeply affected by the horrors of war that he saw firsthand. His poetry was considered to be indecent by some, and he was both praised and vilified during his lifetime. He died in 1892 of tuberculosis.

Some themes in Whitman's writing:

- Imagination versus scientific process
- Individualism

Emily Dickinson has been called the "myth of Amherst" because so little is known of her. She was born in 1830, the second child of Edward and Emily Dickinson. Her family was prominent in Massachusetts and played a major role in the founding of Amherst College. Her father's stern, puritanical control of his family played a pivotal role in the poetry that his daughter eventually wrote. Although he was severe and controlling, he saw that his daughters got a good education. Emily attended Amherst Academy and then Mount Holyoke Female Seminary. She obtained a copy of Emerson's poems in 1850 and began to develop her own beliefs regarding religion and the severe God that her father represented.

Only a few of her poems were published during her lifetime, and she was unknown until after her death. After she withdrew from school, she became more and more reclusive and after the death of her father in 1874, she never left her home. She died of Bright's disease in 1886. Her sister Lavinia found roughly 2,000 poems on small pieces of paper, which were published in several editions. The first full three-volume edition was released in 1955. Dickinson has come to be known for her superb use of concrete language and imagery to express and evoke abstract issues.

Some themes in Dickinson's writing:

- Sanity/insanity
- Doubt
- Death
- Individuality
- Defiance
- Feminism

Gwendolyn Brooks was the first African American to receive a Pulitzer Prize for poetry with her acute images of African Americans in the cities of America. Born in 1917 to a schoolteacher and a janitor, she grew up in Chicago. She was named poet laureate of Illinois in 1978 and was the first female African American honorary fellow of the Modern Language Association. Her family was close-knit, and she tended to spend her time reading when she was a child. She began writing poems when she was very young. She has also had a successful teaching career at several universities including City University of New York, where she was Distinguished Professor. Brooks was writing about the experience of being African American long before it became mainstream. She underwent an evolution in subject matter and thinking about being African American as a result of the civil rights movement. She died of cancer in 2000 at age 83.

Some themes in Brooks' writing:

- Poverty and racism
- Self-respect
- Heritage
- Community
- Family
- African American unity
- The basic humanness in everyone
- African American solidarity
- Pride

Leslie Marmon Silko is a Laguna Native American of mixed ancestry that includes Cherokee, German, English, Mexican, and Pueblo. There were several remarkable women in her life, grandmothers and aunts, who taught her the traditions and stories of the Pueblo. At the same time, her father's role in his tribe also made her aware of the abuses her people had experienced at the hands of the government. The major issue was the land that had been stolen from her people. She believed that she could change things by writing about them.

Some themes in Silko's writing:

- Evil
- Reciprocity
- Individual/community
- Native American traditions
- Native American religion
- Mixed breeds
- Scapegoats
- Racism
- Prejudice

Local color is defined as presenting the peculiarities of a particular locality and its inhabitants. This genre began to be seen primarily after the Civil War, although there were certainly precursors, such as Washington Irving and his depiction of life in the Catskill Mountains of New York. However, the local colorist movement is generally considered to have begun in 1865, when humor began to permeate the writing of those who were focusing on a particular region of the country. Samuel L. Clemens (Mark Twain) is best known for his humorous works about the Southwest such as *The Notorious Jumping Frog of Calaveras County*. The country had just emerged from its "long night of the soul," a time when death, despair, and disaster had preoccupied the nation for almost five years. It's no wonder that artists sought to relieve the grief and pain and lift spirits, nor is it surprising that their efforts brought such a strong response. Mark Twain is generally considered to be not only one of America's funniest writers but also one who wrote great and enduring fiction.

Other examples of local colorists who used many of the same devices are Harriet Beecher Stowe, Bret Harte, George Washington Cable, Joel Chandler Harris, and Sarah Orne Jewett.

Slavery

The best known of the early writers who used fiction as a political statement about slavery is Harriet Beecher Stowe, author of *Uncle Tom's Cabin.* This was her first novel, and it was published first as a serial in 1851 and then as a book in 1852. It brought an angry reaction from people living in the South. This antislavery book infuriated Southerners. Stowe was angered by the 1850 Fugitive Slave Act that made it legal to indict those who assisted runaway slaves. It also took away rights not only of runaways but also of freed slaves. Stowe intended to generate a protest of the law and slavery. *Uncle Tom's Cabin* was the first effort to present the lives of slaves from their standpoint.

The novel is about three slaves, Tom, Eliza, and George, who are together in Kentucky. Eliza and George are married to each other but have different masters. They successfully escape with their little boy, but Tom does not, and is caught. Although he has a wife and children, he is sold, ending up finally with the monstrous Simon Legree, where he dies at last. Stowe cleverly used depictions of motherhood and Christianity to stir her readers. When President Lincoln finally met her, he told her it was her book that started the war.

Many writers used the printed word to protest slavery. Some of them include:

- Frederick Douglass
- William Lloyd Garrison
- Benjamin Lay, a Quaker
- Connecticut theologian Jonathan Edwards
- Susan B. Anthony

Civil Rights

Many of the abolitionists were also early crusaders for civil rights. The 1960s civil rights movement focused attention on the plight of African Americans who had been freed from slavery during the Civil War but continued to face prejudice, violence, and a lack of opportunities and violence. David Halberstam, who had been a reporter in Nashville at the time of the sit-ins by eight young African American college students that initiated the revolution, wrote *The Children*, published in 1998 by Random House, for the purpose of reminding Americans of these students' courage, suffering, and achievements. Congressman John Lewis, Fifth District, Georgia, was one of those eight young men who went on to a life of public service. Halberstam records that when older African American ministers tried to persuade these young people not to pursue their protest, John Lewis responded: "If not us, then who? If not now, then when?"

Some examples of protest literature:

- James Baldwin, *Blues for Mister Charlie*
- Martin Luther King, Jr., *Where Do We Go from Here?*
- Langston Hughes, *Fight for Freedom: The Story of the NAACP*
- Eldridge Cleaver, *Soul on Ice*
- Malcolm X, *The Autobiography of Malcolm X*
- Stokely Carmichael and Charles V. Hamilton, *Black Power*
- Leroi Jones, *Home*

Vietnam

An America that was already divided over the civil rights movement faced even greater divisions over the war in Vietnam. Those who were in favor of the war and who opposed withdrawal saw it as the major front in the war against communism. Those who opposed the war and who favored withdrawal of the troops believed that it would not serve to defeat communism and was a quagmire.

Catch-22 by Joseph Heller was a popular antiwar novel that became a successful movie of the time. *Authors Take Sides on Vietnam*, edited by Cecil Woolf and John Bagguley, is a collection of essays by 168 well-known authors throughout the world. *Where Is Vietnam?*, edited by Walter Lowenfels, consists of 92 poems about the war.

Many writers were publishing works for and against the war, but the genre that had the most impact was rock music. Bob Dylan is an example of the musicians of the time. His music represented the hippie aesthetic and reflected the political and social issues of the time.

Immigration

Immigration has been a popular topic for literature since the time of the Louisiana Purchase in 1804. The recent *Undaunted Courage* by Stephen E. Ambrose is ostensibly the autobiography of Meriwether Lewis but is actually a recounting of the Lewis and Clark expedition. Presented as a scientific expedition by President Jefferson, the expedition was actually intended to provide maps and information for the opening up of the West. A well-known novel of the settling of the west by immigrants from other countries is *Giants in the Earth* by Ole Edvart Rolvaag, himself a descendant of immigrants.

John Steinbeck's novels *Cannery Row* and *Tortilla Flats* glorify the lives of Mexican migrants in California. Amy Tan's *The Joy Luck Club* deals with the problems faced by Chinese immigrants in the late twentieth century.

Leon Uris' *Exodus* deals with the social history that led to the founding of the modern state of Israel. It was published in 1958, only a short time after the Holocaust. It also deals with attempts of concentration camp survivors to get to the land that has become the new Israel. In many ways, it is the quintessential work on the causes and effects of immigration.

E. **Demonstrates knowledge of a substantial body of classic and contemporary British literature**

See also Competency 6.C

The reign of Elizabeth I ushered in a renaissance that led to the end of the medieval age. It was a very fertile literary period. The exploration of the New World expanded the vision of all levels of the social order from royalty to peasant, and the rejection of Catholicism by many in favor of a new Christianity of their own opened up whole new vistas to thought and daily life. The manufacture of cloth had increased, driving many people from the countryside into the cities, and the population of London exploded, creating a metropolitan business center. Printing had been brought to England by William Caxton in the 1470s, and literacy increased from 30 percent in the fifteenth century to over 60 percent by 1530. These seem dramatic changes, and they were, but they occurred gradually.

The Italian renaissance had a great influence on the renaissance in England, and early in the sixteenth century most written works were in Latin. It was assumed that learned people must express their thoughts in that language. However, there began to emerge a determination that vernacular English was valuable in writing, and it began to be defended. Elizabeth's tutor, Roger Ascham, for example, wrote in English.

In 1517, Martin Luther's Ninety-Five Theses, which brought on the Reformation—an attempt to return to pure Christianity—initiated the breakup of western Christendom and eventually the secularization of society and the establishment of the king or queen as the head of this new church. The Reformation also brought about a new feeling that being religious was also being patriotic; it promoted nationalism.

The ascension of Elizabeth to the throne followed a very turbulent period regarding succession, and she ruled for 45 peaceful years, which allowed arts and literature to flourish. Although she herself was headstrong and difficult, she had very shrewd political instincts and entrusted power to solid, talented people, most particularly Cecil, her secretary, and Walsingham, whom she put in charge of foreign policy. She identified with her country as no previous ruler had, and that in itself brought on a period of intense nationalism. She was a symbol of Englishness. The defeat of the Spanish Armada in 1588 was the direct result of the strong support she had from her own nation.

Drama was the principal form of literature in this age. Religious plays had been a part of the life of England for a long time, particularly the courtly life. But in the Elizabethan age, they became more secular and were created primarily for courtly entertainment. By the 1560s, Latin drama, particularly the tragedies of Seneca and the comedies of Plautus and Terence began to wield an influence in England. Courtyards of inns became favorite places for the presentation of plays, but in 1576 the Earl of Leicester's Men, a theatrical company, constructed their own building outside the city and called it The Theatre. Other theatres followed. Each had its own repertory company and performances were not only for profit but also for the queen and her court. It is said that

Shakespeare wrote *The Merry Wives of Windsor* at the specific command of the queen, who liked Falstaff and wanted to see him in love. It was also for the courtly audience that poetry was introduced into drama.

Shakespeare and Marlowe dominated the 1580s and 1590s; at the turn of the century, only a few years before Elizabeth's death, Ben Jonson wrote his series of satirical comedies.

Court favor was notoriously precarious and depended on the whims of the queen and others. Much of the satire of the period reflects the disappointment of writers like Edmund Spenser and John Lyly and the superficiality and treachery of the court atmosphere. "A thousand hopes, but all nothing," wrote Lyly, "a hundred promises, but yet nothing."

Not all literature was dictated by the court. The middle classes developed their own style. Thomas Heywood and Thomas Deloney catered to bourgeois tastes.

The two universities, Oxford and Cambridge, were also sources for the production of literature. The primary aim of the colleges was to develop ministers, since there was a shortage brought on by the break with the Catholic Church. However, most university men couldn't make livings as ministers or academics, so they wrote as a way of earning income. Nashe, Marlowe, Robert Greene, and George Peele all reveal in their writings how difficult this path was. Remuneration came mostly from patrons. Greene had 16 different patrons from 17 books, whereas Shakespeare had a satisfactory relationship with the Earl of Southampton and didn't need to seek other support. Publishers would also sometimes pay for a manuscript, which they would then own. Unfortunately, if the manuscript did not pass muster with all who could condemn it—the court, the religious leaders, prominent citizens—it was the author who was on the hot seat. Very few became as comfortable as Shakespeare did. His success came not only in writing, however, but also from his business acumen.

Writing was seen more as a craft than as an art in this period. There was no great conflict between art and nature, and there was little distinction between literature, sports of the field, or the arts of the kitchen.

Balance and control were important in the England of this day, and this is reflected in writing and in poetry in particular. The sestina, a form in which the last words of each line in the first stanza are repeated in a different order in each of the following stanzas, became very popular. Verse forms ranged from the extremely simple four-line ballad stanza to the rather complicated form of the sonnet to the elaborate and beautiful 18-line stanza of Spenser's *Epithalamion*. Sonnets were called *quatorzains*. The term *sonnet* was used loosely for any short poem. Quatorzains are 14-line poems in iambic pentameter with elaborate rhyme schemes. However, Chaucer's seven-line rhyme royal stanza also survived in the sixteenth century. Shakespeare used it in *The Rape of Lucrece*, for example. An innovation was Spenser's nine-line stanza, called the Spenserian stanza, as used in *The Faerie Queene*.

As for themes, some of the darkness of the previous period can still be seen in some Elizabethan literature, such as in Shakespeare's *Richard II*. At the same time, a spirit of joy, gaiety, innocence, and lightheartedness can be seen in much of the most popular literature and pastoral themes became popular. The theme of the burning desire for conquest and achievement was also significant in Elizabethan thought.

Some important writers of the Elizabethan age

Sir Thomas More (1478–1535)
Sir Thomas Wyatt the Elder (1503–1542)
Sir Philip Sydney (1554–1586)
Edmund Spenser (1552–1599)
Sir Walter Raleigh (1552–1618)
John Lyly (1554–1606)
George Peele (1556–1596)
Christopher Marlowe (1564–1593)
William Shakespeare (1564–1616)
Sir Francis Bacon (1561 – 1626)

The Industrial Revolution in England began with the development of the steam engine. However, this was only one component of the major technological, socioeconomic, and cultural innovations of the early nineteenth century that began in Britain and spread throughout the world. An economy based on manual labor was replaced by one dominated by industry and the manufacture of machinery. The textile industry also underwent very rapid growth and change. Canals were built, roads were improved, and railways were constructed.

Steam power (fueled primarily by coal) and the machinery it powered (primarily in the manufacture of textiles) drove the remarkable amplification of production capacity. All-metal machine tools were introduced by 1820, making it possible to produce more machines.

The dates of the Industrial Revolution vary according to how it is viewed. Some say that it began in the 1780s and wasn't fully underway until the 1830s or 1840s. Others maintain that the beginning was earlier, about 1760, and that it began to manifest visible changes by 1830. The effects spread in Western Europe and North America throughout the nineteenth century, eventually affecting all major countries of the world. The impact on society has been compared to the period when agriculture began to develop and the nomadic lifestyle was abandoned.

The first Industrial Revolution was followed immediately by the Second Industrial Revolution around 1850, when the progress in technology and world economy gained momentum with the introduction of steam-powered ships and railways and eventually the internal combustion engine and electrical power generation.

The most noticeable social effect was the development of a middle class of industrialists and businessmen and a decline in the landed class of nobility and gentry. While working people had more opportunities for employment in the new mills and factories, working conditions were often less than desirable. Exploiting children for labor wasn't new—it had always existed—but it was more apparent and perhaps more egregious as the need for cheap labor increased. In England, laws regarding employment of children began to be developed in 1833. Another effect of industrialization was the enormous shift from hand-produced goods to machine-produced ones and the loss of jobs among weavers and others, which resulted in violence against the factories and machinery beginning in about 1811.

Eventually, the British government took measures to protect industry. Another effect of the Industrial Revolution was the organization of labor. Because laborers were now working together in factories, mines, and mills, they were better able to organize to gain advantages. Conditions were bad enough in these workplaces that the energy to bring about change was significant, and eventually trade unions emerged. Laborers began to use strikes to get what they wanted. The strikes were often violent, and while the managers usually gave in to most of the demands made by strikers, the animosity between management and labor was pandemic.

The mass migration of rural families into urban areas also resulted in poor living conditions, long work hours, extensive use of children for labor, and pollution of the air and water.

Another effect of industrialization of society was the separation of husband and wife. During this period, the mother usually stayed at home and looked after the house and family and the father usually went off to work, a very different configuration from an agriculture-based economy in which the entire family was usually involved in making a living. Eventually, gender roles began to be defined by this new configuration of labor.

The application of industrial processes to printing brought about a great expansion in newspaper and popular book publishing. This, in turn, was followed by rapid increases in literacy and eventually in demands for mass political participation.

Romanticism—the literary, intellectual, and artistic movement that occurred along with the Industrial Revolution—was actually a response to the increasing mechanization of society, an artistic hostility to what was taking over the world. Romanticism stressed the importance of nature in art and language in contrast to the monstrous machines and factories. Blake called them the "dark, satanic mills" in his poem "And Did Those Feet in Ancient Time."

Romanticism followed on the heels of the Enlightenment period and was at least in part a reaction to the aristocratic and political norms of the previous period. Romanticism is sometimes called the Counter-Enlightenment. It stressed strong emotion, made individual imagination the critical authority, and overturned previous social conventions.

Nature was important to the Romantics, whose work elevated the achievements of misunderstood heroic individuals and artists who participated in altering society.

Some Romantic writers:

Johann Wolfgang von Goethe
Walter Scott
Ludwig Tieck
E. T. A. Hoffman
William Wordsworth
Samuel Taylor Coleridge
William Blake
Victor Hugo
Alexander Pushkin
Lord Byron
Washington Irving
John Keats
Percy Bysshe Shelley

World War I, also known as the First World War, the Great War, and the War to End All Wars, raged from July 1914 to the final armistice on November 11, 1918. It was a world conflict between the Allied Powers led by Great Britain, France, Russia, and the United States (after 1917) and the Central Powers, led by the German Empire, the Austro-Hungarian Empire, and the Ottoman Empire. It brought down four great empires: the Austo-Hungarian, German, Ottoman, and Russian. It reconfigured European and Middle Eastern maps.

More than nine million soldiers died on the various battlefields and nearly that many more in the participating countries' home fronts as a result of food shortages and genocide committed under the cover of various civil wars and internal conflicts. However, more people died of the worldwide influenza outbreak at the end of the war and shortly after than died in the hostilities. The unsanitary conditions engendered by the war, severe overcrowding in barracks, wartime propaganda interfering with public health warnings, and migration of so many soldiers around the world contributed to causing a pandemic outbreak of influenza.

The experiences of the war led to a sort of collective national trauma for all the participating countries. The optimism of the 1900s was entirely gone, and those who fought in the war became what is known as the Lost Generation because they never fully recovered from their experiences. For the next few years, memorials continued to be erected in thousands of European villages and towns.

Certainly a sense of disillusionment and cynicism became pronounced and nihilism became popular. The world had never before witnessed such devastation, and the depiction in newspapers and on movie screens made the horrors more personal. War has always spawned creative bursts, and this one was no exception. Poetry, stories, and movies proliferated. In fact, it's still a fertile subject for art of all kinds, particularly literature and movies. In 2008, a young director by the name of Paul Gross created, directed, and starred in *Passchendaele* based on the stories told him by his grandfather, who was haunted all his life by his killing of a young German soldier in this War to End All Wars.

Some literature based on World War I:

"The Soldier," poem by Rupert Brooke
Goodbye to All That, autobiography of Robert Graves
"Anthem for Doomed Youth" and "Strange Meeting," poems by Wilfred Owen, published posthumously by Siegfried Sassoon in 1918
"In Flanders Fields," poem by John McCrae
Three Soldiers, novel by John Dos Passos
Journey's End, play by R. C. Sherriff
All Quiet on the Western Front, novel by Erich Maria Remarque
Death of a Hero, novel *by* Richard Aldington
Memoirs of an Infantry Officer, novel by Siegfried Sassoon
Sergeant York, movie directed by Howard Hawks

The dissolution of the British Empire, the most extensive empire in world history and for a time the foremost global power, began in 1867 with its transformation into the modern Commonwealth. Dominion status was granted to the self-governing colonies of Canada in 1867, to Australia in 1902, to New Zealand in 1907, to Newfoundland in 1907, and to the newly created Union of South Africa in 1910. Leaders of the new states joined with British statesmen in periodic Colonial Conferences, the first of which was held in London in 1887.

In 1948, Ireland became a republic, fully independent from the United Kingdom, and withdrew from the Commonwealth. Ireland's constitution claimed the six counties of Northern Ireland as a part of the Republic of Ireland until 1998. The issue over whether Northern Ireland should remain in the United Kingdom or join the Republic of Ireland has divided Northern Ireland's people and led to a long and bloody conflict known as the Troubles.

The rise of anti-colonial nationalist movements in the subject territories and the changing economic situation of the world in the first half of the twentieth century challenged an imperial power now increasingly preoccupied with issues nearer home. The empire's end began with the onset of World War II, when a deal was reached between the British government and the Indian independence movement whereby India would cooperate and remain loyal during the war but after which it would be granted independence. Following India's lead, nearly all of the other colonies would become independent over the next two decades.

In the Caribbean, Africa, Asia, and the Pacific, postwar decolonization was achieved with almost unseemly haste in the face of increasingly powerful nationalist movements, and Britain rarely fought to retain any territory.

Some representative literature:

Heart of Darkness, novel by Joseph Conrad
Passage to India, novel by E. M. Forster
"Gunga Din," poem by Rudyard Kipling
Burmese Days, novel by George Orwell
"Shooting an Elephant," essay by George Orwell

F.   Demonstrates knowledge of a substantial body of classic and contemporary world literature

See Competency 6.C

G.   Demonstrates knowledge of a substantial body of young adult literature

Prior to twentieth-century research on child development and child/adolescent literature's relationship to that development, books for adolescents were primarily didactic. They were designed to be instructive of history, manners, and morals.

Middle Ages

As early as the eleventh century, Anselm, the Archbishop of Canterbury, wrote an encyclopedia designed to instill in children the beliefs and principles of conduct acceptable to adults in medieval society. Early monastic translations of the Bible and other religious writings were written in Latin, for the edification of the upper class. Fifteenth-century hornbooks were designed to teach reading and religious lessons. William Caxton printed English versions of *Aesop's Fables*, Malory's *Le Morte d'Arthur*, and stories from Greek and Roman mythology. Though printed for adults, tales of adventures of Odysseus and the Arthurian knights were also popular with literate adolescents.

Renaissance

The Renaissance saw the introduction of inexpensive chapbooks, small in size and 16 to 64 pages in length. Chapbooks were condensed versions of mythology and fairy tales. Designed for the common people, chapbooks were imperfect grammatically but were immensely popular because of their adventurous contents. Though most of the serious, educated adults frowned on the sometimes vulgar little books, they received praise from Richard Steele of *Tatler* fame for inspiring his grandson's interest in reading and pursuing his other studies.

Meanwhile, the Puritans' three most popular reads were the Bible, John Foxe's *Book of Martyrs*, and John Bunyan's *Pilgrim's Progress*. Though venerating religious martyrs and preaching the moral propriety that was to lead to eternal happiness, the stories of the *Book of Martyrs* were often lurid in their descriptions of the fate of the damned. Not written for children and difficult reading even for adults, *Pilgrim's Progress* was as attractive to adolescents for its adventurous plot as for its moral outcome. In Puritan America, the *New England Primer* set forth the prayers, catechisms, Bible verses, and illustrations meant to instruct children in the Puritan ethic. The seventeenth-century French used fables and fairy tales to entertain adults, but children found them enjoyable as well.

Seventeenth Century

The late seventeenth century brought the first concern with providing literature that specifically targeted the young.

Pierre Perrault's *Fairy Tales*, Jean de la Fontaine's retellings of famous fables, Mme. d'Aulnoy's novels based on old folktales, and Mme. de Beaumont's "Beauty and the Beast" were written to delight as well as instruct young people. In England, publisher John Newbury was the first to publish a series of books for children. These included a translation of Perrault's *Tales of Mother Goose; A Little Pretty Pocket-Book*, "intended for instruction and amusement" but decidedly moralistic and bland in comparison to the previous century's chapbooks; and *The History of Little Goody Two-Shoes*, allegedly written by Oliver Goldsmith for a juvenile audience.

Eighteenth Century

By and large, into the eighteenth century adolescents were finding their reading pleasure in adult books: Daniel Defoe's *Robinson Crusoe*, Jonathan Swift's *Gulliver's Travels*, and Johann Wyss's *Swiss Family Robinson*. More books were being written for children, but the moral didacticism, though less religious, was nevertheless ever present. The short stories of Maria Edgeworth, the four-volume *The History of Sandford and Merton* by Thomas Day, and Martha Farquharson's 26-volume *Elsie Dinsmore* series dealt with pious protagonists who learned restraint, repentance, and rehabilitation from sin. Two bright spots in this period of didacticism were Jean Jacques Rousseau's *Emile* and *The Tales of Shakespeare*, Charles and Mary Lamb's simplified versions of Shakespeare's plays. Rousseau believed that a child's abilities were enhanced by a free, happy life, and the Lambs subscribed to the notion that children were entitled to more entertaining literature in language comprehensible to them.

Nineteenth Century

Child/adolescent literature truly began its rise in nineteenth-century Europe. Hans Christian Andersen's *Fairy Tales* were fanciful adaptations of the somber versions written by the Grimm brothers in the previous century. Andrew Lang's series of colorful fairy books contain the folklores of many nations and are still part of the collections of many modern libraries. Clement Moore's "A Visit from St. Nicholas" is a cheery, nonthreatening child's view of the night before Christmas. The humor of Lewis Carroll's books about Alice's adventures, Edward Lear's poems with caricatures, and Lucretia Nole's stories of the Philadelphia Peterkin family were full of fancy and not a smidgen of morality. Other popular Victorian novels introduced the modern fantasy and science fiction genres: William Makepeace Thackeray's *The Rose and the Ring*, Charles Dickens' *The Magic Fishbone*, and Jules Verne's *Twenty Thousand Leagues Under the Sea*. Adventure to exotic places became a popular topic: Rudyard Kipling's *Jungle Books*, Verne's *Around the World in Eighty Days*, and Robert Louis Stevenson's *Treasure Island* and *Kidnapped*. In 1884, the first English translation of Johanna Spyri's *Heidi* appeared.

North America was also finding its voices for adolescent readers. American Louisa May Alcott's *Little Women* and Canadian L. M. Montgomery's *Anne of Green Gables* ushered in the modern age of realistic fiction. American youth were enjoying the adventures of Tom Sawyer and Huckleberry Finn. For the first time, children were able to read books about real people just like themselves.

Twentieth Century

The literature of the twentieth century is extensive and diverse, and as in previous centuries much influenced by the adults who write, edit, and select books for youth consumption. In the first third of the century, suitable adolescent literature dealt with children from good homes with large families. These books projected an image of a peaceful, rural existence. Though the characters and plots were realistic, the stories maintained focus on topics that were considered emotionally and intellectually proper. Popular at this time were Laura Ingalls Wilder's *Little House on the Prairie* series and Carl Sandburg's biography *Abe Lincoln Grows Up*. English author J. R. R. Tolkien's fantasy *The Hobbit* prefaced modern adolescent readers' fascination with the works of Piers Antony, Madeleine L'Engle, and Anne McCaffrey.

Studies in the late nineteenth and early twentieth centuries by behaviorists and developmental psychologists significantly affected the manner in which the education community and parents approached the selection of literature for children.

The cognitive development studies of Piaget, the epigenic view of personality development by Erik Erikson, the formulation of Abraham Maslow's hierarchy of basic needs, and the social learning theory of behaviorists like Alfred Bandura contributed to a greater understanding of child/adolescent development even as these theorists contradicted one another's findings. Though few educators today totally subscribe to Piaget's inflexible stages of mental development, his principles of both qualitative and quantitative mental capacity, his generalizations about the parallels between physical growth and thinking capacity, and his support of the adolescent's heightened moral perspective are still used as measures by which to evaluate child/adolescent literature.

Piaget's Four Stages of Mental Development

1. The **sensorimotor stage** (birth to age two) deals with the pre-language period of development. The child is most concerned with coordinating movement and action. Words begin to represent people and things.

2. **The preoperational stage** is the period spanning ages two through 7. It is broken into several substages, including the following:

    i) *Preconceptual phase* (ages 2 through 4): Most behavior is based on subjective judgment.

    ii) *Intuitive phase* (ages 4 through 7): Children use language to verbalize their experiences and mental processes.

3. The **concrete operational stage** (ages 7 through 11) is when children begin to apply logic to concrete things and experiences. They can combine performance and reasoning to solve problems.

4. The **formal operational stage** (ages 12 to 15) is when adolescents begin to think beyond the immediate and to theorize. They apply formal logic to interpreting abstract constructions and to recognizing experiences that are contrary to fact.

Though Piaget presented these stages as progressing sequentially, a given child might enter any period earlier or later than most children. Furthermore, a child might perform at different levels in different situations. Thus, a 14-year-old female might be able to function at the formal operational stage in a literature class, but function at a concrete operational level in mathematical concepts.

Piaget's Theories Influence Literature

Most middle school students have reached the concrete operational level. By this time they have left behind their egocentrism for a need to understand the physical and social world around them. They become more interested in ways to relate to other people. Their favorite stories become those about real people rather than animals or fairy tale characters. The conflicts in their literature are internal as well as external. Books like Paula Fox's *The Stone-Faced Boy*, Betsy Byards's *The Midnight Fox*, and Lois Lenski's *Strawberry Girl* deal with a child's loneliness, confusion about identity or loyalty, and poverty.

Preadolescents are becoming more cognizant of and interested in the past, thus their love of adventure stories about national heroes like Davy Crockett, Daniel Boone, and Abraham Lincoln and biographies/autobiographies of real-life heroes like Jackie Robinson and Cesar Chavez. At this level, children also become interested in the future; thus, their love of both fantasy and science fiction.

Seven- to eleven-year-olds also internalize moral values. They are concerned with their sense of self and are willing to question rules and adult authority. In books such as Beverly Cleary's *Henry Huggins* and *Mitch and Amy*, the protagonists are children pursuing their own desires with the same frustrations as other children. When these books were written in the 1960s, returning a found pet or overcoming a reading disability were common problems.

From ages 12 to 15, adolescents advance beyond the concrete operational level and begin developing communication skills that enable them to articulate attitudes and opinions and to exchange knowledge. They can recognize and contrast historical fiction with pure history and biography. They can identify the elements of literature and their relationships within a specific story. As their thinking becomes more complex, early adolescents become more sensitive to others' emotions and reactions. They become better able to suspend their disbelief and enter the world of literature, thus expanding their perceptions of the real world.

Concerning adolescents' moral judgment, Piaget noted that after age 11, children stopped viewing actions as either "right" or "wrong." The older child considers both the intent and the behavior in its context. A younger child would view an accidental destruction of property in terms of the amount of damage. An older child would find major damage that was unintentional less wrong than minor damage done with malice.

Kohlberg's Theories of Moral Development

Expanding on Piaget's thinking, Lawrence Kohlberg developed a hierarchy of values. Though progressive, the stages of Kohlberg's hierarchy are not clearly aligned to chronological age. The six stages of development correlate to three levels of moral judgment.

Level I. Moral values reside in external acts rather than in persons or standards.

> *Stage 0. Premoral:* No association of actions or needs with sense of right or wrong.
>
> *Stage 1. Obedience and punishment orientation:* Child defers to adult authority. The child's actions are motivated by a desire to stay out of trouble.
>
> *Stage 2. Right action/self-interest orientation:* Performance of right deeds results in needing satisfaction.

Level II. Moral values reside in maintaining conventions of right behavior.

> *Stage 3. Good person orientation:* The child performs right actions to receive approval from others, conforming to the same standards.

Stage 4. *Law and order orientation:* Doing one's duty and showing respect for authority contributes to maintaining social order.

Level III. Moral values reside in principles separate from the persons or agencies that enforce these principles.

Stage 5. *Legalistic orientation:* The rules of society are accepted as correct but alterable. Privileges and duties are derived from social contact. Obedience to society's rules protects the rights of self and others.

Stage 6. *Conscience orientation:* Ethical standards, such as justice, equality, and respect for others, guide moral conduct more than legal rules.

Though these stages represent a natural progression of values to actions relationships, persons may regress to an earlier stage in certain situations; an adolescent already operating at Stage 5 may regress to Stage 3 in a classroom in which nonconformity is met with disapproval or punishment. An adult operating at Stage 6 may regress to Stage 4 when obligated by military training or confronted with a conflict between self-preservation and the protection of others.

Values clarification education based on Piaget's and Kohlberg's theories implies that development is inherent in human socialization. Becoming a decent person is a natural result of human development.

Social Learning Theory

Much of traditional learning theory has resulted from the work of early behaviorists, like B. F. Skinner, and has been refined by modern theorists such as Albert Bandura. Behaviorists believe that intellectual, and therefore behavioral, development cannot be divided into specific stages. They believe that behavior is the result of conditioning experiences, a continuum of rewards and punishments. Environmental conditions are viewed as greater stimuli than inherent qualities. Thus in social learning theory the consequences of behavior—that is, the rewards or punishments—are more significant in social development than are the motivations for the behavior.

Bandura also proposed that a child learns vicariously through observing the behavior of others, whereas the developmental psychologists presumed that children developed through actual self-experience.

The Humanistic Theory of Development

No discussion of child development would be complete without a review of Abraham Maslow's hierarchy of needs, from basic physiological needs to the need for self-actualization. The following list represents those needs in the hierarchy that most affect children.

1. **Need for physical well-being.** In young children the provisions for shelter, food, clothing, and protection by significant adults satisfy this need. In older children, this satisfaction of physical comforts translates to a need for material security and may manifest itself in struggles to overcome poverty and maintain the integrity of home and family.

2. **Need for love.** The presumption is that every human being needs to love and be loved. With young children this reciprocal need is directed at and received from parents and other family members, pets, and friends. In older children and adolescents this need for love forms the basis for romance and peer acceptance.

3. **Need to belong.** Beyond the need for one-on-one relationships, a child needs the security of being an accepted member of a group. Young children identify with family, friends, and schoolmates. They are concerned with having happy experiences and being accepted by people they love and respect. Later in life they associate with community, country, and perhaps world groups. Adolescents become more aware of a larger world order and thus develop concerns about issues facing society, such as political or social unrest, wars, discrimination, and environmental issues. They seek to establish themselves with groups that accept and share their values. They become more team oriented.

4. **Need to achieve competence.** A human's need to interact satisfactorily with his or her environment begins with the infant's exploration of his or her immediate surroundings. Visual and tactile identification of objects and persons provides confidence to perform further explorations. To become well adjusted, the child must achieve competence to feel satisfaction. Physical and intellectual achievements become measures of acceptance. Frustrations resulting from physical or mental handicaps are viewed as hurdles to be overcome if satisfaction is to be achieved. Older children view the courage to overcome obstacles as part of the maturing process.

5. **Need to know.** Curiosity is the basis of intelligence. The need to learn is persistent. To maintain intellectual security, children must be able to find answers to their questions to stimulate further exploration of information to satisfy that persistent curiosity.

6. **Need for beauty and order.** Aesthetic satisfaction is as important as the need for factual information. Intellectual stimulation comes from satisfying curiosity about the fine, as well as the practical, arts. Acceptance for one's accomplishments in dance, music, drawing, writing, or performing or appreciation of the arts leads to a sense of accomplishment and self-actualization.

Theory of Psychosocial Development

Erik Erikson, a follower of Sigmund Freud, presented the theory that human development consists of maturation through a series of psychosocial crises. The struggle to resolve these crises helps a person achieve individuality as he or she learns to function in society.

Maturation occurs as the individual moves through a progression of increasingly complex stages. The movement from one stage to the next hinges on the successful resolution of the conflicts encountered in that stage, and each of the stages represents a step in identity formation. Stage 1 (trust versus distrust), Stage 2 (achieving autonomy), and Stage 3 (developing initiative) relate to infants and young/middle children. Stages 4 and 5 relate to late childhood through adolescence.

Stage 4: Becoming Industrious. Late childhood, according to Erikson, occurs between ages 7 and 11. Having already mastered conflicts that helped them overcome mistrust of unfamiliar persons, places, and things, children have become more independent in caring for themselves and their possessions and have overcome their sense of guilt at behavior that creates opposition with others. They are ready to assert themselves in suppressing feelings of inferiority. Children at this stage learn to master independent tasks and to work cooperatively with other children. They increasingly measure their own competence by comparing themselves to their peers.

Stage 5: Establishing Identity. From age 11 through the teen years, a person's conflicts arise from his or her search for identity, as an individual and as a member of society. Because internal demands for independence and peer acceptance sometimes oppose external demands for conformity to rules and standards, friction with family, school, and society in general occur during these years. Adolescents must resolve issues such as the amount of control they will concede to family and other rule-enforcing adults as they search for other acceptance models. In their quest for self-identity, they experiment with adult behaviors and attitudes. At the end of their teen years, they should have a well- established sense of identity.

Theory of Multiple Intelligences

Howard Gardner's research in the 1980s has been influential in helping teachers understand that human beings process information differently and, therefore, communicate their knowledge through different modes of operation. It is important to present language and literature in visual, auditory, tactile, and kinesthetic ways to allow all children to develop good skills through their own mode of learning. Then, children must be allowed to perform through the strength of their intelligence.

The movement toward learning academies in the practical and fine arts and in the sciences is a result of our growing understanding of all aspects of child development.

Modern Society's Role in Child Development

Despite their differences, there are many similarities in the theories of child development. However, most of these theories were developed prior to the social unrest of the 1970s. In industrialized Western society, children are increasingly excluded from the activities of work and play with adults, with education instead becoming their main occupation. This exclusion tends to prolong childhood and adolescence and thus inhibit development as visualized by theorists. For adolescents in the United States, this prolonging results in slower social and intellectual maturation, contrasted to increasing physical maturity. Adolescents today deal with drugs, violence, communicable diseases, and a host of social problems that were of minimal concern 50 years ago. Even preadolescent children are dealing with poverty, disease, broken homes, abuse, and drugs.

Influence of Theories on Literature

All of these development theories and existing social conditions influence the literature created and selected for and by child/adolescent readers.

Child/adolescent literature, whether nonfiction or fiction, has always been didactic to some degree. Until the twentieth century, "kiddie" lit was also morally prescriptive. Written by adults who determined either what they believed children needed or liked or what they should need or like, most books, stories, poems, and essays dealt with experiences or issues that would make children into better adults. The fables, fairy tales, and epics of old set the moral/social standards of their times while entertaining the child in every reader/listener. These tales are still popular because they have a universal appeal. Except for the rare exceptions discussed earlier in this section, most books were written for literate adults. Educated children found their pleasure in the literature that was available.

Benefits of Research

One benefit of the child development and learning theory research is that it provides guidelines for writers, publishers, and educators to follow in the creation, marketing, and selection of good reading materials. MacMillan introduced children's literature as a separate publishing market in 1918. By the 1930s, most major publishers had a children's department. Though arguments have existed throughout this century about quality versus quantity, there is no doubt that children's literature is a significant slice of the market pie.

Children's books are a reflection of both developmental theories and social changes. Reading provides children with the opportunity to become more aware of societal differences, to measure their behavior against the behavior of realistic fictional characters or the subjects of biographies, to become informed about events of the past and present that will affect their futures, and to acquire a genuine appreciation of literature.

Furthermore, there is an obligation for adults to provide instruction and entertainment that all children in our democratic society can use. As parents and educators we have an obligation to guide children in the selection of books that are appropriate to their reading ability and interest levels. Of course, there is a fine line between guidance and censorship. As with discipline, parents learn that to make forbidden is to make more desirable. To publish a list of banned books is to make them suddenly attractive. Most children/adolescents left to their own selections will choose books on topics that interest them and are written in language they can understand.

Social changes since World War II have significantly affected adolescent literature. The civil rights movements, feminism, the protest of the Vietnam War, and issues surrounding homelessness, neglect, teen pregnancy, drugs, and violence all have given rise to contemporary fiction that helps adolescents understand and cope with the world they live in.

Popular books for preadolescents deal more with establishing relationships with members of the opposite sex and learning to cope with their changing bodies, personalities, or life situations, as in Judy Blume's *Are You There, God? It's Me, Margaret*. Adolescents are still interested in the fantasy and science fiction genres as well as popular juvenile fiction. Middle school students still read the *Little House on the Prairie* series and the mysteries of the Hardy Boys and Nancy Drew. Teens value the works of Emily and Charlotte Brontë, Willa Cather, Jack London, William Shakespeare, Mark Twain, and J. R. R. Tolkien as much as those of Piers Anthony, S. E. Hinton, Suzanne Collins, Madeleine L'Engle, Stephen King, J. K. Rowling, and Stephenie Meyer because they're fun to read whatever their underlying literary worth may be.

Older adolescents enjoy the writers in these genres:

- Fantasy: Piers Anthony, Ursula K. LeGuin, Anne McCaffrey

- Horror: V. C. Andrews, Stephen King

- Juvenile fiction: Judy Blume, Robert Cormier, Rosa Guy, Virginia Hamilton, S. E. Hinton, M. E. Kerr, Harry Mazer, Norma Fox Mazer, Richard Newton Peck, Cynthia Voigt, Paul Zindel

- Science fiction: Isaac Asimov, Ray Bradbury, Arthur C. Clarke, Frank Herbert, Larry Niven, H. G. Wells

These classic and contemporary works combine the characteristics of multiple theories. Functioning at the concrete operations stage (Piaget), being of the "good person" orientation (Kohlberg), still highly dependent on external rewards (Bandura), and exhibiting all five needs previously discussed from Maslow's hierarchy, eleven to twelve-year-olds should appreciate the following titles, grouped by reading level. These titles are also cited for interest at that grade level and do not reflect high-interest titles for older readers who do not read at grade level. Some high interest titles will be cited later.

Reading level 6.0 to 6.9

Barrett, William. *Lilies of the Field*
Cormier, Robert. *Other Bells for Us to Ring*

Dahl, Roald. *Danny, Champion of the World*; *Charlie and the Chocolate Factory*
Lindgren, Astrid. *Pippi Longstocking*
Lindbergh, Anne. *Three Lives to Live*
Lowry, Lois. *Rabble Starkey*
Naylor, Phyllis. *The Year of the Gopher*; *Reluctantly Alice*
Peck, Robert Newton. *Arly*
Speare, Elizabeth. *The Witch of Blackbird Pond*
Sleator, William. *The Boy Who Reversed Himself*

For seventh and eighth grades

Most seventh- and eighth-grade students, according to learning theory, are still functioning cognitively, psychologically, and morally as sixth graders. As these are not inflexible standards, there are some twelve- and thirteen-year-olds who are much more mature socially, intellectually, and physically than the younger children who share the same school. They are becoming concerned with establishing individual and peer group identities, and this can present conflicts with established authority and rigid rules. Some at this age are still tied firmly to the family and its expectations, while others identify more with those their own age or older.

Enrichment reading for this group must help them cope with life's rapid changes or provide escape and thus must be either realistic or fantastic depending on the child's needs. Adventures and mysteries (the Hardy Boys and Nancy Drew series) are still popular today. Preteens also become more interested in biographies of contemporary figures than those of legendary figures of the past.

Reading level 7.0 to 7.9

Armstrong, William. *Sounder*
Bagnold, Enid. *National Velvet*
Barrie, James. *Peter Pan*
London, Jack. *White Fang*; *Call of the Wild*
Lowry, Lois. *Taking Care of Terrific*
McCaffrey, Anne. The *Dragonsinger* series
Montgomery, L. M. *Anne of Green Gables* and sequels
Steinbeck, John. *The Pearl*
Tolkien, J. R. R. *The Hobbit*
Zindel, Paul. *The Pigman*

Reading level 8.0 to 8.9

Cormier, Robert. *I Am the Cheese*
McCullers, Carson. *The Member of the Wedding*
North, Sterling. *Rascal*
Twain, Mark. *The Adventures of Tom Sawyer*
Zindel, Paul. *My Darling, My Hamburger*

For ninth grade

Depending upon the school environment, a ninth grader may be top dog in a junior high school or underdog in a high school. Much of ninth graders' social development and thus their reading interests become motivated by their peer associations. Ninth graders are technically adolescents operating at the early stages of formal operations in cognitive development. Their perception of their own identity is becoming well defined, and they are fully aware of the ethics required by society. These students are more receptive to the challenges of classic literature but still enjoy popular teen novels.

Reading level 9.0 to 9.9

>Brown, Dee. *Bury My Heart at Wounded Knee*
>Defoe, Daniel. *Robinson Crusoe*
>Dickens, Charles. *David Copperfield*
>Greenberg, Joanne. *I Never Promised You a Rose Garden*
>Kipling, Rudyard. *Captains Courageous*
>Mathabane, Mark. *Kaffir Boy*
>Nordhoff, Charles. *Mutiny on the Bounty*
>Shelley, Mary. *Frankenstein*
>Washington, Booker T. *Up From Slavery*

For tenth through twelfth grades

All high school sophomores, juniors, and seniors can handle most other literature except for a few of the most difficult titles like *Moby-Dick* or *Vanity Fair*. However, since many high school students do not progress to the eleventh- or twelfth-grade reading level, they will still have their favorites among authors whose writings they can understand.

Many will struggle with assigned novels but still read high-interest books for pleasure. A few high-interest titles are listed below without reading level designations, though most are 6.0 to 7.9.

>Bauer, Joan. *Squashed*
>Borland, Hal. *When the Legends Die*
>Danzinger, Paula. *Remember Me to Herald Square*
>Duncan, Lois. *Stranger with My Face*
>Hamilton, Virginia. *The Planet of Junior Brown*
>Hinton, S. E. *The Outsiders*
>Paterson, Katherine. *The Great Gilly Hopkins*

Teachers of students at all levels must be familiar with the materials offered by the libraries in their own schools. Only then can they guide their students into appropriate selections for their social age and reading level development.

Adolescent literature, because of the age range of readers, is extremely diverse. Fiction for the middle group, usually ages 10–11 to 14–15, deals with issues of coping with internal and external changes in their lives. Because children's writers in the twentieth and twenty-first centuries have produced increasingly realistic fiction, adolescents can now find problems dealt with honestly in novels and short stories.

Teachers of middle/junior high school students see the greatest change in interests and reading abilities. Fifth- and sixth-graders, included in elementary grades in many schools, are viewed as older children, while seventh and eighth graders are seen as preadolescents. Ninth-graders, who are sometimes the highest class in junior high school and sometimes the lowest class in high school, definitely view themselves as teenagers. Their literature choices will often be governed more by interest than by ability; thus the wealth of high-interest, low-readability books that has flooded the market in recent years. Tenth- through twelfth-graders will still select high-interest books for pleasure reading but are also easily encouraged to stretch their abilities by reading more classics.

Because of rapid social changes, topics that once did not interest young people until they reached their teens—such as suicide, gangs, and homosexuality—are now subjects of books for younger readers. The plethora of high-interest books reveals how desperately schools have failed to produce on-level readers and how the market has adapted to that need. However, these high-interest books are now readable for younger children whose reading levels are at or above normal. No matter how tastefully written, some content is inappropriate for younger readers. The problem becomes not so much steering them toward books that they have the reading ability to handle but encouraging them toward books whose content is appropriate to their levels of cognitive and social development. A fifth-grader may be able to read V. C. Andrews' book *Flowers in the Attic* but not possess the social/moral development to handle the deviant behavior of the characters.

At the same time, because of the complex changes affecting adolescents, the teacher must be well versed in learning theory and child development and competent to teach the subject matter of language and literature.

H. Demonstrates knowledge of various critical approaches to literature

Facts, Opinions, and Arguments

Facts are statements that are verifiable. Opinions are statements that must be supported to be accepted. Facts are used to support opinions. For example, "Jane is a bad girl" is an opinion. However, "Jane hit her sister with a baseball bat" is a fact upon which the opinion is based. Judgments are opinions—decisions or declarations based on observation or reasoning that express approval or disapproval. Facts report what has happened or exists and come from observation, measurement, or calculation. Facts can be tested and verified whereas opinions and judgments cannot. They can only be supported with facts.

Most statements cannot be so clearly distinguished. "I believe that Jane is a bad girl" is not a fact. The speaker knows what he or she believes. However, it obviously includes a judgment that could be disputed by another person who might believe otherwise. Judgments are not usually so firm. They are, rather, plausible opinions that provoke thought or lead to factual development.

An argument is a generalization that is proven or supported with facts. If the facts are not accurate, the generalization remains unproven. Using inaccurate information to support an argument is called a *fallacy* in reasoning. Some factors to consider in judging whether the facts used to support an argument are accurate are as follows:

1. Are the facts current or are they out of date? For example, if the proposition "birth defects in babies born to drug-using mothers are increasing," then the data must include the latest that is available.

2. Another important factor to consider in judging the accuracy of a fact is its source. Where was the data obtained, and is that source reliable?

3. The calculations on which the facts are based may be unreliable. It's a good idea to perform your own calculations before using a piece of derived information.

Even facts that are true and have a sharp impact on the argument may not be relevant to the case at hand. To continue the example above:

1. Health statistics from an entire state may have no relevance, or little relevance, to a particular county or zip code. Statistics from an entire country cannot be used to prove very much about a particular state or county.

2. An analogy can be useful in making a point, but the comparison must match up in all characteristics or it will not be relevant. Analogy should be used very carefully. It is often just as likely to destroy an argument as it is to strengthen it.

The significance of a fact may not be sufficient to strengthen an argument. For example, of the millions of immigrants in the United States, using a single family's situation to support a position on immigration reform does not strengthen the argument for that position (even though those single-example arguments are often used to support one approach or another). Such a story may achieve a positive reaction, but it will not prove that one position is better than another. If enough cases were cited from a variety of geographical locations, the information might be more significant.

How many facts are enough? Generally speaking, three strong supporting facts are sufficient to establish the thesis of an argument. For example:

Conclusion: All green apples are sour.

- When I was a child, I bit into a green apple from my grandfather's orchard, and it was sour.

- I once bought green apples from a roadside vendor, and when I bit into one, it was sour.

- My grocery store had a sale on green Granny Smith apples last week, and I bought several only to find that they were sour when I bit into one.

Although this argument is supported by three facts, the sample is still insufficient. Some basic research into green apples will uncover types of green apples that are not sour.

Sometimes more than three arguments are too many. On the other hand, it's not unusual to hear public speakers, particularly politicians, cite a long litany of facts to support their positions.

A very good example of the omission of facts in an argument is the resume of an applicant for a job. The applicant is arguing that he or she should be chosen for a particular job. The application form will ask for information about past employment, and the applicant may omit unfavorable dismissals from jobs in the past. Employers are usually suspicious of periods of time during which the applicant has not listed an employer.

A writer makes choices about which facts will be used and which will be discarded in developing an argument. Those choices may exclude anything that is not supportive of the point of view the writer is taking. It's always a good idea for the reader to do some research to spot the omissions and to ask whether they have impact on the strength of the writer's argument.

No judgment is either black or white. If the argument seems too neat or too compelling, there are probably facts that might be relevant that have not been included.

See also Competency 4.I

Tone

A piece of writing is an integrated whole. It's not enough to just look at the various parts; the total entity must be examined. It should be considered in two ways:

- As an emotional expression of the author
- As an artistic embodiment of a meaning or set of meanings

This is what is sometimes called **tone** in literary criticism.

It's important to remember that the writer is a human being with his or her own individual bents, prejudices, and emotions. A writer is telling the readers about the world as he or she sees it and will give voice to certain phases of his or her own personality. By reading a writer's works, we can know the personal qualities and emotions of the writer embodied in the work itself. However, it's important to remember that not all the writer's characteristics will be revealed in a single work. Like everyone, writers change and may have very different attitudes at different times in their lives.

Sometimes a writer will be influenced by a desire to have a piece of work published, to appear to be current, or to satisfy the interests and desires of the readers he or she hopes to attract. These influences can destroy a work or make it less than it might be. Sometimes the best works are not commercial successes in the generation when they were written; rather, they are discovered at a later time and by another generation.

There are three places to look for tone:

- Choice of form: tragedy or comedy; melodrama or farce; parody or sober lyric.
- Choice of materials: characters who have human qualities that are attractive; others that are repugnant. What an author shows in a setting will often indicate what his or her interests are.
- The writer's interpretation: it may be explicit—telling us how he or she feels. It may also be implicit—giving his or her feelings for a character through the description. For example, the use of *smirked* instead of *laughed*; or *minced*, *stalked*, or *marched* instead of *walked*.

The reader is asked to join the writer in the feelings expressed about the world and the things that happen in it. The tone of a piece of writing is important in a critical review of it.

Style

Style in literature means a distinctive manner of expression and applies to all levels of language, beginning at the phonemic level—word choices, alliteration, assonance, and so on; moving to the syntactic level—length of sentences, choice of structure and phraseology, patterns, and so on; and extending beyond the sentences to paragraphs and chapters. Readers should ask: What is distinctive about this writer's use of these elements?

Style is often the writer's signature. The reader does not need to be told that William Faulkner wrote a story to know it because his style is so distinctive that it is immediately recognizable. Even the writing of Toni Morrison, which could be said to be Faulknerian, cannot be mistaken for the work of Faulkner himself.

In Steinbeck's *Grapes of Wrath*, for instance, the style is quite simple in the narrative sections, and the dialogue is dialectal. Because the emphasis is on the story—the narrative—Steinbeck's style is straightforward, for the most part. He just tells the story.

However, there are interchapters in which he varies his style. He uses symbols and combines them with description that is realistic. He sometimes shifts to a crisp, repetitive pattern to underscore the beeping and speeding of cars. By contrast, some of those interchapters are lyrical, almost poetic.

These shifts in style reflect the attitude of the author toward the subject matter. He intends to make a statement, and he uses a variety of styles to strengthen the point.

TEACHER CERTIFICATION STUDY GUIDE

COMPETENCY 007   **THE TEACHER UNDERSTANDS STRATEGIES FOR READING LITERARY TEXTS AND PROVIDES STUDENTS WITH OPPORTUNITIES TO FORMULATE, EXPRESS, AND SUPPORT RESPONSES TO LITERATURE**

A.   **Demonstrates knowledge of various types of responses to literary texts and encourages a variety of responses in students**

Writing about an author's use of plot should begin with determining what the conflicts are. In a naturalist story, the conflicts may be between the protagonist and a hostile or indifferent world. Sometimes the conflicts are between two characters, the protagonist and the antagonist, and sometimes the conflicts are internal—between two forces within an individual character that have created a dilemma. For example, a Catholic priest may be devoted and committed to his role in the church that calls for a celibate life yet at the same time be deeply in love with a woman.

Once the conflicts have been determined, the pattern of action will hinge on how the story comes out—who (or what) wins and who (or what) loses. If the protagonist struggles throughout the story but emerges triumphant in the end, the pattern is said to be rising. In contrast, if the story is about the downfall of the major character, the pattern can be said to be falling. If there is no winner in the end, the pattern is flat. This is an important point for a writer to make because it is crucial to all other aspects of an analysis of a work of fiction.

The pattern of the plot is also an important consideration. Where is the climax going to occur? Is denouement necessary? Does the reader need to see the unwinding of all the strands? Many stories fail because a denouement is needed but not supplied.

Characters are developed in many ways. Sometimes the writer simply tells the reader what kind of person a character is. More often, however, the reader is left to deduce a character's qualities from dialogue with others, from what other characters think or say about him or her, or from description—what the character looks like (for example, tall, short, thin, plump, dark-haired, gray-haired). The techniques a writer uses to define character are called characterization, and a student writer will usually deal with characterization when writing an analysis.

Setting can be a period of time—the 1930s, for example. It can also be a place, either a real place like a particular city or a fictional place like a farm or a mansion. It can be emotional—for example, some of Truman Capote's stories are set in an atmosphere of fear and danger, and the effectiveness of the story depends on that setting. An analysis should deal with the *function* of the setting in the story. For example, if it is set in a particular period of time, such as *The Great Gatsby* (set in the 1920s), would it be a different story if it were set in a different period of time? A setting can sometimes function as a symbol, so the writer should be looking for that as a possibility.

Theme in a work of fiction is similar to a thesis in an essay. It's the *point* the story makes. In a story, it may be spoken by one of the characters, but more often it is left to the writer to create.

Uncovering the theme of a piece of fiction requires careful reading and should take into account all aspects of the story. Different analysts will come to different conclusions about what a story means. Very often the thesis of an analytical essay will be the student writer's declaration of the theme according to his or her own well-reasoned opinion.

Point of view seems simple on the surface, but often it is not. In fact, Wallace Hildick wrote *Thirteen Types of Narrative* to explain point of view in literature. One of the most common is first-person narrator objective, in which the person telling the story only records his or her observations of what is happening. In this point of view, the only clues as to what the characters are like come from the narrator. The attitude of the narrator toward the theme or the characters will be an important part of the story and should be dealt with in an analysis. Sometimes, it's apparent that the narrator's view does not square with reality, in which case the narrator becomes unreliable and the reader must make an effort to determine what is real and what is not. If a writer uses this device, it's extremely important that the analyst point it out and examine what it does for the story.

Third-person objective is another common point of view. In this point of view, there is no narrator. The story is told by an unseen observer. The reader does not know what anyone is thinking, only what is being said and described.

Third-person omniscient point of view is also fairly common. In this point of view, the story is being told by an unseen observer, but the observer is able to know what at least one person is thinking. If the narrator known only what one or a few of the characters are thinking, this is called limited omniscient point of view.

Point of view is extremely powerful in controlling the way a story is perceived and must be dealt with in a written analysis.

B.   Knows strategies for motivating students to read literature and for promoting their appreciation of the value of literature

Reading for enjoyment makes it possible to go to places in the world we will never be able to visit, or perhaps when we learn about the enchantments of a particular place, we will set a goal of going there someday. When *Under the Tuscan Sun* by Frances Mayes was published, it became a bestseller. It also increased tourism to Italy. Many of the readers of that book visited Italy for the first time in their lives.

In fiction, we can vicariously experience what we will never encounter. We delve into feelings that are similar to our own or that are so far removed from our own that we are filled with wonder and curiosity by these new feelings. We read in part because we're curious—curious to visit, experience, and know new and different things. The reader lives with a crowd of people and a vast landscape. Life is constantly being enriched by reading, and the mind is constantly being expanded by reading. To read is to grow. Sometimes the experience of reading a particular book or story is so delicious that we go back and read it again and again.

How do we model this wonderful gift for our students? We can bring those interesting stories into our classrooms and share the excitement we feel when we discover them. We can relate things that make us laugh so students may see the humor and laugh with us. We can vary the established curriculum to include something we are reading that we want to share. The tendency of students today is to receive all or most of their information from television or the Internet. It's important for the teacher to help students understand that television and the Internet are not substitutes for reading. They should be an accessory to, an extension of, and a springboard for reading.

Another thing teachers can do to inspire students to become readers is to assign a book that you have never read before and read along with them, chapter by chapter. Run a contest in which the winner gets to pick a book that you and your students will read chapter by chapter. If you are excited about it and are experiencing satisfaction from the reading, that excitement will be contagious. Be sure that the discussion sessions allow for students to relate what they are thinking and feeling about what they are reading. Lively discussions and the opportunity to express their own feelings will lead to more spontaneous reading.

You can also hand out a reading list of your favorite books and spend some time telling the students what you liked about each. Make sure the list is diverse. It's good to include nonfiction along with fiction. Don't forget that a good biography or autobiography may encourage students to read beyond thrillers and detective stories.

When the class is discussing the latest movie, whether formally as a part of the curriculum or informally and incidentally, if the movie is based on a book, this is a good opportunity to demonstrate how much more can be derived from reading than from watching. How do the two combined make the experience more satisfying and worthwhile?

Share with your students the excitement you feel about reading. Successful writers are usually good readers. The two go hand in hand.

Students who have access to books and who read regularly learn to read more easily. They keep improving their reading skills throughout their school years, perform better on language tests, are better writers, develop oral skills and literacy in a second language more easily, have better levels of reading comprehension, have a larger vocabulary, and have more general knowledge. How can we encourage reading and an enjoyment of reading?

Tips to Encourage Independent Reading for Pleasure

Remember, books won't work by themselves. As a teacher, you have to make sure students read books by setting aside time regularly for reading. For example:

Have a DEAR period: Drop Everything and Read
Everyone can participate in a DEAR period and read for 15 minutes. This often works well right at the beginning of the school day, every day.

SSR period: Sustained silent reading
Have everyone choose a book and read without interruption for 20 to 30 minutes. Ideally this should take place daily but even twice a week will show results.

Independent reading sessions
Set aside one day a week for learners to select new books, read independently or in pairs, and have time to respond to and discuss the books they have read. This should take place weekly. Break time, after school, and free periods are good opportunities to read.

Read with children
Taking books home is a very good option as learners can read to and with other family members. Even if children can read alone, they will still benefit from being read to.

Encourage reading of any suitable and relevant written material if books are not accessible. Try newspaper or magazine articles, street signs, food packaging labels, posters—anything can be used, provided it is at the correct level.

Encourage readers to make their own material and/or bring additional material to school to read.

Having books in a classroom is one of the easiest and most effective ways of increasing reading, linguistic, and cognitive development. No other single variable can be shown to carry the same significance.

Once regular reading habits have been established, independent reading should be encouraged. Reading independently:

- allows learners to read, reread, and engage with a text at their own pace
- allows learners to choose what subjects they want to read, which motivates them to read
- impacts language development in the areas of vocabulary and syntax
- impacts knowledge of sight words and phonics
- is important for second-language learners as it provides a wealth of real language input

Reading for pleasure should be encouraged simultaneously with teaching reading and basic literacy. Reading for pleasure is therapeutic and enlightening, and it paves the way for developing a culture of reading and of lifelong learning.

C. **Knows how to draw from wide reading in American, British, world, and young adult literature to guide students to explore and select independent reading based on their individual needs and interests**

See Competencies 6.C, 6.D, 6.E, 6.F, and 7.B

D. **Knows how to promote students' interest in literature and facilitate their reading and understanding**

See Competency 7.B

E. **Uses technology to promote students' engagement in and comprehension of literature**

See Competencies 10.G and 11.E

F. **Knows strategies for creating communities of readers and for promoting conversations about literature and ideas**

See Competencies 7.B and 10.D

G. **Understands and teaches students strategies to use for analyzing and evaluating a variety of literary texts, both classic and contemporary**

When we analyze a literary text, we use the construction and various elements of the text in order to discern its meaning. Most authors construct a literary work with some eye to meaning; a message to impart about the nature of things. To analyze a literary text is very often to increase in both comprehension of its meaning and its art. Analyzing a literary text brings us into the mind of the author, even if he or she lived long ago, and gives readers a window into a different time, place, and perspective that nevertheless speaks to a universal human community and commonality. Analyzing an author's work tells why or how or how well he or she chose and utilized the elements and structure to shed light or offer a new perspective.

Analyzing Poetry

Poetry and Form

When we speak of *form* with regard to poetry, we usually mean one of three things: the pattern of the sound and rhythm; the visible shape the poem takes; or rhyme and free verse.

Sound and rhythm

It helps to know the history of poetry. Poetry was passed down in oral form almost exclusively until the invention of the printing press and was often set to music. A rhymed story is much easier to commit to memory.

Adding a tune makes it even easier to remember, so it's not a surprise that much of the earliest literature—epics and odes—is rhymed and was probably sung. When we speak of the pattern of sound and rhythm, we are referring to two things: verse form and stanza form.

The verse form is the rhythmic pattern of a single verse. An example would be any meter: blank verse, for instance, is iambic pentameter. A stanza is a group of a certain number of verses (lines) that have a rhyme scheme. If the poem is written, there is usually white space between the verses although a short poem may be only one stanza. If the poem is spoken, there will be a pause between stanzas.

The visible shape the poem takes

In the seventeenth century, some poets shaped their poems to reflect the theme. A good example is George Herbert's *Easter Wings*. Since that time, poets have occasionally played with this device; it is, however, generally viewed as nothing more than a demonstration of ingenuity. The rhythm, effect, and meaning are often sacrificed by forcing the poem to fit into the shape.

Rhyme and free verse

Poets also use devices to establish forms that will underscore the meanings of their poems. A very common one is alliteration. When the poem is read (poetry is intended to be read), the repetition of a sound may not only underscore the meaning but also give pleasure to the reading. Following a strict rhyming pattern can add intensity to the meaning of the poem in the hands of a skilled and creative poet. However, the meaning can be drowned out by the steady beat-beat-beat of the rhyming pattern. Shakespeare skillfully used the regularity of rhyme in his poetry, breaking the rhythm at certain points to effectively underscore a point. For example, in Sonnet 130, "My mistress' eyes are nothing like the sun," the rhythm is primarily iambic pentameter. It lulls the reader (or listener) to accept that this poet is following the standard conventions for love poetry, which in Shakespeare's day reliably used rhyme and more often than not iambic pentameter to express feelings of romantic love along conventional lines. However, in Sonnet 130, the last two lines sharply break from the monotonous pattern, forcing the reader or speaker to pause:

> And yet, by heaven, I think my love as rare
> As any she belied with false compare.

Shakespeare's purpose is clear: he is not writing a conventional love poem; the object of his love is not the conventional woman written about in other poems of the period. This is a good example in which a poet uses form to underscore meaning.

Poets eventually began to feel constricted by traditional rhyming conventions and began to break away and make new rules for poetry.

When poetry was always rhymed, it was easy to define it. When free verse, or poetry written in a flexible form, came upon the scene in France in the 1880s, it quickly began to influence English-language poets such as T. S. Eliot, whose memorable poem *The Waste Land* had an alarming but desolate message for the modern world. It's impossible to imagine that it could have been written in the soothing, lulling rhymed verse of previous periods. Those who first began writing in free verse in English were responding to the influence of the French *vers libre*. However, it should be noted that it could be loosely ascribed to the poetry of Walt Whitman, writing in the mid-nineteenth century, as can be seen in the first stanza of *Song of Myself*:

> I celebrate myself, and sing myself,
> And what I assume you shall assume,
> For every atom belonging to me as good belongs to you.

When poetry was no longer defined as a piece of writing arranged in verses that had a rhyme scheme of some sort, distinguishing poetry from prose became a point of discussion. Merriam-Webster's *Encyclopedia of Literature* defines poetry as follows: "Writing that formulates a concentrated imaginative awareness of experience in language chosen and arranged to create a specific emotional response through its meaning, sound and rhythm."

A poet chooses the form of his or her poetry deliberately, based on the emotional response he or she hopes to evoke and the meaning he or she wishes to convey. Robert Frost, a twentieth-century poet who chose to use conventional rhyming verse to make his point, is a memorable and often-quoted modern poet. Who can forget his closing lines in "Stopping by Woods on a Snowy Evening"?

> And miles to go before I sleep,
> And miles to go before I sleep.

Would they be as memorable if the poem had been written in free verse?

Poetic devices

See also Competency 6.B

Slant rhyme: Slant rhyme occurs when the final consonant sounds are the same but the vowels are different; occurs frequently in Irish, Welsh, and Icelandic verse. Examples include: *green* and *gone*, *that* and *hit*, *ill* and *shell*.

Alliteration: Alliteration occurs when the initial sounds of a word, beginning either with a consonant or a vowel, are repeated in close succession. Examples include: Athena and Apollo, Nate never knows, People who pen poetry.

Note that the words only have to be close to one another, not in immediate succession; alliteration that repeats and attempts to connect a number of words is little more than a tongue-twister. The function of alliteration, like rhyme, might be to accentuate the beauty of language in a given context or to unite words or concepts through a kind of repetition. Alliteration, like rhyme, can follow specific patterns. Sometimes the repeated consonants aren't always the initial ones, but they are generally the stressed syllables.

Alliteration is less common than rhyme, but because it is less common, it can call our attention to a word or line in a poem that might not have the same emphasis otherwise.

Assonance: If alliteration occurs at the beginning of a word and rhyme at the end, assonance takes the middle territory. Assonance occurs when the vowel sound within a word matches the same sound in a nearby word, but the surrounding consonant sounds are different. *Tune* and *June* are rhymes; *tune* and *food* are assonant. The function of assonance is frequently the same as end rhyme or alliteration; all serve to give a sense of continuity or fluidity to the verse. Assonance might be especially effective when rhyme is absent: It gives the poet more flexibility, and it is not typically used as part of a predetermined pattern. Like alliteration, it does not determine the structure or form of a poem; rather, it is ornamental.

Narrative Poetry

The greatest difficulty in analyzing narrative poetry is that it partakes of many genres. It can have all the features of poetry: meter, rhyme, verses, stanzas, and so on, but it can also have all the features of prose—both fictional and nonfictional prose. It can have a protagonist, characters, conflicts, action, plot, climax, theme, and tone. It can also be a persuasive discourse and have a thesis (real or derived) and supporting points. The arrangement of an analysis will depend to a great extent upon the peculiarities of the poem itself.

In an epic, the conflicts take place in the social sphere rather than a personal life, and an epic has a historical basis or one that is accepted as historical. The conflict is between opposed nations or races and involves diverging views of civilization that are the foundation of the challenge. Often it involves pitting a group that conceives of itself as a higher civilization against a lower civilization and, more often than not, divine will determines that the higher one will win, exerting its force over the lower, barbarous, and profane enemy. Examples are the conflict of Greece with Troy, Rome with Carthage, the Crusaders with the Saracen, or Milton's omnipotent God versus Satan. In analyzing these works, protagonist and antagonist need to be clearly identified, the conflicts established, and the climax and an outcome that sets the world right in the mind of the writer clearly shown.

At the same time, the form of the epic as a poem must be considered. What meter, rhyme scheme, verse form, and stanza form have been chosen to tell this story? Is it consistent? If it varies, where does it vary and what does the variation do for the poem/story? What about figures of speech? Is there alliteration or onomatopoeia?

The epic is a major literary form historically although it had begun to fall out of favor by the end of the seventeenth century. There have been notable efforts to produce an American epic, but they always seem to slide over into prose. Some would say that the novel *Moby–Dick* is an American epic.

Narrative poetry has been very much a part of the output of modern American writers apart from attempts to write epics. Many of Emily Dickinson's poems are narrative in form and retain the features that we look for in the finest of American poetry. The first two verses of "A Narrow Fellow in the Grass" illustrate the use of narrative in a poem:

> A narrow fellow in the grass
> Occasionally rides;
> You may have met him—did you not,
> His notice sudden is.
>
> The grass divides as with a comb,
> A spotted shaft is seen;
> And then it closes at your feet
> And opens further on. . . .

This is certainly narrative in nature and has many of the aspects of prose narrative. At the same time, it is a poem with rhyme, meter, verses, and stanzas, and it can be analyzed as such.

Sonnet

The sonnet is a fixed-verse form of Italian origin, which consists of 14 lines that are typically five-foot iambics rhyming according to a prescribed scheme. Popular since its creation in the thirteenth century in Sicily, it spread at first to Tuscany, where Petrarch adopted it. The Petrarchan sonnet generally has a two-part theme. The first eight lines, the octave, state a problem, ask a question, or express an emotional tension. The last six lines, the sestet, resolve the problem, answer the question, or relieve the tension. The rhyme scheme of the octave is abbaabba; that of the sestet varies.

Sir Thomas Wyatt and Henry Howard, Earl of Surrey, introduced this form into England in the sixteenth century. It played an important role in the development of Elizabethan lyric poetry, leading to the development of a distinctive English sonnet, which was composed of three quatrains, each with an independent rhyme scheme, and ended with a rhymed couplet. A form of the English sonnet created by Edmund Spenser combines the English form and the Italian. The Spenserian sonnet follows the English quatrain and couplet pattern but resembles the Italian in its rhyme scheme, which is linked: abab bcbc cdcd ee. Many poets wrote sonnet sequences in which several sonnets were linked together, usually to tell a story.

Considered to be the greatest of all sonnet sequences is one of Shakespeare's. These sonnets are addressed to a young man and a "dark lady"; their love story is overshadowed by the underlying reflections on time and art, growth and decay, and fame and fortune.

The sonnet continued to develop, more in subject matter than in form. When John Donne in the seventeenth century used the form for religious themes, some of which are almost sermons, or for personal reflections ("When I consider how my light is spent"), there were no longer any boundaries on the themes a sonnet could contain.

The sonnet's flexibility is demonstrated in the wide range of themes and purposes for which it has been used—from frivolous concerns to statements about time and death. Wordsworth, Keats, and Elizabeth Barrett Browning used the Petrarchan form of the sonnet. A well-known example is Wordsworth's "The World Is Too Much With Us." Rainer Maria Rilke's *Sonnets to Orpheus* (1922) are also well-known twentieth-century sonnets.

Analysis of a sonnet should focus on the form—does it fit a traditional pattern or does it break from tradition? If so, why did the poet choose to make that break? Does it reflect the purpose of the poem? What is the theme? What is the purpose? Is it narrative? If so, what story does it tell, and is there an underlying meaning? Is the sonnet form appropriate for the subject matter?

Limerick

The limerick probably originated in County Limerick, Ireland, in the eighteenth century. It is a form of short, humorous verse, often nonsensical and often ribald. Its five lines rhyme aabbaa with three feet in all lines except the third and fourth, which have only two. Rarely presented as serious poetry, this form is popular because almost anyone can write it.

Analysis of a limerick should focus on its form. Does it conform to a traditional pattern or does it break from the tradition? If so, what impact does that have on the meaning? Is the poem serious or frivolous? Does it try to be funny but fail to achieve its purpose? Is there a serious meaning underlying the frivolity?

Cinquain and Haiku

A cinquain is a poem with a five-line stanza. Adelaide Crapsey (1878–1914) called a five-line verse form a cinquain and invented a particular meter for it. Similar to the haiku, there are two syllables in the first and last lines and four, six, and eight in the middle three lines. It has a mostly iambic cadence. Her poem, "November Night," is an example:

Listen…
With faint dry sound
Like steps of passing ghosts,
the leaves, frost-crisp'd, break from the trees
And fall.

Haiku is a very popular unrhymed form that is limited to 17 syllables arranged in three lines thus: five, seven, and five syllables. This verse form originated in Japan in the seventeenth century where it is accepted as serious poetry and is Japan's most popular form. Originally, Haikus dealt with the season, the time of day, and the landscape; as the form has come into more common use, the subjects have become less restricted. The imagist poets and other English writers used the form or imitated it. Haikus are often used in classrooms to introduce students to the writing of poetry.

Analysis of a cinquain or a haiku should focus on form first. Does the haiku conform to the 17-syllable requirement, and are the syllables arranged in a five, seven, and five pattern? For a cinquain, does it have only five lines? Does the poem distill the words so as much meaning as possible can be conveyed? Does it treat a serious subject? Is the theme discernable? Short forms like these seem simple to dash off; however, they are not effective unless the words are chosen and pared so the meaning intended is conveyed. The impact should be forceful, and creating this impact with so few words can take more effort, skill, and creativity than achieving the same impact using a longer poetic form. This impact should be taken into account in student writers' analyses.

Analyzing Prose

The analysis of prose, similar to the analysis of poetry, also calls for attention to structural elements so as to discern meaning, purpose, and themes. The author's intentions are gleaned through the elements he or she uses and how they are used.

The elements of both short and long fiction include plot, characters, setting, and point of view.

Plot

The plot is the sequence of events (it may or may not be chronological) that the author chooses to represent the story to be told--both the underlying story and the externals of the occurrences the author relates. An author may use "flashbacks" to tell the back story (or what went before the current events begin). Often, authors begin their stories *in media res*, or in the middle of things, and, over time, supply the details of what has gone before to provide a clearer picture to the reader of all the relevant events.

Sometimes authors tell parallel stories in order to make their points. For example, in Count Leo Tolstoy's classic *Anna Karenina*, the unhappy extramarital affair of Anna Karenina and Count Vronsky is contrasted with the happy marriage of Lev and Kitty through the use of alternating chapters devoted to each couple. The plot consists of the progress of each couple: Anna and Count Vronsky into deeper neurosis, obsession, and emotional pain, and Lev and Kitty into deeper and more meaningful partnership through growing emotional intimacy, parenthood, and caring for members of their extended family.

In good novels each part of the plot is necessary and has a purpose. For example, in *Anna Karenina*, a chapter is devoted to a horse race Count Vronsky participates in. This might seem like mere entertainment, but, in fact, Count Vronsky is riding his favorite mare, and, in a moment of carelessness in taking a jump, puts the whole weight of his body on the mare's back, breaking it. The horse must be shot. Vronsky loved and admired the mare, but being overcome by a desire to win, he kills the very thing he loves. Similarly, Anna descends into obsession and jealousy as their affair isolates her from society and separates her from her child, and ultimately kills herself. The chapter symbolizes the destructive effect Vronsky's love, coupled with inordinate desire, has upon what and whom he loves.

Other authors use repetitious plot lines to reveal the larger story over time. For example, in Joseph Heller's tragic-comedy *Catch-22*, the novel repeatedly returns to a horrific incident in an airplane while flying a combat mission. Each time the protagonist, Yossarian, recalls the incident, more detail is revealed. The reader knows from the beginning that this incident is key to why Yossarian wants to be discharged from the army, but it is not until the full details of the gruesome incidents are revealed late in the book that the reader knows why the incident has driven Yossarian almost mad. Interspersed with comedic and ironic episodes, the book's climax (the full revealing of the incident) remains powerfully with the reader, showing the absurdity, insanity, and inhumanity of war. The comic device of Catch-22, a fictitious army rule from which the title is derived, makes this point in a funny way: Catch-22 states that a soldier cannot be discharged from the army unless he is crazy; yet, if he wants to be discharged from the army, he is not crazy. This rule seems to embody the insanity, absurdity, and inhumanity of war.

Characters

Characters usually represent or embody an idea or ideal acting in the world. For example in the Harry Potter series, Harry Potter's goodness, courage and unselfishness as well as his capacity for friendship and love make him a powerful opponent to Voldemort, whose selfishness, cruelty, and isolation make him the leader of the evil forces in the epic battle of good versus evil. Memorable characters are many-sided: Harry is not only brave, strong, and true, he is vulnerable and sympathetic: orphaned as a child, bespectacled, and often misunderstood by his peers, Harry is not a stereotypical hero.

Charles Dickens's Oliver Twist, in the book of the same title, is the principle of goodness, oppressed and unrecognized, unleashed in a troubled world. Oliver encounters a great deal of evil, which he refuses to cooperate with, and also a great deal of good in people who have sympathy for his plight. In contrast to the gentle, kindly, and selfless Maylies who take Oliver in, recognizing his goodness, are the evil

Bill Sykes and Fagin—thieves and murderers—who are willing to sell and hurt others for their own gain. When Nancy, a thief in league with Sykes and Fagin, essentially "sells" herself to help Oliver, she represents redemption from evil through sacrifice.

Setting

The setting of a work of fiction adds a great deal to the story. Historical fiction relies firmly on an established time and place: Johnny Tremain takes place in revolutionary Boston; the story could not take place anywhere else or at any other time. Ray Bradbury's *The Most Dangerous Game* requires an isolated, uninhabited island for its plot. Settings are sometimes changed in a work to represent different periods of a person's life or to compare and contrast life in the city or life in the country.

Point of View

The point of view is the perspective of the person who is the focus of the work of fiction: a story told in the first person is from the point of view of the narrator. In more modern works, works told in the third person usually concentrate on the point of view of one character or else the changes in point of view are clearly delineated, as in *Cold Mountain* by Charles Frazier, who names each chapter after the person whose point of view is being shown. Sudden, unexplained shifts in point of view—i.e., going into the thoughts of one character after another within a short space of time—are a sign of amateurish writing.

See also Competencies 4.C, 4.G, 4.H, and 4.I

H.   Applies effective strategies for helping students view literature as a source for exploring and interpreting human experience

It's no coincidence the study of ancient civilizations relies on these civilizations' art just as much as their more concrete, technological achievements to understand their way of life. A society's creative output is a direct glimpse into the heart and soul of the people. We can gather so much more about the Middle Ages, for example, by looking at the literature of the time than by studying a goblet owned by a king. Why is this? Literature is the result of people expressing themselves or their experience of life in words.

Pass this philosophy along to students by using historical literature as a way to peek into each author's experience. Ask students questions such as, "What does the tone of this piece say about the way of life for the author?" or "How is the way of life depicted in this story different from your own life experience?" Getting students to think about literature as a way to document a certain period's human experience may inspire them to document their own!

I. Applies effective strategies for engaging students in exploring and discovering the personal and societal relevance of literature

See Competency 7.H

Pre-teaching about the time period in which a piece of literature was written and providing social and historical information that affected the literature, or noting the effects the literature had upon its epoch is an effective strategy for demonstrating the societal relevance of literature.

Reading-response journals are also an effective strategy to engage students in exploring and discovering the personal relevance of literature as they record their own emotional responses to the literature, relate the literature to their own lives, admire or disavow characters and their choices, or imagine alternative, more satisfying endings.

See Competency 6.D, particularly The Realistic Period.

J. Promotes students' understanding of relationships among literary works from various times and cultures

Literary allusions are drawn from classical mythology, national folklore, and religious writings with which the reader is assumed to be familiar so he or she can recognize the comparison between the subject of the allusion and the person, place, or event in the current reading. Children and adolescents who have knowledge of proverbs, fables, myths, epics, and the Bible can understand these allusions and thereby appreciate their reading to a greater degree than those who cannot recognize them.

Fables and Folktales

This literary group of stories and legends was originally orally transmitted to the common populace to provide models of exemplary behavior or deeds worthy of recognition and homage.

In fables, animals talk, feel, and behave like human beings. The fable always has a moral, and the animals illustrate specific people or groups without directly identifying them. For example, in Aesop's Fables, the lion is the king and the wolf is the cruel, often unfeeling noble class. In the fable of "The Lion and the Mouse," the moral is that "Little friends may prove to be great friends." In "The Lion's Share," it is "Might makes right." Many British folktales—such as *How Robin Hood became an Outlaw* and *St. George: Slaying of the Dragon*—stress the correlation between power and right.

Classical Mythology

Much of the mythology from which allusions in modern English writings are drawn is a product of ancient Greece and Rome because these myths have been widely translated for centuries. Some Norse myths are also well known. These stories provide insight into the order and ethics of life as ancient heroes overcame the terrors of the unknown and brought meaning to thunder and lightning, to the changing of the seasons, to the magical creatures of the forests and seas, and to the myriad of natural phenomena that can frighten humankind. There is often a childlike quality in the emotions of supernatural beings with which children can identify. Many good translations of myths exist for readers of varying abilities, but Edith Hamilton's *Mythology* is the most definitive reading for adolescents.

Fairy Tales

Fairy tales are lively fictional stories involving children or animals that come in contact with supernatural beings through magic. Fairy tales provide happy solutions to human dilemmas. The fairy tales of many nations are peopled by trolls, elves, dwarfs, and pixies, child-sized beings capable of fantastic accomplishments.

Among the most famous are "Beauty and the Beast," "Cinderella," "Hansel and Gretel," "Snow White and the Seven Dwarfs," "Rumpelstiltskin," and "Tom Thumb." In each tale, the protagonist survives prejudice, imprisonment, ridicule, or even death to receive justice in a cruel world.

Older readers encounter a kind of fairy-tale world in Shakespeare's *The Tempest* and *A Midsummer Night's Dream*, which use pixies and fairies as characters. Adolescent readers today are fascinated by the creations of fantasy realms in the works of Piers Anthony, Ursula K. LeGuin, and Anne McCaffrey. An extension of interest in the supernatural is science fiction that uses current knowledge to predict the possible course of the future.

Angels (or sometimes fairy godmothers) play a role in some fairy tales, and Milton in *Paradise Lost* and *Paradise Regained* also used symbolic angels and devils.

Biblical stories provide many allusions. Parables, which are moralistic tales like fables but have human characters, include the stories of the Good Samaritan and the Prodigal Son. References to the treachery of Cain and the betrayal of Christ by Judas Iscariot are oft-cited examples.

American Folktales

American folktales are divided into two categories: imaginary tales (tall tales) and real tales (legends).

Imaginary tales, also called **tall tales**, are humorous tales based on nonexistent, fictional characters developed through blatant exaggeration.

For example, John Henry is a two-fisted steel driver who beats a steam drill in competition. Rip Van Winkle sleeps for 20 years in the Catskill Mountains and upon awakening cannot understand why no one recognizes him.

Paul Bunyan, a giant lumberjack, owns a great blue ox named Babe and has extraordinary physical strength. He is said to have plowed the Mississippi River, and the impressions of Babe's hoof prints created the Great Lakes.

Real tales, also called **legends**, are based on real persons who accomplished the feats that are attributed to them even if they are slightly exaggerated. For example, for more than 40 years, Johnny Appleseed (John Chapman) roamed Ohio and Indiana planting apple seeds. Daniel Boone—scout, adventurer, and pioneer—blazed the Wilderness Trail and made Kentucky safe for settlers. Paul Revere, a colonial patriot, rode through the New England countryside warning of the approach of British troops.

K. Promotes students' ability to analyze how literary elements and devices contribute to meaning and to synthesize and evaluate interpretations of literary texts

It's no accident that **plot** is sometimes called action. If the plot does not *move*, the story quickly dies. Therefore, the successful writer of stories uses a wide variety of active verbs in creative and unusual ways. If a reader is kept on his or her toes by the movement of the story, the experience of reading it will be pleasurable. That reader will probably want to read more of this author's work. Careful, unique, and unusual choices of active verbs will bring about that effect.

William Faulkner is a good example of a successful writer whose stories are lively and memorable because of his use of unusual active verbs. It's wise to look at the verbs in an analysis of plot. However, the development of believable conflicts is also vital. If there is no conflict, there is no story. What devices does a writer use to develop the conflicts, and are they real and believable?

Character is portrayed in many ways: for example, description of physical characteristics, dialogue, interior monologue, the thoughts of the character, and the attitudes of other characters toward this one. Descriptive language depends on the writer's ability to recreate a sensory experience for the reader. If the description of the character's appearance is a visual one, then the reader must be able to *see* the character. What's the shape of the nose? What color are the eyes? How tall or how short is this character? Is the character thin or chubby? How does the character move? How does the character walk? The writer must choose terms that will create a picture for the reader.

It's not enough to say the character's eyes are blue, for example. What shade of blue? Often the color of eyes is compared to something else to enhance the reader's ability to visualize the character. A good test of characterization is the reader's level of emotional involvement in the character. If the reader is to become involved, the description must provide an actual experience—seeing, smelling, hearing, tasting, or feeling.

Dialogue will reflect characteristics. Is it clipped? Is it highly dialectal? Does a character use a lot of colloquialisms? The ability to portray the speech of a character can make or break a story. The kind of person the character is in the mind of the reader is dependent on impressions created by description and dialogue. How do other characters feel about this one, as revealed by their treatment of him or her, their discussions of him or her with one another, or their overt descriptions of the character? For example, "John, of course, can't be trusted with another person's possessions." In analyzing a story, it's useful to discuss the devices used to produce character.

Setting may be visual, temporal, psychological, or social. Descriptive words are often used here also. In Edgar Allan Poe's description of the house in "The Fall of the House of Usher" as the protagonist/narrator approaches it, the air of dread and gloom that pervades the story is caught in the setting and sets the stage for the story. A setting may also be symbolic, as it is in Poe's story, in which the house is a symbol of the family that lives in it. As the house disintegrates, so does the family.

The language used in all of these aspects of a story—plot, character, and setting—creates the **mood** of a story. Poe's first sentence establishes the mood of "The Fall of the House of Usher": "During the whole of a dull, dark, and soundless day in the autumn of the year, when the clouds hung oppressively low in the heavens, I had been passing alone, on horseback, through a singularly dreary tract of country; and at length found myself, as the shades of the evening drew on, within view of the melancholy House of Usher."

To *interpret* means essentially to read with understanding and appreciation. It is not as daunting as it can seem. Simple techniques for interpreting literature are as follows:

- **Ambiguity:** Ambiguity is any writing whose meaning cannot be definitively determined by its context. Ambiguity may be introduced accidentally, confusing the readers and disrupting the flow of reading. If a sentence or paragraph jars upon reading, there is lurking ambiguity. It is particularly difficult to spot ambiguities in your own writing.

- **Connotation:** Connotation refers to the ripple effect surrounding the implications and associations of a given word, distinct from the denotative or literal meaning. Connotation is used when a subtle tone is preferred. It may stir up a more effective emotional response than if the author had used blunt, denotative diction.

- **Symbolism:** A symbol is something that stands for something else. In most cases, it stands for something that has a deeper meaning than its literal denotation. Symbols can have personal, cultural, or universal associations. An understanding of symbols can be used to unearth a meaning the author might have intended but not expressed, or even something the author never intended at all.

- **Rhythm:** Rhythm refers to the "beat" between the words chosen and the smoothness, rapidity, or disjointedness of the way those words are written. Sentences that are too long may disrupt the rhythm of a piece, as may sentences that are too short. Reading text out loud is an easy way to impart understanding of literary rhythm.

- **Rhyme:** Using rhyme can be especially effective at generating reader response. Think about the success Dr. Seuss had with his rhyming style. Rhyme is tricky, though; used ineffectively or unnecessarily, it can break up the entire rhythm of the piece or fog the reader's understanding of it. Rhyme should be used when it is purely beneficial to the format of the piece. Make sure it is not forcing you to use more words than needed and that each verse is moving the story forward.

- **Diction:** Diction is simply the right word in the right spot for the right purpose. The hallmark of a great writer is precise and memorable diction.

- **Imagery:** Imagery engages one or more of the five senses. An author might use imagery to give the reader a greater, more descriptive picture of the scene he or she is trying to depict. Imagery may conjure up a past experience that the reader has had (the smell of the ocean, the feeling of a childhood blanket), thereby enriching the reader's mental picture of the scene.

- **Context:** This includes the author's feelings, beliefs, past experiences, goals, needs, and physical environment. Incorporate an understanding of how these elements may have affected the writing to enrich an interpretation of it.

- **Questions:** Asking questions, such as "How would I react in this situation?" may shed further light on how you feel about the work.

L. **Knows effective strategies for teaching students to formulate, express, and support responses to various types of literary texts**

The first principle in writing an analysis of a literary selection is a thorough reading and understanding of the work. Once the student feels that he or she clearly understands the author's intent, he or she must determine a thesis statement for his or her analysis. For example, if one were analyzing Mitch Albom's *The Five People You Meet in Heaven*, the thesis for the analysis might be as follows: "The theme of this story is that living to serve others gives meaning to the end of one's life."

The student can make a point that is meaningful by focusing on a particular aspect of the story. For example, the *style* of a writer like Ernest Hemingway is so unusual and significant that the thesis might focus on that aspect of one of his stories. Setting may also play a special role in a story and might make a good thesis for analysis. In fact, any aspect of the story can be useful for this kind of paper. This choice is important and will drive how the analysis is developed.

Once the thesis is decided, the next steps fall in line. The first step is a search for passages that support or relate to the thesis. Even before the student has chosen a thesis, he or she should have been taking notes, possibly on the pages of the book itself.

Once the thesis is determined, then the student can go back through the work, looking at the notes already made but adding or adjusting them to make sure adequate material is available to support the thesis of the analysis. At this point, the student should compile and organize the notes in a document for easy reference. Specifics and details are important to make the analysis complete and effective. In this second reading, the thesis might change—either to an entirely different one or to a variation of the first one.

It's not enough to just present illustrative material; it must be organized in such a way that it is logical and reasonable to the reader of the analysis. To achieve this, the student should make a preliminary outline of the final paper. This outline does not have to follow the progression of the book; the passages in the book should be used in the order that best supports the analysis.

The student should remember that an analysis is a recursive process. Nothing is set in stone until the paper is ready to be handed in. The student will notice things during the second and third readings that were not apparent the first time through, and he or she must feel free to make changes that make the thesis clearer or stronger. Even the thesis or the aspect of the story that will be the focus of the analysis is open to change until the last stage of the writing process. Students sometimes have difficulty coming to a decision, so they should be encouraged to set time limits on themselves for making the decisions and completing the various steps required to write a successful paper.

Helping students become successful writers of literary analyses depends on several factors. They should have plenty of experience in analysis in class. The short story is a good way to help students become confident that they can do this kind of writing, which requires independent reasoning. Using the short story as the basis for a writing course gives students more opportunities to go through the analyzing process and to practice their analytical skills. The role of the teacher is not only to continually teach the principles but also to encourage independent thinking in these matters, which often means accepting some less-than-perfect analyses.

Ultimately, the analysis should be the student's convictions as a result of reading and understanding the text. This is a good opportunity to help students begin to take responsibility for what they write—an important objective for a writing course.

M. **Demonstrates an understanding of informal and formal procedures for monitoring and assessing students' comprehension of literary texts**

See Competency 4.M

N. **Knows how to use assessment results to plan and adapt instruction that addresses students' strengths, needs, and interests and that builds on students' current skills to increase their proficiency in comprehending literary texts**

See Skill 4.M

DOMAIN III. WRITTEN COMMUNICATION

COMPETENCY 008 THE TEACHER UNDERSTANDS AND PROMOTES WRITING AS A RECURSIVE, DEVELOPMENTAL, INTEGRATIVE, AND ONGOING PROCESS AND PROVIDES STUDENTS WITH OPPORTUNITIES TO DEVELOP COMPETENCE AS WRITERS

A. **Understands recursive stages in the writing process and provides students with explicit instruction, meaningful practice, and effective feedback as they engage in all phases of the writing process**

Writing is a process that involves stages, and those stages involve a certain amount of repetition—that is, going back in a circular way rather than proceeding in a linear fashion. These are the recursive stages of writing: prewriting, drafting, revising, editing, and publishing. The process itself lends itself well to teacher feedback if teachers provide effective feedback at each stage of the process rather than only grading students on finished papers.

Prewriting is planning a first draft. Prior to writing a first draft, a student needs to prewrite for ideas and details on a given topic and decide how the essay will be organized. Students should be guided to develop at least three main points and at least two to three details to support each main point. There are several types of graphic organizers that may be used, including making an outline once the student has done a preliminary review of literature and made notes. Determining the purpose and audience of the written document are part of prewriting. Note-taking from resources is important and especially effective if the notes are being taken to provide information for an outline.

Formal outlines inhibit effective writing. However, a loosely constructed outline can be an effective device for note-taking that will yield the information for a worthwhile statement about a topic. Sentence outlines are better than topic outlines because they require the writer to do some thinking about the direction a subtopic will take.

After the prewriting phase is completed, the teacher should review the students' work and process, re-direct and correct if necessary, look for tangents, and decide whether purpose, audience, main points are being addressed and whether appropriate literature or nonliterary texts are being consulted.

The writing at this next stage is likely to be highly individualized. However, successful writers tend to just write, keeping in mind the purpose of the paper, the point that is going to be made in it, and the information that has been turned up in the research. Student writers need to understand that this first draft is just that—the first one. It takes more than one draft to write a worthwhile statement about a topic. This is what successful writers do. It's sometimes helpful to read the various drafts of a story by a well-known writer. Students writers should be encouraged that this is only a first draft. Teachers should read the students' first drafts and give feedback with an eye to the next phase: revisions.

Revising the first draft includes considering how well the purpose of the writing, the audience, and the main theme have been addressed and removing any extraneous, repetitive information or adding in information where it is needed. These large structural issues need to be addressed in revising the first draft, as do flow, style, logic, word choice, and the use of literary or persuasive devices. The teacher's feedback is invaluable at this stage as the written work proceeds toward the editing phase.

The next phase is editing, which is concerned with the mechanics of expression, correcting grammar, spelling, punctuation, clumsy sentences, etc. The students' editing of their work should be checked by the teacher and feedback given as to its accuracy, as well as anything missed pointed out. In addition to mechanics, spelling, punctuation, and grammar, editing is rereading objectively, testing the effectiveness of the arrangement and the line of reasoning. The kinds of changes that will need to be made are rearranging the parts, adding necessary information that is missing, and deleting information that doesn't fit or contribute to the accomplishment of the purpose. The teacher will be able to provide a more objective and practiced eye for feedback at this stage than the student writer.

Conferencing with fellow students and the teacher may yield important feedback at this stage, resulting in a final draft which is checked once again for mechanical errors and then made ready for presentation or publication, whereupon the feedback circle will extend beyond the teacher and possibly beyond the classroom.

B.   Understands writing as a process that allows students to construct meaning, examine thinking, reflect, develop perspective, acquire new learning, and influence the world around them

Writing and reading are complementary skills. Writing is the partner of reading, as reading and writing skills develop simultaneously in children. As reading is a mental process of constructing meaning, so is writing.

The process of writing exercises thought as an active, participatory process not only in constructing but even creating meaning. Writing is a process that allows a student to explore thinking in more depth; it is a process that stimulates reflection that goes beneath the surface and often reveals new perspectives, in addition to being a perspective-taking activity in itself. Journaling is self-revealing and often therapeutic; writing in response to readings makes the reader plumb deeper depths of understanding, challenge conscious thinking with unconscious revelation, and engage in reflection, calling upon personal stores of knowledge, experience, and understanding and interacting with those stores with the new information and fresh perspectives transmitted through reading.

The National Commission on Writing is quoted in a 2007 report to the Carnegie Foundation as saying: "If students are to make knowledge their own, they must struggle with the details, wrestle with the facts, and rework raw information and dimly understood concepts into language they can communicate to someone else. In short, if students are to learn, they must write."

As an interactive process, writing raises questions for examination and suggests new explorations and a need for additional information. As students study both literary and nonliterary texts that have had impact on the world, the power of the pen is revealed. The sayings that "the pen is mightier than the sword" and that "nothing is more powerful than an idea whose time has come" become a reality when impactful writings are studied an reflected upon. Studying such written works as Thomas Paine's revolutionary writings, the texts of Frederick Douglass's speeches and articles, and the works of social critics such as Upton Sinclair and others allows students to see how the process of writing has the power to change history. Students may realize that their own writings can have impact upon the world too; even a simple Letter to the Editor of a newspaper can have some social significance.

Teachers may remind students that writing can allow them to express thoughts they might not otherwise put forth or even be aware of. Furthermore, when those thoughts are put down on paper, the choice is up to the students whether they want to share them with their peers or keep them as private notes. Occasional free-writing periods may loosen up reluctant writers, especially if they are informed that they need not turn in their work. This security may break down the inhibitions that most students have when writing in a classroom setting. Encourage students to save their writing, describing the enjoyment they will have when looking back on it when they are older.

Many students see writing as a painful task, but they should be reminded that writing is not used solely for essays and reports. Think about the joy of signing yearbooks and reading the written messages of others. Writing a screenplay for a movie can be an exciting adventure. Communicating with friends through the written word is often a cure for loneliness when friends are not near. This and other psychological releases in the process of writing are important to emphasis. It can be cathartic to write an angry note to vent frustration at someone (whether the note is sent or not). The creative process is often psychologically integrating, and writing may be a creative process. Students may be assured that the more they write, the better they will get at writing. As an example of the interrelatedness of reading and writing, students may be informed that the fear and avoidance people may feel at the prospect of a blank page or empty compute file (known as writer's block) is best cured by reading something on the topic to be addressed and then attempting to write again.

C. **Applies writing conventions, including sentence and paragraph construction, spelling, punctuation, usage, and grammatical expression, and provides students with explicit instruction in using them during the writing process**

See Competency 3.D

D.   Applies criteria for evaluating written work and teaches students effective strategies for evaluating their own writing and the writings of others

See Competency 8.A

Sometimes students see editing and evaluating their work as simply catching errors in spelling or word use. Students need to reframe their thinking about revising and editing. They should ask the following questions:

- Is the reasoning coherent?
- Is the point established?
- Does the introduction make the reader want to read this discourse?
- What is the thesis? Is it proven?
- What is the purpose? Is it clear? Is it useful, valuable, interesting?
- Is the style of writing so wordy that it exhausts the reader and interferes with engagement?
- Is the writing so spare that it is boring?
- Are the sentences too uniform in structure?
- Are there too many simple sentences?
- Are too many of the complex sentences the same structure?
- Are the compounds truly compounds or are they unbalanced?
- Are parallel structures truly parallel?
- If there are characters, are they believable?
- If there is dialogue, is it natural or stilted?
- Is the title appropriate?
- Does the writing show creativity or is it boring?
- Is the language appropriate? Is it too formal? Too informal? If jargon is used, is it appropriate?

Studies have clearly demonstrated that this is the most fertile area in teaching writing. If students can learn to revise their own work effectively, they are well on their way to becoming effective, mature writers. Word processing software is an important tool for teaching this stage in the writing process. Microsoft Word has tracking features that make the revision exchanges between teachers and students more effective than ever before.

E.   Structures peer conference opportunities that elicit constructive, specific responses and that promote students' writing development

Viewing writing as a process allows teachers and students to see the writing classroom as a cooperative workshop in which students and teachers encourage and support one another in each writing endeavor. Listed below are some techniques that help teachers facilitate and create a supportive classroom environment.

1. Create peer response/support groups that are working on similar writing assignments. The members help one another in all stages of the writing process—prewriting, writing, revising, editing, and publishing.

2. Provide several prompts to give students the freedom to write on a topic of their choice. Writing should be generated out of personal experience, and students should be introduced to in-class journals. One effective way to get into writing is to let students write often and freely about their own lives, without having to worry about grades or evaluation.

3. Respond in the form of a question whenever possible. Teachers/facilitators should respond non-critically and use positive, supportive language.

4. Respond to formal writing by acknowledging the student's strengths and focusing on the composition skills demonstrated by the writing. A response should encourage the student by offering praise for what the student has done well.

5. Give the student a focus for revision and demonstrate that the process of revision has applications in many other writing situations.

6. Provide students with readers' checklists so that they can write observational critiques of others' drafts and can revise their own papers at home using the checklists as a guide.

7. Pair students so that they can give and receive responses. Pairing students keeps them aware of the role of an audience in the composing process and in evaluating stylistic effects.

8. Focus critical comments on specific aspects that can be observed in the writing. Comments like "I noticed you use the word 'is' frequently" will be more helpful than "Your introduction is dull" and will not tend to demoralize the writer.

9. Provide the group with a series of questions to guide them through the group writing sessions.

F. **Understands and promotes the use of technology in all phases of the writing process and in various types of writing, including writing for research and publication**

See Competencies 10.G and 11.E

G. **Applies strategies for helping students develop voice and style in their writing**

There are at least 13 possible choices for point of view (voice) in literature as demonstrated and explained by Wallace Hildick in his *13 Types of Narrative* (London: MacMillan and Co., 1968). However, for purposes of helping students write essays about literature, three—or possibly four—are adequate. Teaching students to use this aspect of a piece of literature to write about it not only is an analytic exercise but also helps them research how a writer's choices impact the overall effect of the work.

Point of view or *voice* means "angle of vision," or the eyes through which the reader sees the action. The most common point of view is third-person objective. If the story is seen from this point of view, the reader watches the action, hears the dialogue, and reads descriptions, and from all of those must deduce characterization—what sort of person a character is. In this point of view, an unseen narrator tells the reader what is happening, using the third person: he, she, it, and they. The effect of this point of view is usually a feeling of distance from the plot. More responsibility is on the reader to make judgments than in other points of view. However, the author may intrude and evaluate or comment on the characters or the action.

The voice of the first-person narrator is often used also. The reader sees the action through the eyes of an actor in the story who is also telling the story. In writing about a story that uses this voice, the narrator must be analyzed as a character. What sort of person is this? What is this character's position in the story—observer, commentator, actor? Can the narrator be believed, or is he or she biased? The value of this voice is that, while the reader is able to follow the narrator around and see what is happening through that character's eyes, the reader is also able to feel what the narrator feels. For this reason, the writer can involve the reader more intensely in the story itself and move the reader by invoking feelings—pity, sorrow, anger, hate, confusion, disgust, and so on. Many of the most memorable novels are written in first-person point of view.

Another voice often used is called *omniscient* because the reader is able to get into the mind of more than one character or sometimes all the characters. This point of view can also bring greater involvement of the reader in the story. By knowing what a character is thinking and feeling, the reader is able to empathize when a character feels great pain and sorrow, which tends to make a work memorable. However, knowing what a character is thinking makes it possible to get into the mind of a pathological murderer and may elicit horror or disgust.

Omniscient point of view can be broken down into third-person omniscient and first-person omniscient. In third-person omniscient, the narrator is not seen or known or acting in the story but is able to watch and record not only what is happening or being said but also what characters are thinking. In first-person omniscient, the narrator plays a role in the story but can also record what other characters are thinking. It is possible, of course, that the narrator is a pathological murderer, which creates an effect quite different from a story in which the thoughts of the murderer are known but the narrator is standing back and reporting the murderer's behavior, thoughts, and intents.

Point of view or voice is a powerful tool in the hands of a skillful writer. The questions to be answered in writing an essay about a literary work are: What point of view has this author used? What effect does it have on the story? If it had been written in a different voice, how would the story be different?

Most, but not all, credible literary works are consistent in point of view, so consistency is another aspect that should be analyzed. Does the point of view change? Where does it vary? Does it help or hurt the effect of the story?

When writing personal notes or letters, the writer needs to keep the following key matters in mind:

- Once the topic is determined, the writer must determine the appropriate tone to introduce and express it. Is humor appropriate? Seriousness? Bluntness or subtlety? Does the situation call for formal or informal language? The answers to these questions will depend, in good part, on the writer's relationship to the reader.
- Does the writer's introduction clearly explain the topic/situation to a reader who doesn't know or feel everything that the reader knows or feels? Don't assume that the writer and reader are on the same page. Make a checklist to make sure that all key information is clearly and concisely expressed.
- If a note or letter involves a request, what type of response/result does the writer desire? Devise a strategy or strategies for achieving a desired outcome.
- If a note or letter involves a complaint about the reader, the writer will need to decide whether to ask for particular amends or to let the reader decide what, if anything, to do. If no amends are requested, the writer may wish to suggest ideas that would help avoid similar conflicts in the future. Asking the reader for his or her opinion is also a possibility.
- If a timely response to any note or letter is needed, the writer must mention this.

Give students in-class opportunities to write a variety of personal notes and letters, whether involving real-life or hypothetical situations. Invitations, thank-you notes, complaints, requests for favors, or personal updates are a few of the options available. Have students experiment with a variety of tones and strategies on a particular piece of personal correspondence. For example, write a complaint letter in a blunt tone, then write the same complaint in a humorous tone; compare and contrast the drafts. Structure in-class activities to allow for peer feedback.

A final note: Remind students that email messages, even if intended for just one reader, may eventually reach a much wider audience. In recent years there have been numerous instances of writers finding themselves in embarrassing situations or legal troubles due to their personal emails being circulated on the Internet. If a writer is addressing a sensitive, unpleasant, or controversial matter, he or she should consult state laws to determine whether personal privacy laws protect correspondence. If the law protects such correspondence from being circulated by the addressee, then the writer may wish to mention this in his or her message. Otherwise, clarity, concision, and civility in written works provide a writer all the protection that he or she will likely need.

See also Competency 7.A

H. **Demonstrates an understanding of informal and formal procedures for monitoring and assessing students' writing competence**

- Have students write a short story, essay, or other specified genre of writing.
- Assess students' ability to write about a given body of knowledge in a logical and critical way.
- Observe their ability to use language resources appropriate for the required task.
- Use a rating system, such as a scale from 1 to 4 (where 1 = unsatisfactory and 4 = excellent).
- Monitor their use of source material.
- Evaluate the structure and development of their writing.
- Ensure that their writing style is appropriate for the task assigned.
- Check for grammatical correctness.
- Provide follow-up support for any weaknesses detected.

I. **Uses assessment results to plan and adapt instruction that addresses students' strengths, needs, and interests and that builds on students' current skills to increase their writing proficiency**

Consider the following exercises to encourage students to write and to develop their writing proficiency:

- Keep an idea book to jot down ideas that come to mind.
- Write in a daily journal.
- Write down whatever comes to mind; this is called free writing. Students do not stop to make corrections or interrupt the flow of ideas. A variation of this technique is focused free writing—free writing on a specific topic—to prepare for writing an essay.
- Make a list of all ideas connected with a topic; this is called brainstorming. Make sure students know that this technique works best when they let their minds work freely. After completing the list, students should analyze the list to look for a pattern or way to group the ideas.
- Ask the questions Who? What? When? Where? When? and How? Help the writer approach a topic from several perspectives.
- Create a visual map on paper to gather ideas. Cluster circles and lines to show connections among ideas. Students should try to identify the relationships that exist among their ideas. If they cannot see the relationships, have them pair up, exchange papers, and have their partners look for some related ideas.
- Observe details of sight, hearing, taste, touch, and taste.
- Visualize by making mental images of something and writing down the details in a list.

After students have practiced each of these writing strategies, ask them to pick out the ones they prefer and discuss how they might use the techniques to help them with future writing assignments.

It is important for students to remember that they can use more than one writing strategy at a time. Also, they may find that different writing situations may suggest certain techniques.

Teaching students how to plan, revise, and edit their compositions strongly impacts the quality of student writing in a positive way. Therefore, the recursive process of writing should be assessed at each phase, and students should be given feedback to address their specific needs.

Students' abilities in writing summaries should be assessed, as this is an important writing improvement strategy. Do students effectively glean the main points of a piece, and are they able to express these points succinctly?

Students' writing improves with specific product goals, so assessing how well students meet goals in writing is an important way to plan and adapt further instruction. For example, requiring specific structural elements in a composition rather than giving a general direction allow for clear assessment of whether students are meeting goals.

COMPETENCY 009   THE TEACHER UNDERSTANDS EFFECTIVE WRITING AND TEACHES STUDENTS TO WRITE EFFECTIVELY IN A VARIETY OF FORMS AND FOR VARIOUS AUDIENCES, PURPOSES, AND CONTEXTS

A.   Understands and teaches the distinguishing features of various forms of writing

The writer must be cognizant of his or her own strengths and weaknesses and continually work to hone the way sentences are written, words are chosen, and descriptions are crafted until they are razor-sharp. The best advice to the aspiring writer: Read the works of successful writers. If a writer wants to write a bestseller, then that writer needs to be reading bestsellers.

Writing Poetry

Writing poetry in the twenty-first century is quite a different thing from writing it in earlier periods. There was a time when a poem was required to fit a certain pattern or scheme. Poetry was once defined as a piece of writing that used end-rhymes, among other conventions. Today, rhymed poems make up only a small percentage of worthwhile and successful poetry.

The first skill to work on for the budding poet is descriptive writing, defined as language that appeals to one or more of the five senses. A good poem makes it possible for the reader to experience an emotional event—seeing a mountain range as the sun rises, watching small children on a playground, smelling the fragrance of a rose, hearing a carillon peal a religious tune at sunset, feeling fine silk under one's fingers. Creating language that makes that experience available to the readers is only the first step, however, because the ultimate goal is to evoke an emotional response—feeling the horror of the battleground, weeping with the mother whose child was drowned, exulting with a winning soccer team. It's not enough to tell the reader what it's like. It's necessary to *show* the reader.

The aspiring poet should know the possibilities as well as the limitations of this genre. A poem can tell a story, for instance, but the emotional response is more important than the story itself. Edgar Allen Poe, in an 1842 review of Hawthorne's *Twice-Told Tales* in *Graham's Magazine,* had important advice for the writer of poetry: ". . . the unity of effect or impression is a point of the greatest importance." Even though he considered the tale or short story the best way to achieve this, he wrote several memorable poems, and much of his prose writing is considered to be as close to poetry as to prose by most critics. He also wrote in 1847, in an expansion of his critique of Hawthorne's works, that ". . . true originality . . . is that which, in bringing out the half-formed, the reluctant, or the unexpressed fancies of mankind, or in exciting the more delicate pulses of the heart's passion, or in giving birth to some universal sentiment or instinct in embryo, thus combines with the pleasurable effect of *apparent* novelty, a real egoistic delight."

Playwriting

Playwriting uses many of the same skills that are necessary to successful story writing. In addition to those skills, there are many more required of the writer who wishes his or her story to be told on stage or on film. The point of view, of course, is always objective unless the writer uses the Shakespearean device of the soliloquy, in which a player steps forward and gives information about what's going on. The audience must figure out the meaning of the play on the basis of the actions and speeches of the actors.

A successful playwright is expert in characterization. What a character is like is determined by dialogue, appearance (costume, makeup, and so on), behavior, and actions. A successful playwright also understands motivation. If a character's behavior cannot be traced to motivating circumstances, the audience will probably find the action incoherent—a major barrier to positive reception of the play.

The writing in a play must be very carefully honed. Absolutely no excess words can be used in a successful play. It takes very little time to lose an audience; every word counts. The playwright should concentrate on saying the most possible with the fewest words possible.

Setting is an important feature of the play. Most plays have only one setting because changing settings in the middle is difficult and disrupting. This calls for a very special kind of writing. The entire action of the play must either take place within the setting or be brought forth in that setting by the reporting or recounting of what is going on outside the setting by one or more of the characters. The writer must determine what the setting will be. The actual building and creation of the set is in the hands of another kind of artist—one who specializes in set creation.

The plot of most plays is rising; that is, the conflicts are introduced early in the play and continue to develop and intensify over the course of the play. As a general rule, the climax is the last thing that happens before the final curtain falls, but not necessarily. Plots of plays demonstrate the same breadth of patterns that are found in stories. For example, a play may end with nothing resolved. Denouement is less likely to follow a climax in a play than in a story, but epilogues do sometimes occur.

See also Competencies 6.H and 7.A

B.   Applies and teaches skills and strategies for writing effectively in a variety of forms and for a variety of audiences, purposes, and contexts

Once a topic is assigned or chosen, the next step is to begin to gather supporting materials. Those materials may come from the writer's own experience, in which case the best way to collect them is in prewriting. Prewriting is simply putting on paper whatever is there by way of past experience relevant to the topic; observations concerning it; articles or books that the writer has read on the topic; and any media (such as film or television) presentations that have to do with the topic. The writer needs to keep in mind the need to make a statement about the topic—to declare something about it. Very often, once the writer has gone through this exercise, getting his or her own ideas and thoughts down on paper, a thesis or several theses may emerge. If not, then it is time to do active research on the topic.

It's better to write more than one thesis statement before beginning research if possible. A successful writer, however, will set a point when a single one must be chosen so the development of the paper may proceed. Once that decision has been made, the narrowing process begins.

The writer should be asking such questions as "Is the scope too broad to cover in a 500-word paper?" For example, the thesis statement "Democracy is the best form of government," will take a book or even several books to develop. However, the thesis statement "Democracy is the best form of government for Iraq" is more doable. Even so, some narrowing of the predicate may still be in order. "The development of a democratic government will solve the problems of cultural and religious divisions in Iraq" may be a thesis that could be developed in one classroom assignment.

Remember that the introduction and conclusion should be written after the paper is developed so the writer will know what is being introduced and concluded. The writer should decide whether the reasoning will be inductive, from particular to general, or deductive, from general to particular. Will the pattern be inductive—evidence presented first and the thesis stated at the end? Will the thesis—the generalization—be presented first, followed by the proofs and evidence?

Will the introduction offer background information or be an anecdote or other device that will help lead the reader into the thesis and proofs? Or will it simply be designed to grab the reader's interest? It can also be used to establish the credibility of the writer. In the conclusion, will the reasoning be restated briefly with emphasis on the point of the paper, or will it also be anecdotal? Whatever form the conclusion takes, it should reinforce the point the paper makes and leave the reader with a favorable impression.

News Reporting and Editorials

Freedom of the press is essential to democracy. In this form of government, representatives are elected by the people and are responsible to them, and the people are entitled to know what those representatives are doing. The only way that can happen is if the press is free to report the news in an unbiased manner. If the mayor of a city has a conflict of interest that is profiting him or her, the people need to know. If an elected representative is arrested for driving under the influence, that representative's constituency has a right to know. It's the only way unbiased management of the public interest can occur.

For these reasons, news media have an obligation to keep themselves unencumbered and unbiased. Most news reporters pride themselves on their objectivity.

News stories are usually assumed to be unbiased. It can be argued, of course, that no one can be entirely unbiased and that it's the nature of the written word that those biases may creep into the reporting of news. Even so, the professional reporter and/or editor will exercise the strength necessary to keep his or her own biases out of the reporting as much as possible.

Editorializing is an entirely different thing. Most newspapers, for instance, have an editorial position, which will often correspond to a political party. A newspaper may, for instance, declare itself to be Republican. This does not mean that the newspaper will favor the party of choice in news reporting. It does, however, mean that editorial materials will probably be slanted in that direction. In a time of election, a newspaper will often come out for one candidate over another and try to influence its readership to follow suit. A newspaper will often take a side when an issue is on the docket at time of election or even at other times. An editorial will frequently state an opinion about a matter that concerns the newspaper's readership.

News reporters generally become excellent writers because they get a lot of practice, which is a principle most writing teachers try to employ with their students. Also, news writing is instructive in skills for writing clearly and coherently. Reporters generally write in one or two modes: straight reporting or feature writing. In both modes, the writer must be concerned with accuracy and objectivity. The reporter does not write his or her opinions. He or she does not write persuasive discourse. The topic is typically assigned, although some experienced reporters have the opportunity to seek out and develop their own stories.

Investigative reporting is sometimes seen as a distinct form of writing, although technically, all reporters are investigative. That is, they research the background of the story they're reporting, using as many means as are available. For example, the wife of a conservative, model minister murders him pre-meditatively and in cold blood. The reporter reports the murder and the arrest of the wife, but the story is far from complete until some questions are answered, the most obvious one being "why?" The reporter is obligated to try to answer that question and to do so will interview as many people as will talk to him about the lives of both the minister and wife, such as their parents, members of the church, and their neighbors.

The reporter will also look at newspaper archives in the town where the murder took place as well as in newspapers in any town in which the husband and/or wife had lived previously. High-school yearbooks are sources that are often explored in these cases.

When Bob Woodward and Carl Bernstein, reporters for *The Washington Post,* began to break the Watergate story in 1972 and 1973, they set new standards for investigative reporting and had a strong influence on journalistic writing. Most reporters wanted to be Woodward and Bernstein and became more aggressive than reporters had been in the past. Even so, the basic techniques and principles still apply. The reporting of these two talented journalists demonstrated that while newspapers keep communities aware of what's going on, they also have the power to influence it.

A good news story is written as an "inverted pyramid." That is, the reasoning is deductive. The thesis or point is stated first and is supported with details. The reasoning moves from general to specific. The lead sentence might be, "The body of John Smith was found in the street in front of his home with a bullet wound through his skull." The headline will be a trimmed-down version of that sentence and shaped to grab attention. It might read: "Murdered man found on Spruce Street." The news article might fill several columns, the first details having to do with the finding of the body; the next with the role of the police; the next with the victim's life; and then the scope will broaden to details about his family, friends, neighbors, and so on. If he held a position of prominence in the community, those details will broaden further and include information about his relationships with fellow workers and his day-to-day contacts in the community. The successful reporter's skills include the ability to do thorough research, to maintain an objective stance (not to become involved personally in the story), and to write an effective inverted pyramid.

Feature writing is more like writing an informative essay, although it may also follow the inverted pyramid model. This form of reporting focuses on a topic designed to be interesting to at least one segment of the readership—for example, sports enthusiasts, travelers, vacationers, families, women, or food lovers. The article will focus on one aspect of the area of interest such as a particular experience for the vacationing family. The first sentence might read something like this: "Lake Lure offers a close-to-home relaxing weekend getaway for families in East Tennessee." The development can be an ever-widening pyramid of details focused particularly on what the family can experience at Lake Lure but also including directions for how to get there.

While the headline is intended to contain in capsule form the point that an article makes, this can sometimes result in a disconnection between headline and article. Well-written headlines provide a guide for the reader as to what is in the article; they will also be attention-grabbers. This requires a special kind of writing.

Business Letters and Email

Email has revolutionized business communications. It has most of the advantages of business letters and the added ones of immediacy, lower costs, and convenience. Very long reports can be attached to an email, or a two-line message can be sent and a response received immediately, bringing together the features of the postal system and the telephone.

Business-related, professional email should be composed with as much care as letters. Carefully written professional correspondence, whether on paper or electronic, can be powerful. It can alienate, convince, persuade, entice, motivate, and/or create goodwill.

As with any other communication, it's worthwhile to learn as much as possible about the receiver. This may be complicated if there will be more than one receiver of the message; in these cases, it's best to write in a way that can be understood by the receiver with the least knowledge if that can be achieved without "writing down" to any of those who will read and be affected or influenced by the letter. It may be better to send more than one form of the letter to the various receivers in some cases.

Purpose is the most powerful consideration in writing a business letter. What is the letter expected to accomplish? Is it intended to get the receiver to act or to act in a specific manner? Are you hoping to see some action take place as the result of the letter? If so, you should clearly define for yourself what the purpose is before you craft the letter, and it's good to include a deadline for the response.

Reasons for using a letter as the channel of communication include the following:

1. It's easy to keep a record of the transaction.
2. The message can be edited and perfected before it is transmitted.
3. It facilitates the handling of details.
4. It's ideal for communicating complex information.
5. It's a good way to disseminate mass messages at a relatively low cost.

The parts of a business letter are: date line, inside address, salutation, subject line*, body, complimentary close, company name*, signature block, reference initials*, enclosure notation*, copy notation*, and postscript*.
Aspects of the letter denoted with an asterisk above are not required but sometimes useful. Email includes many of these elements by default, such as the date line, subject line, and signature block.

Business letters typically use formal language. They should be straightforward and courteous. The writing should be concise, and special care should be taken to leave out no important information. Clarity is very important; otherwise, it may take more than one exchange of letters or phone calls to get the message across.

Letters of Complaint

A complaint is a specific kind of business letter. It can come under the classification of a "bad news" business letter, and there are some guidelines that are helpful when writing this kind of letter. A positive writing style can overcome much of the inherent negativity of a letter of complaint.

No matter how in the right you may be, maintaining self-control and courtesy and avoiding demeaning or blaming language is the best way to be effective. Abruptness, condescension, or harshness of tone will not achieve your purpose, particularly if you are requesting a positive response such as reimbursement for a defective product or some help righting a wrong that may have been done to you. It's important to remember that you want to solve the specific problem and to retain the goodwill of the receiver if possible.

Induction is better than deduction for this type of communication. Beginning with the details and building to the statement of the problem generally has the effect of softening the bad news. It's also useful to begin with an opening that will serve as a buffer. The same is true for the closing. It's good to leave the reader with a favorable impression by writing a closing paragraph that will generate good rather than bad will.

C. Understands and teaches how a writer's purpose and audience define appropriate language, writing style, and text organization

Listening to students sitting on the steps that lead into the building that houses their classrooms, teachers will hear dialogue that may not even be understandable to them. The student who is writing to his or her peers will need to know and understand the peculiarities of that discourse to use them effectively. This is a good example for students of what it means to tailor language for a particular audience and for a particular person.

This is a good time to teach the concept of jargon. Writing to be read by a lawyer is a different thing from writing to be read by a medical doctor. Writing to be read by parents is different from writing to be read by the administrator of the school. Not only are the vocabularies different, but also the formality/informality of the discourse will need to be adjusted.

Determining what the language should be for a particular audience, then, hinges on two things: vocabulary and formality/informality. The most formal language does not use contractions or slang. The most informal language will certainly use contractions and the slang that is appropriate for the particular audience. Formal language will use longer sentences and will not sound like a conversation. The most informal language will use shorter sentences—not necessarily simple sentences—and will sound like a conversation.

Novels use formal language only when it is spoken by a character who would speak that way, such as a lawyer or a school superintendent, or is the voice of a third-person narrator. It's jarring to read a novel that has a construction worker using formal language. Using examples of various characters and their dialogues from fiction is useful in helping students understand this crucial aspect of writing.

D. Provides students with explicit instruction, meaningful practice opportunities, and effective feedback as the students create different types of written works

Most teachers have the experience of carefully preparing writing assignments that seem to miss the mark. What seemed clear and straightforward in preparation didn't turn out to be so for the students. Because students learn the most about writing by writing, the ability to create effective assignments that lead students to creatively use and practice the strategies you're teaching them is crucial if they are to experience the growth we look forward to seeing when the course is over. Fortunately, there are some guidelines for writing such assignments.

From the time students enter middle school, the goals of the English curriculum must include the production of the kind of writing that will be required when they enter college, which will include writing for a variety of audiences such as faculty in various departments, the general public, and the workplace. Objectives will include the ability to write in several genres and for different audiences.

The goals and objectives must be realizable. The effective writing teacher will perfect the ability to write achievable, worthwhile goals and objectives. No class should begin before the teacher has a clear concept of what will be true in terms of student understanding and performance once the class has ended. The same thing can be said of the various stages through which the course will go. Many teachers write their assignments before the class begins and then make adjustments in those assignments to fit the progress of a particular group of students. Whatever approach the teacher takes, the class should be envisioned as a complete entity and outcomes should be anticipated before it begins.

Sequencing the Assignments

The rhetorical mode with which students have the most experience is persuasion. They have become quite expert at persuading their parents to give them what they want or to let them do what they want to do. They begin practicing these skills almost as soon as they can speak, so this is a good place to start and a good place to end. Remember that critical-thinking skills can and should be taught, and they apply most directly to this mode. This is not to say that other modes should be neglected; however, they do need to be set in the structure of the persuasive mode. Certainly comparison/analysis is one way of making a point clear.

Descriptive writing is often used to move an audience emotionally, and this is a good time to help students understand the ethical aspects of persuasion—that emotion as a persuader is only one tool, not the only tool, as many religious and political speakers and writers seem to believe. Establishing credibility is important for any writer/speaker, and students can be led to understand its use in the persuasion process. Exposition—the explaining, informative mode—is vital to effective persuasion, as is definition.

Persuasive writing provides an excellent opportunity to teach thesis, support, critical thinking, and use of examples. The skeleton of an argument is a good way for students to see how the thinking and writing process works. An analysis of a poem, a story, or an essay is persuasive in nature: It states an opinion about the work and then uses examples from the work itself as support.

Assignments should never be made orally, and they should be straightforward. It's good to give students the outline as soon as the class begins to meet. This doesn't mean that it is set in stone. No two classes progress in exactly the same way, and the teacher needs the freedom and flexibility to make adjustments as the class moves through the semester. Even so, giving students some insight into what is to come can be helpful for some and is likely to lead them to be more cooperative. Also, creating an outline that they will have in their hands will help the teacher think more critically about outcomes and goals.

Some teachers who are very good writers of prompts will link all the essays in a writing class together, perhaps beginning with observation that will make no attempt to make a point. Using that observation, the sequence can move forward, teaching each of the skills and tools that are available in writing to make a statement, writing that someone will want to read. The final essay, then, can take the assignments and work of the semester and demonstrate their use in a worthwhile piece of writing that will display what has been learned.

Here are some guidelines for effective prompts:

- Fit the prompt into a sequence that is understood and seen by the students as one step toward a final goal.
- Make clear what the student is expected to do, and be sure that the mode being worked on in this assignment is clear.
- Be specific about how the assignment is to be completed and presented. If an informal tone is expected, then the assignment should say so. Include such things as whether outside sources are to be used, whether the assignment is to be typed or sent electronically, what the due date is, the required length, and so on.
- Give guidelines about purpose—what the paper is supposed to do and who the audience is.
- Specify criteria to be used in assessing the paper.

Writing is a very complex skill. There is no way to make it simple.

Trying to teach and test everything at once will inevitably lead to failure on the teacher's part as well as on the students'. Teaching the complexities in stages and then linking them together has the best chance of changing the writing behaviors of students in a positive way—the best objective a writing class can achieve.

E.   **Promotes students' ability to compose effectively**

Enhancing Interest:

- Start out with an attention-grabbing introduction. This sets an engaging tone for the entire piece and will be more likely to pull in the reader.
- Use dynamic vocabulary and varied sentence beginnings. Keep the readers on their toes. If they can predict what you are going to say next, switch it up.
- Avoid using clichés (as cold as ice, the best thing since sliced bread, nip it in the bud). These are easy shortcuts, but they are not interesting, memorable, or convincing.

Ensuring Understanding:

- Avoid using the words *clearly*, *obviously*, and *undoubtedly*. Often, things that are clear or obvious to the author are not as apparent to the reader. Instead of using these words, make your point so strongly that it is clear on its own.
- Use the word that best fits the meaning you intend, even if the word is longer or a little less common. Try to find a balance or go with a familiar yet precise word.
- When in doubt, explain further.

Maintaining Focus:

- **Focus on a main point.** The point should be clear to readers, and all sentences in the paragraph should relate to it.

- **Start the paragraph with a topic sentence.** This should be a general, one-sentence summary of the paragraph's main point, relating both back toward the thesis and forward toward the content of the paragraph. (A topic sentence is sometimes unnecessary if the paragraph continues a developing idea clearly introduced in a preceding paragraph or if the paragraph appears in a narrative of events in which generalizations might interrupt the flow of the story.)

- **Stick to the point.** Eliminate sentences that do not support the topic sentence.

Be flexible. If there is not enough evidence to support the claim your topic sentence is making, do not fall into the trap of wandering or introducing new ideas within the paragraph. Either find more evidence or adjust the topic sentence to correspond to the evidence that is available.

Introductions

It's important to remember that in the writing process, the introduction should be written last. Until the body of the paper has been determined—thesis and development—it's difficult to make strategic decisions regarding the introduction. The Greek rhetoricians called this part of a discourse *exordium*, a "leading into." The basic purpose of the introduction, then, is to lead the reader into the discourse. It can let the reader know what the purpose of the discourse is, and it can condition the audience to be receptive to what the writer wants to say. It can be very brief or it can take up a large percentage of the total word count. Aristotle said that the introduction could be compared to the flourishes that flute players make before their performance—an overture in which the musicians display what they can play best to gain the favor and attention of the audience for the main performance.

To do this, we must first of all know what we are going to say; who the readership is likely to be; what the social, political, and economic, climate is; what preconceived notions the audience is likely to have regarding the subject; and how long the discourse is going to be.

There are many ways to do this:

- Show that the subject is important.
- Show that although the points we are presenting may seem improbable, they are true.
- Show that the subject has been neglected, misunderstood, or misrepresented.
- Explain an unusual mode of development.
- Forestall any misconception of the purpose.
- Apologize for a deficiency.
- Arouse interest in the subject with an anecdotal lead-in.
- Ingratiate oneself with the readership.
- Establish one's own credibility.

The introduction often ends with the thesis, the point or purpose of the paper. However, this is not set in stone. The thesis may open the body of the discussion, or it may conclude the discourse. The most important thing to remember is that the purpose and structure of the introduction should be deliberate if it is to serve the purpose of leading the reader into the discussion.

Conclusions

It's easier to write a conclusion after the decisions regarding the introduction have been made. Aristotle taught that the conclusion should strive to do five things:

1. Inspire the reader with a favorable opinion of the writer.
2. Amplify the force of the points made in the body of the paper.
3. Reinforce the points made in the body.
4. Rouse appropriate emotions in the reader.
5. Restate in a summary way what has been said.

The conclusion may be short or it may be long depending on its purpose in the paper. Recapitulation, a brief restatement of the main points or of the thesis is the most common form of effective conclusions. A good example is the closing argument in a court trial.

Text Organization

In studies of professional writers and how they produce their successful works, it has been revealed that writing is a process that can be clearly defined, although in practice it must have enough flexibility to allow for creativity. The teacher must be able to define the various stages that a successful writer goes through to make a statement that has value. There must first be a discovery stage, in which ideas, materials, supporting details, and so on are deliberately collected. These may come from many possible sources: the writer's own experience and observations, deliberate research of written sources, interviews of live persons, television presentations, or the Internet.

The next stage is organization, in which the purpose, thesis, and supporting points are determined. Most writers will put forth more than one possible thesis and in the next stage, the writing of the paper, settle on one as the result of trial and error. Once the paper is written, the editing stage is necessary and is probably the most important stage. Editing is not just polishing. At this point, decisions must be made regarding whether the reasoning is cohesive. The writer should consider questions such as the following: Does it hold together? Is the arrangement the best possible one, or should the points be rearranged? Are there holes that need to be filled in? What form will the introduction take? Does the conclusion lead the reader out of the discourse, or is it inadequate or too abrupt?

It's important to remember that the best writers engage in all of these stages recursively. They may go back to discovery at any point in the process, or they may go back and rethink the organization. To help students become effective writers, the teacher needs to give them adequate practice in the various stages and encourage them to engage deliberately in the creative thinking that makes writers successful.

F. **Provides students with professionally written, student-written, and teacher-written models of writing**

To find good professional models for your students, check professional journals, textbooks, the workplace, or your own hard drive. Student-authored samples can be found on the web or taken from your or other teachers' files.

Guide your students in analyzing models to understand the methodology behind the form. This can be done through class discussion or homework assignments that guide analysis of the model before students try their own hand at writing in that form.

Professionally Written Models

Analyzing professional models provides a window into how professionals write up their research and findings. When analyzing the model in class:

- Ask students to outline the model.
- Have the class construct a chart that lists *purpose, necessary information, key components*, and *format* for each section of the model.
- Have students answer a list of homework questions about the model. Questions might include:
    - What's the primary purpose of the piece of writing? What are possible secondary purposes?
    - Who is the audience? What assumptions about the audience does the author seem to have?
    - What is the logic behind the overall organization?
    - What is the function or purpose of each part?
    - What information do you need to write each section? How do you get it?
    - What do you notice about the language, style, and length of each part?

- o How does the author refer to outside sources? What documentation is used?
- Have students work in small groups to compare their responses to the homework questions. (If the samples are long or involved, ask each group to focus on a different section or aspect of the model.)

Student-Written Models

In addition to providing professional models, many teachers like to use student-authored samples of a particular form. Student samples are often good but not perfect and show students what they can achieve.

Here are several possible teaching strategies:

- Have students discuss what works well and what could use more work in the student samples.
- If you use more than one sample (or both student and professional models), ask students to compare the two: What are the similarities? What are the significant differences?
- Have students revise a particularly problematic student-authored sample and then discuss the results. (Such an assignment works best with shorter samples. For longer samples, assigning work on a specific part may be more fruitful.)

Your insights and tips (*do's* and *don'ts*) throughout these activities can greatly aid students' understanding and ability to work with their own material.

G. **Demonstrates knowledge of factors that influence student writing**

See Competency 2.A

H. **Analyzes and teaches the use of literary devices in writing**

Imagery can be described as a word or sequence of words that refers to any sensory experience—that is, anything that can be seen, tasted, smelled, heard, or felt. While writers of prose may also use imagery, it is most distinctive of poetry. The poet intends to make an experience available to the reader. To do that, he or she must appeal to one of the senses. The most often used sense is vision. The poet will deliberately paint a scene in such a way that the reader can see it. However, the purpose is not simply to stir the visceral feeling but also to stir the emotions. A good example is "The Piercing Chill" by Taniguchi Buson (1715–1783):

> The piercing chill I feel:
> My dead wife's comb, in our bedroom,
> Under my heel . . .

In only a few short words, the reader can feel many things: the shock that might come from touching the corpse, a physical sense of death, the contrast between her death and the memories he has of her when she was alive. Imagery might be defined as speaking of the abstract in concrete terms, a powerful device in the hands of a skillful poet.

A **symbol** is an object or action that can be observed with the senses and that suggests many other things. The lion is a symbol of courage; the cross a symbol of Christianity; the color green a symbol of envy. These examples are simple, because society pretty much agrees on the one-to-one meaning of them. Symbols used in literature are usually of a different sort. They tend to be private and personal; their significance is only evident in the context of the work in which they are used. A good example is the huge pair of spectacles on a signboard in Fitzgerald's *The Great Gatsby*. They are interesting as a part of the landscape, but they also symbolize divine myopia. A symbol can have more than one meaning, and the meaning may be as personal as the memories and experiences of the particular reader. In analyzing a poem or a story, it's important to identify the symbols and their possible meanings.

Looking for symbols is often challenging, especially for novice readers. However, these suggestions may be useful: First, pick out all the references to concrete objects, such as a newspaper or a black cat. Note any that the writer emphasizes by describing in detail, by repeating, or by placing at the very beginning or ending of a poem. Ask yourself: What is the piece of writing about? What does it add up to? Paraphrase the piece and determine whether the meaning depends upon certain concrete objects. Then ponder what the concrete object symbolizes in this particular piece of writing. A symbol may be a part of a person's body, such as the eye of the murder victim in Poe's story *The Tell-Tale Heart*, or a look, a voice, or a mannerism.

A symbol is not an abstraction such as truth, death, or love; in narrative, a well-developed character who is not at all mysterious; or the second term in a metaphor. In Emily Dickinson's poem "The Lightning is a yellow Fork," the symbol is the lightning, not the fork.

An **allusion** is very much like a symbol, and the two sometimes tend to run together. An allusion is defined by Merriam Webster's *Encyclopedia of Literature* as "an implied reference to a person, event, thing, or a part of another text." Allusions are based on the assumption that there is a common body of knowledge shared by poet and reader and that a reference to that body of knowledge will be immediately understood. Allusions to the Bible and classical mythology are common in Western literature on the assumption that they will be immediately understood. This is not always the case, of course. T. S. Eliot's *The Waste Land* requires research and annotation for understanding.

The use of allusion is a sort of shortcut for poets. They can use an economy of words and count on meaning to come from the reader's own experience.

Figurative language is also called figures of speech. Listing all possible figures of speech is beyond the scope of this list. However, for purposes of analyzing poetry, a few are sufficient.

1. **Simile:** Direct comparison between two things; for example, "My love is like a red, red rose."

2. **Metaphor:** Indirect comparison between two things. The use of a word or phrase denoting one kind of object or action in place of another to suggest a comparison between them. While poets use them extensively, they are also integral to everyday speech.

3. **Parallelism:** The arrangement of ideas in phrases, sentences, and paragraphs that balance one element with another of equal importance and similar wording. Here is an example from Francis Bacon's *Of Studies:* "Reading maketh a full man, conference a ready man, and writing an exact man."

4. **Personification:** Human characteristics attributed to an inanimate object, an abstract quality, or an animal. For example, John Bunyan included characters named Death, Knowledge, Giant Despair, Sloth, and Piety in *The Pilgrim's Progress.* The *arm* of a chair is a form of personification.

5. **Euphemism:** The substitution of an agreeable or inoffensive term for one that might offend or suggest something unpleasant. Many euphemisms are used to refer to death to avoid using the word, such as "passed away," "crossed over," or "passed."

6. **Hyperbole:** Deliberate exaggeration for dramatic or comic effect. Here is an example from Shakespeare's *The Merchant of Venice*:

    > Why, if two gods should play some heavenly match
    > And on the wager lay two earthly women,
    > And Portia one, there must be something else
    > Pawned with the other, for the poor rude world
    > Hath not her fellow.

7. **Climax:** A number of phrases or sentences are arranged in ascending order of rhetorical forcefulness. Here is an example from Melville's *Moby–Dick*:
   All that most maddens and torments; all that stirs up the lees of things; all truth with malice in it; all that cracks the sinews and cakes the brain; all the subtle demonisms of life and thought; all evil, to crazy Ahab, were visibly personified and made practically assailable in Moby–Dick.

8. **Bathos:** A ludicrous attempt to portray pathos—that is, to evoke pity, sympathy, or sorrow. It may result from inappropriately dignifying the commonplace, using elevated language to describe something trivial, or greatly exaggerating pathos.

9. **Oxymoron:** A contradiction in terms deliberately employed for effect. It is usually seen in a qualifying adjective whose meaning is contrary to that of the noun it modifies, such as "wise folly."

10. **Irony:** Expressing something other than and often opposite of the literal meaning, such as words of praise when blame is intended. In poetry, it is often used as a sophisticated or resigned awareness of contrast between what is and what ought to be and expresses a controlled pathos without sentimentality. It is a form of indirection that avoids overt praise or censure. An early example is the Greek comic character Eiron, a clever underdog who by his wit repeatedly triumphs over the boastful character Alazon.

11. **Alliteration:** The repetition of consonant sounds in two or more neighboring words or syllables. In its simplest form, it reinforces one or two consonant sounds. Here is an example from Shakespeare's Sonnet 12:

    When I do **c**ount the **c**lock that **t**ells the **t**ime.

    Some poets use more complex patterns of alliteration by creating consonants both at the beginning of words and at the beginning of stressed syllables within words. Here is an example from Shelley's "Stanzas Written in Dejection Near Naples":

    The **C**ity's voi**c**e it**s**elf is **s**oft like **So**litude's

12. **Onomatopoeia:** The naming of a thing or action by a vocal imitation of the sound associated with it, such as *buzz* or *hiss*, or the use of words whose sound suggests their sense. Here is a good example from "The Brook" by Tennyson:

    I chatter over stony ways,
    In little sharps and trebles,
    I bubble into eddying bays,
    I babble on the pebbles.

13. **Malapropism:** A verbal blunder in which one word is replaced by another similar in sound but different in meaning. This term comes from Sheridan's Mrs. Malaprop in *The Rivals* (1775). Thinking of the geography of contiguous countries, she spoke of the "geometry" of "contagious countries."

Poets use figures of speech to sharpen the effect and meaning of their poems and to help readers see things in ways they have never seen them before. Marianne Moore observed that a fir tree has "an emerald turkey-foot at the top." Her poem makes us aware of something we probably had never noticed before. The sudden recognition of the likeness yields pleasure in the reading.

Figurative language allows for the statement of truths that more literal language cannot. Skillfully used, a figure of speech will help the reader see more clearly and focus upon particulars. Figures of speech add many dimensions of richness to our reading and understanding of a poem; they also allow many opportunities for worthwhile analysis. The approach to take in analyzing a poem on the basis of its figures of speech is to ask the following questions: What does it do for the poem? Does it underscore meaning? Does it intensify understanding? Does it increase the intensity of our response?

I.   Teaches students skills and strategies for using writing as a tool for reflection, exploration, learning, problem solving, and personal growth

See Competencies 8.A, 8.B, and 9.B

J.   Understands and teaches writing as a tool for inquiry, research, and learning

See Competencies 5.H and 5.1K

K.   Teaches students to evaluate critically the sources they use for their writing

When evaluating sources, first go through this checklist to make sure the source is even worth reading:

- Title (How relevant is it to your topic?)
- Date (How current is the source?)
- Organization (What institution is this source coming from?)
- Length (How in depth does it go?)

Check for signs of bias:

- Does the author or publisher have political ties or religious views that could affect his or her objectivity?
- Is the author or publisher associated with any special-interest groups that might only see one side of an issue, such as Greenpeace or the National Rifle Association?
- How fairly does the author treat opposing views?
- Does the language of the piece show signs of bias?

Keep an open mind while reading, and don't let opposing viewpoints prevent you from absorbing the text. Remember that you are not judging the author's work; you are examining its assumptions, assessing its evidence, and weighing its conclusions.

L.   Provides instruction about plagiarism, academic honesty, and integrity as applied to students' written work and their presentation of information from different sources, including electronic sources

Plagiarism, whether intentional or accidental, has ethical implications, and anyone who writes needs to have a clear understanding of what it is. Basically, it means passing off the words or ideas of another person as one's own without giving proper credit to the source.

It's acceptable to paraphrase someone else's words as long as you provide a citation—that is, announce where and whom it came from.

Remember, though, that any exact words or phrases that come from the original work must be set off in quotation marks and the point in the original where it came from must be indicated. These rules apply to all words and ideas, whether they are written, from a speech, from a television or radio program, from email messages, from interviews, or from conversations. It's critical to be careful about lifting any such information from a website because today there are very powerful search engines that identify plagiarism, and many people who provide information on the Internet use them to make sure their words and information are not being stolen. Potential fines for plagiarism are very steep.

Lifting another person's words or ideas and presenting them as one's own is no different from thievery. Many people who wouldn't think of stealing property think nothing of presenting the words and ideas of others as their own.

A second kind of unethical misuse of information is falsely reporting or attributing words or ideas. This can be putting words in another's mouth or bending what was said to create a false impression. Sometimes simply failing to report the context in which something was said becomes false reporting. So many misuses of the printed and spoken word have taken place in a world that is constantly flooded with communications from all directions that students sometimes feel that it is acceptable to commit these misuses themselves. The writing classroom is an ideal forum for teaching and discussing what is ethical and moral in the use of language from a source and what is not.

M. **Understands and teaches students the importance of using acceptable formats for communicating research results and documenting sources**

Guidelines for Documenting Sources

- Keep a record of any sources consulted during the research process.
- As you take notes, avoid unintentional plagiarism.
- Summarize and paraphrase in your own words without the source in front of you.
- Cite anything that is not common knowledge. This includes direct quotes as well as ideas or statistics.

Blueprint for Standard Attribution

1. Begin the sentence with, "According to _____,"
2. Proceed with the material being cited, followed by the page number in parentheses.
3. Include the source information in a bibliography or works cited page.
   (Last name, first name. *Book Title*. Location: Publisher, year.)

Example

In-text citation:

According to Steve Mandel, "our average conversational rate of speech is about 125 words per minute" (78).

Works cited entry:

Mandel, Steve. *Effective Presentation Skills*. Menlo Park, California: Crisp Publications, 1993.

N.   **Demonstrates an understanding of informal and formal procedures for monitoring and assessing students' writing development**

See Competency 8.H

O.   **Uses assessment results to plan and adapt instruction that addresses students' strengths, needs, and interests and that builds on students' current skills to increase their writing proficiency**

See Competency 8.I

TEACHER CERTIFICATION STUDY GUIDE

DOMAIN IV.   ORAL COMMUNICATION AND MEDIA LITERACY

COMPETENCY 010   THE TEACHER UNDERSTANDS PRINCIPLES OF ORAL COMMUNICATION AND PROMOTES STUDENTS' DEVELOPMENT OF LISTENING AND SPEAKING SKILLS

A.   Understands similarities and differences between oral and written language and promotes students' awareness of these similarities and differences

Although widely different in many aspects, written and spoken English share a common basic structure or syntax (subject, verb, and object) and the common purpose of fulfilling the need to communicate—but there, the similarities end.

Spoken English follows the basic word order mentioned above (subject, verb object) as does written English. We would write as we would speak: "I sang a song." It is usually only in poetry or music that that word order or syntax is altered: "Sang I a song." However, beyond that, spoken English, unless in a formal context, is freed from the constraints and expectations imposed upon the written word.

Because of these restraints, in the form of rules of grammar and punctuation, learning to read and write occupy years of formal schooling, whereas learning to speak is a natural developmental stage, much like walking, that is accomplished before we begin the process of learning to write what we speak.

These rules are imposed upon the written language in part out of necessity. Written English is an isolated event. The writer must use an expected, ordered structure, complete with proper spacing and punctuation, to be understood by an audience that he or she may never see.

In contrast, the speaker of English can rely on hand gestures, facial expressions, and tone of voice to convey information and emotions beyond what is conveyed in his or her words alone. In addition, speaking is sometimes not an isolated event. In these cases, the speaker has a listener who can interrupt, ask questions, or provide additional information, ensuring that the communication is understood.

Thus, spoken English is a much more fluid form of communication than written English and is more directly suited to meeting the needs of a particular audience. This gives rise to regional dialects and forms of expressions that with time and usage may find their way into formal written English.

However, with technology, there are new avenues for communication that are resulting in a synthesis of spoken and written communication: text messaging and online dialogues. In these forms, written English is not bound by the formal rules of spelling, grammar, and punctuation—rather, it is free to more closely mimic its spoken counterpart.

Want to shout your answer? USE ALL CAPS! Saying something with a smile? Then show it! ☺ The limited space on mobile phones and the immediacy of Internet communication has also led to adaptations in spelling, where, for example, "text message" becomes "txt msg." Other abbreviated spellings and expressions have gained such popular usage that in 2005, the world's first dxNRE & glosRE (dictionary and glossary), "transl8it!" (Translate It!) was published to help in the translation of standard English into text speak. Although these unorthodox forms of communication may frighten formal grammarians, this brave new world of communicating, as employed online and via mobile phones, is far from being the death knell for standard English. Rather, it is one more indication of the versatility of the English language and the ingenuity and creativity of the individuals who employ it.

B. Understands and helps students understand the role of cultural factors in oral communication

Political correctness is a new concept discussed frequently in the twenty-first century. It has always existed, of course. The successful speaker of the nineteenth century understood and was sensitive to audiences. However, that speaker was typically a man and the only audience that was important was a male audience and, more often than not, the only important audience was a white one.

Many things have changed in discourse since the nineteenth century just as the society in which the speaker lives has changed, and the speaker who disregards the existing conventions for political correctness usually finds him- or herself in trouble. Rap music makes a point of ignoring those conventions, particularly with regard to gender, and is often the target of very hostile attacks. Rap performers, however, often intend to be revolutionary and have developed their own audiences, and many have become wealthy by exploiting those newly developed audiences based primarily on thumbing their noses at establishment conventions.

Even so, the successful speaker must understand and be sensitive to what is current in political correctness. The "n word" is a case in point. There was a time when that term was thrown about at will by politicians and other public speakers—but no more. Nothing spells the end of a politician's career more certainly than using that term in his or her campaign or public addresses.

References to gender have become particularly sensitive in the twentieth century as a result of the women's rights movement, and the speaker who disregards these sensitivities does so at his or her peril. The generic *he* is no longer acceptable, and this requires a strategy to deal with pronominal references without repetitive he/she, his or her, and so on. There are several ways to approach this: Switch to a passive construction that does not require a subject; switch back and forth, using the male pronoun in one reference and the female pronoun in another one, being sure to sprinkle them reasonably evenly; or switch to the plural.

C. Facilitates effective student interaction and oral communication, including group discussions and individual presentations

Debates and panel discussions fall under the umbrella of formal speaking, and the rules for formal speaking should apply here, although lapsing into conversation language is sometimes acceptable. Swear words should be avoided in these situations.

A **debate** presents two sides of a debatable thesis—pro and con. Each side will post a hypothesis, prove it, and defend it. A formal debate is a sort of formal dance with each side following a strictly defined format. However, within those guidelines, debaters are free to develop their arguments and rebuttals as they choose. The successful debater prepares by developing very thoroughly both sides of the thesis, for example, "Students should be able to use vouchers to attend private schools" and "Students should not be able to use vouchers to attend private schools." Debaters must be thoroughly prepared to argue their own side, but they must also have a strategy for rebutting the opposing side's arguments. All aspects of critical thinking and logical argument are employed, and the successful debaters will use ethical appeal (their own credibility) and emotional appeal to persuade the judges who will determine who wins—that is, the side that best establishes its thesis, proves it logically, and also *persuades* the audience to come over to its position.

A **panel** is typically composed of experts who explain and defend a particular topic. Often, panels will include representatives from more than one field of study and more than one position on the topic. Typically, each will have a limited amount of time to make an opening statement either presenting explanatory material or arguing a point of view. Then the meeting will be opened up to the audience for questions. A moderator will keep order and will control the time limits on the opening statements and responses and will sometimes intervene and ask a panel member who was not the target of a particular question from the audience to elaborate or rebut the answer of the panel member who was questioned. Panels are usually limited to four or five people, although in special cases they may be much larger.

D. Understands and teaches various forms of oral discourses and their characteristics and provides effective opportunities for practice

Presenting

The content of material to be presented orally plays a big role in how it is organized and delivered. For example, a literary analysis or a book report will be organized inductively, laying out the details and then presenting a conclusion, which will usually be what the author's purpose, message, and intent are.

If the analysis is focusing on multiple layers in a story, more specific details about the layers will probably follow the preliminary conclusion. Keeping in mind that the speaker will want to keep the audience's attention, if the content has to do with difficult-to-follow facts and statistics, a visual presentation (possibly created using presentation software such as PowerPoint) may be used as a guide to the presentation. The speaker can also intersperse interesting anecdotes, jokes, or humor from time to time so the listeners don't fall asleep.

It's also important to take the consistency of the audience into account when organizing a presentation. If the audience can be counted on to have a high level of interest in what is being presented, little would need to be done in the way of organizing and presenting to hold interest. In contrast, if many of those in the audience are there because they have to be, or if the level of interest is not very high, something like a visual presentation can be very helpful. In these cases, the lead-in and introduction need to be structured not only to be entertaining and interest-grabbing but also to create interest in the topic. No matter the audience, it's important to keep the presentation lively and to be careful not to "speak down" to them. Carefully written introductions aimed specifically at a particular audience will go a long way to attract their interest in the topic.

No speaker should stand up to make a presentation if he or she has not carefully determined the purpose of the presentation. If the speaker is not focused on the purpose, the audience will quickly lose interest. To organize for a particular purpose, some of the decisions to be made are where a statement of the purpose will occur in the presentation—beginning, middle, or end—and whether displaying the purpose on a chart, a slide, or a banner will enhance the presentation. The purpose might be the lead-in for a presentation if it can be counted on to grab the interest of the listeners, in which case, the organization will be deductive. If it seems better to save the purpose until the end, the organization will be inductive.

The occasion always plays an important role in the development and delivery of a presentation. A celebration speech when the company has achieved an important accomplishment will be organized around congratulating those who were most responsible for the accomplishment and giving some details about how it was achieved and perhaps about the competition for the achievement. The presentation will be upbeat and not too long. In contrast, if bad news is being presented, it will probably be the CEO who is making the presentation and the bad-news announcement will come first, followed by details about the news itself and how it came about, and it will probably end with a pep talk and encouragement to do better the next time.

Communication skills are crucial in a collaborative society. In particular, a person cannot be a successful communicator without being an active listener. Focus on what others say, rather than planning what to say next. By listening to everything another person is saying, you may pick up on natural cues that lead to the next conversation move without so much effort.

Facilitating Conversation

It is acceptable to use standard opening lines to facilitate a conversation. Don't agonize over trying to come up with witty one-liners, as the main obstacle in initiating conversation is just making the first statement. After that, the real substance begins. A useful technique may be to make a comment or ask a question about a shared situation. This may be anything from the weather to the food you are eating to a new policy at work. Use an opener you are comfortable with, because most likely your partner in conversation will be comfortable with it as well.

Stimulating Higher-Level Critical Thinking through Inquiry

Many people rely on questions to communicate with others. However, most fall back on simple clarifying questions rather than open-ended inquiries. Try to ask open-ended, deeper-level questions, since those tend to have the greatest reward and lead to a greater understanding. In answering those questions, more complex connections are made and more significant realizations are achieved.

The successful conversationalist is a person who keeps up with what's going on around the world and ponders the meanings of events and developments. That person also usually reads about the topics that are of the most interest to him or her, both in printed materials and online. In addition, the effective conversationalist has certain areas that are of particular interest that he or she has probed in some depth. An interest in human behavior is usually one of this person's interests. Why do people behave as they do? Why do some succeed and some fail? This person will also be interested in and concerned about social issues, not only in the immediate community but also on a wider scale, and will have ideas for solving some of those problems.

With all of this, the most important thing a good conversationalist can do is to *listen*, not just waiting until the other person quits speaking so he or she can take the floor again but actually listening to learn what the other person has to say and also to learn more about that other person. Following a gathering, the best thing a person can think about another is that he or she was interested enough to listen to others' ideas and opinions, and that is the person who will be remembered the longest and with the most regard.

It's acceptable to be passionate about one's convictions in polite conversation; it is not acceptable to be overbearing or unwilling to hear and consider another's point of view. It's important to keep one's emotions under control in these circumstances even if others do not.

E. **Understands and teaches skills for speaking to diverse audiences for various purposes and provides students with effective opportunities to apply these skills in a variety of contexts**

See Competencies 2.C and 9.C

F. **Understands and teaches strategies for preparing, organizing, and delivering different types of oral presentations, including informative and persuasive messages and literary interpretations**

Preparing to speak on a topic should be seen as a process that has three stages: **Discovery, Organization,** and **Editing**.

Discovery

There are many possible sources for the information that will be used to create an oral presentation. The first step in the discovery process is to settle on a topic or subject. Answer the question: What is the speech going to be about? For example, the topic or subject could be immigration. In the discovery stage, one's own knowledge, experience, and beliefs should be the first source, and notes should be taken as the speaker probes this source. The second source might be interviews with friends and possibly experts. The third source will be research, what has been written or said publicly on this topic. Research can become overwhelming, so a plan for the collecting of source information should be well organized with set time limits for each part.

Organization

At this point, the presenter needs to make several decisions. The first is what the *purpose* of the speech is. Does the speaker want to persuade the audience to believe something or to act on something, or does the speaker simply want to present information that the audience might not have? Once that decision is made, a thesis should be developed. What point does the speaker want to make? What are the points that will support that point? In what order will those points be arranged? Introductions and conclusions should be written last. The purpose of the introduction is to draw the audience into the topic. The purpose of the conclusion is to polish off the speech, making sure the thesis is clear, reinforcing the thesis, or summarizing the points that have been made.

Editing

This is the most important stage in preparing a speech. Once decisions have been made in the discovery and organization stages, it's good to allow time to let the speech rest for a while and to go back to it with fresh eyes. Objectivity is extremely important, and the speaker should be willing to make drastic changes if they are needed. It's difficult to let go of one's own composition, but good speechmakers are able to do that. However, editing can get out of hand, and it should be limited. The speaker must recognize that at some point, the decisions must be made and he or she must be committed to the speech as it stands to deliver the message with conviction.

The concept of recursiveness is very useful to speechwriters. That is, everything must be written at the outset with full knowledge that it can be changed. The willingness to go backward, even to the discovery stage, is what makes a good speechwriter.

G. **Understands and teaches skills and strategies for using technology in oral presentations**

The student should be able to produce visual images, messages, and meaning to communicate with others using technology. For example, the student should be able to produce a PowerPoint presentation to enhance an oral presentation, perhaps make or upload a YouTube digital video as an adjunct to an oral presentation, to illustrate a point or to add information and interest, and should be able to access and upload public domain or copyright-free images.

Appropriate backgrounds for any PowerPoint slides should be chosen for readability and for thematic consistency. Students should be instructed in this or given feedback once the presentation is over.

The old adage "One picture is worth a thousand words" holds true, and using digital images makes it simple for students to present appropriate pictures to the class to enhance their oral presentations. Copyright law often allows for "fair use" of images for a one-time educational purpose, the range of images from which students may select is broad.

Visuals should make a point; they should not just be "thrown in" randomly for distraction. Humorous representations are acceptable as long as they are related to the topic.

Selection of font color and size is an important oral presentation skill when using technology—readability for the audience is the primary consideration. Using contrasting colors, such as yellow and blue (a blue background is common in PowerPoint presentations; a yellow typeface could be used for text).

PowerPoint panels should not contain reams of text: bullet points that condense and summarize points being made orally are better than text-crowded slides.

H. **Understands and teaches strategies for evaluating the content and effectiveness of spoken messages and provides effective opportunities for practice**

Questions: Ask students what strategies the spoken message uses, how well those strategies respond to the requirements of the situation, and how well the speaker responded to spontaneous occurrences, questions, or problems.

Perception checking: This is a feedback technique. It refers to the effort to understand the feelings behind the words. Ask students to describe their impressions of the speaker's feelings. They should not relay any feelings of approval or disapproval.

Paraphrasing: When students paraphrase, it is significant to stress that the resulting summary reflects what the spoken message meant to the student, not what it was intended to mean. Have students practice different types of paraphrasing, such as restating the original statement in more specific terms, restating it in more general terms, or using an example.

I. **Understands and teaches skills for active, purposeful listening in various situations and provides effective opportunities for practice**

See Competency 10.D

J. **Demonstrates an understanding of informal and formal procedures for monitoring and assessing students' oral communication skills**

Language Skills to Evaluate:

- The ability to talk at length with few pauses and fill time with speech
- The ability to call up appropriate things to say in a wide range of contexts
- The size and range of a student's vocabulary and syntax skills
- The coherence of a student's sentences and the ability to speak in reasoned and semantically dense sentences
- Knowledge of the various forms of interaction and conversation for various situations
- Knowledge of the standard rules of conversation
- The ability to be creative and imaginative with language and express oneself in original ways
- The ability to invent and entertain and to take risks in linguistic expression

Methods of Evaluation:

- Commercially designed language assessment products
- Instructor observation using a rating scale from 1 to 5 (where 1 = limited proficiency and 5 = high proficiency)
- Informal observation of students' behaviors

K. **Uses assessment results to plan and adapt instruction that addresses students' strengths, needs, and interests and that builds on students' current skills to increase proficiency in oral communication**

See Competencies 3.G

TEACHER CERTIFICATION STUDY GUIDE

COMPETENCY 011 THE TEACHER UNDERSTANDS AND TEACHES BASIC PRINCIPLES OF MEDIA LITERACY AND PROVIDES STUDENTS WITH OPPORTUNITIES TO APPLY THESE PRINCIPLES IN INTERACTIONS WITH MEDIA

A. Understands different types and purposes of media

Media's impact on today's society is immense, constantly increasing, and changing. Parents' roles as verbal and moral teachers are diminishing in response to the much more stimulating guidance of the television set, computer monitor, laptop, iPad, or other computer tablets, and smartphones.

Adolescence, which used to be the time for going out and exploring the world firsthand, is now consumed by the allure of television, the Internet, popular music, smartphones, and video games. Through popular media, young adults are exposed to sexual situations and violence. However, media's impact on society is also beneficial and progressive. Its effect on education in particular provides both special challenges and opportunities for teachers and students.

For example, Internet access through a number of devices allows instant access to unlimited data, reams of information, and connects people across all cultures through shared interests. Much Internet content is visual, and sites such as YouTube, Vimeo, and others utilize video, many of which may be instructive. However, the Internet also uses a great deal of text, potentially increasing reading time for students. Easy and almost instant access to books through handheld reading devices also encourages reading. Research and information-seeking skills may be developed through the use of Google and other search engines. Texting through cell phones may help students' understand the importance of the written word in communication and help them practice clear and concise composition. Twitter, with its emphasis on short messages, may be used as an exercise in editing, condensing, summarizing, and the effective use of famous and useful quotations. If classes are interested in social causes, Facebook is often a virtual gathering place for similarly interested groups. A class can create its own Facebook page and learn social media etiquette and what is appropriate to post in an open forum like the Internet, where information never completely disappears.

Media, when used in a productive way, enriches instruction and can make it more individualized, interesting, accessible, and economical. There are also many educational software programs that the teacher may use to enhance student interest and learning.

B. Analyzes and teaches about the influence of the media and the power of visual images

More money is spent each year on advertising toward children than educating them. Thus, the media's strategies are considerably well thought out and effective. Media targeting children employ large, clear letters, bold colors, simple line drawings, and popular symbols to announce upcoming events, push ideas, and advertise products. By using attractive photographs, brightly colored cartoon characters, or instructive messages, they increase sales, win votes, or stimulate learning. The graphics are designed to communicate messages clearly, precisely, and efficiently. Some even target subconscious yearnings for sex and status.

Because so much effort is being spent on influencing students through media tactics, just as much effort should be devoted to educating those students about media awareness. A teacher should explain that media artists and the aspect they choose to portray, as well as the ways in which they portray what they have chosen, reflect their attitudes and understandings. The artistic choices they make are not entirely based on creative license—they also reflect an imbedded meaning the artist wants to represent. Colors, shapes, and positions are sometimes meant to arouse basic instincts for food, sex, and status, and are often used to sell cars, clothing, or liquor.

C. Demonstrates awareness of ethical and legal factors to consider in the use and creation of media products

When using movies or television, photographs, videos, paintings, audio recordings, diagrams, or maps in the classroom, the teacher must be aware of the ethical and legal factors associated with multimedia works. Today's technology enables us to conveniently access many different media. However, the ease of access provided by modern digital technology may result in the use of works without full understanding of rights and responsibilities. Creating and using unauthorized copies of audio and visual works in either digital or non-digital format is not appropriate and may be illegal.

Facts about Copyright

1. A work, in whatever medium, is protected by copyright law unless it has been placed in the public domain. Owners of copyrights hold exclusive right to the reproduction and distribution of their work.
2. Unauthorized use and distribution of copyrighted works is illegal. Copyright law protects creators and publishers, just as patent law protects inventors.
3. Unauthorized use and distribution of copyrighted works can harm the entire academic community. If unauthorized use and distribution proliferate in a school, the institution may incur a legal liability. Also, the institution may find it more difficult to negotiate agreements that would make copyrighted products more widely and less expensively available to members of the academic community.
4. Unauthorized use and distribution of copyrighted works can deprive creators and publishers of a fair return on their work and inhibit the creation of new works. Respect for the intellectual and creative work and property of others has always been essential to the mission of educational institutions. As members of the academic community, we value the free exchange of ideas.

Just as we do not tolerate plagiarism, we do not condone the unauthorized use and distribution of intellectual and creative work.

Using a copyrighted work for educational purposes may be permitted under a legal doctrine known as *fair use*, but use for educational purposes is not permitted automatically. If in doubt, check with the copyright holder.

There are generally four factors that courts use to determine whether a particular use of a copyrighted work is fair use. These factors are for guidance and are not necessarily exhaustive:

- The purpose and character of the use, including whether such use is commercial in nature or is for nonprofit educational purposes; educational purpose is more likely to be considered fair use.
- The nature of the copyrighted work; that is, the extent to which the work is factual or creative. The more factual and less creative a work is (for example, a news report compared to a song), the more likely a use of the work is to fall under purview of the fair use doctrine—all else being equal.
- The amount and substantiality of the portion used in relation to the copyrighted work as a whole. Usually, only short passages of a literary work that do not convey or express the core of the work are permitted under fair use. For the specific case of single visual images, this criterion is often difficult to meet, in that small subsets of an image are not always useful; visual images are usually used in their entirety.
- The effect of the use on the potential market for or value of the copyrighted work. For a claim of fair use to hold, the owner or creator of the work should not suffer significant monetary damages from that particular use.

D.   **Applies and teaches skills for responding to, interpreting, analyzing, and critiquing a variety of media**

To stimulate analysis of media strategies, ask students such questions as:

- Where/when do you think this picture was taken/film was shot/piece was written?
- Would you like to have lived at this time in history, or in this place?
- What objects are present?
- What do the people presented look like? Are they happy or sad?
- Who is being targeted?
- What can you learn from this piece of media?
- Is it telling you something is good or bad?
- What message is being broadcasted?

E.   **Understands and facilitates the production of media messages**

Media literacy means that students are able to understand, analyze, weigh, and also create messages in a variety of media contexts. The most important element of media literacy is understanding what messages are conveyed, including subliminal ones, and to what purpose. This applies regardless of the medium to be considered. Being able to produce their own media messages effectively means that students understand how media is used to convey meaning.

Factors to consider include the following.

Classroom Organization

Only a few students at a time can work with any media technology, but they can all be involved in planning, brainstorming and research. There are many different ways of dividing up tasks in a media production: Groups can work on separate sections of the project, including research, scripting, writing, editing, and so on.

Scale and Format

It's best to produce a one-minute digital recording or audio file that has been well thought out, scripted and/or storyboarded, well recorded within the limitations of available equipment, and carefully edited down from a manageable amount of material.

Your pupils should be familiar with the conventions and formats of the mainstream media, but they don't always need to follow them: They should make their own judgment about what's appropriate for their own project. If the class is starting a blog or a Facebook page, conventions used by established bloggers and companies may be studied as models.

Ownership

It may sound elementary, but there's often a temptation to impose one's own creative ideas on the class if they're not coming up with any or to take over on the equipment to save time. Following the guidelines here will make it more likely that pupils will be able to undertake all the work and make their own decisions. They will have learned more about media processes, and they will feel that they own the finished product.

Students need to do the following:

Analyze examples

Most students watch television, but they might not watch documentaries. If they're going to make one, they'll need to look critically at examples and to identify important features and their functions in the program.

Studying advertising is an important component of media literacy and understanding media messages, from television commercials to Internet pop-ups. Guiding students in analyzing advertising hones their media literacy skills and also instructs them in effective messaging.

Many pupils only listen to pop music, so they will have no idea of how talk radio programs like those on National Public Radio are structured unless you give them the opportunity to listen to some and analyze them.

Develop skills

A sure way to discourage pupils is to send them out with the equipment but with insufficient preparation. Time spent on preliminary exercises, on honing their interviewing techniques in the classroom, or on practicing with the equipment will result in much better results when they come to gather material for the final product. Students should practice, examine their results, and practice again until they are comfortable with the equipment and skills they need.

Plan

Students should have a clear idea of the finished product they are aiming for before being let loose with the equipment. Even if some of the material to be gathered is unpredictable—such as an interview or coverage of a live event—some form of script or outline is essential.

Planning is a crucial part of the production process; it's often the part of the project that offers the most opportunities for practicing language and other skills.

Evaluate

Finishing the video, audio recording or photographic display isn't the end of the story. Students should evaluate their work. Did it meet the objectives they set at the planning stage? How could it have been improved? They could show their work to another class or to parents to get their feedback as well.

F.   **Guides students to evaluate their own and others' media productions**

Possible Criteria to Guide Evaluation

- What important question motivated this research or project?
- Have students mapped out or "chunked" the information they want to present before beginning the project?
- Have students storyboarded the information they want to present before beginning the project?
- Did the students take their material from several different sources and perspectives?
- Are the sources appropriate for the way they are used?
- Are the sources of the information and media cited?
- Is there a balance between design and content?
- Is the content presented in a well-organized and meaningful way?
- Is it easy to navigate through the multimedia project?

- Are ideas and concepts connected with hypertext links?
- Did the students choose their text and media well to support their point of view or illustrate their concepts?
- Can the students articulate their criteria used to select the information and media they included in their project?
- Did the students select media appropriate to its purpose?

G. **Demonstrates an understanding of informal and formal procedures for monitoring and assessing students' media literacy**

Teachers should note how students use their comprehension skills to analyze how words, images, graphics, and sounds work together in various forms to impact meaning. Can students compare and contrast how events are presented and information is communicated by visual images as opposed to printed text? Are students able to analyze how media messages use visual and sound techniques (background music, shooting from various camera angles, shooting only certain subjects, organization of material, etc.) to convey subliminal messages? Do students understand the concept of "framing", where, out of journalistic necessity and an attempt to make meaning out of large amounts of information, media wittingly and unwittingly contribute to stereotypes of an accepted narrative about various groups and nations? Students should be asked to successfully compare and contrast the differences between coverage of an event in varied media (on the Internet, on television, through blogs, talk shows, etc.) and also compare and contrast coverage of the same event from varying perspectives of liberal, conservative, etcetera.

Even students who will not be going on to college will be required to use technological tools to deal with their worlds. They will be filling out forms on a computer and communicating with many people via website and email that they have dealt with face-to-face or via telephone in the past. The demands on the writing teacher are no longer simply teaching thinking/writing skills, but also teaching students skills that will connect them to the technological world of the twenty-first century.

Students need to know how to get on the Internet, where to find email (there are a number of mail programs, such as Microsoft Outlook); how to compose an email in order to be understood; and some of the etiquette required for effective email communications. Job applications are often filled out on a website.

Students need to know how to interact on Acrobat, which includes finding the icon that permits text insertion. They also need to know how to conduct searches, so they need to be aware of what "search" means, what Boolean terms are, what the major search engines are, and how to use them.

In most colleges nowadays, themes are exchanged on a website set up specifically for the school. The students need to be prepared to present their themes electronically and exchange messages with their teachers in this way, so they need to understand Microsoft Word well enough to be able to read and respond to comments on Word's tracking function and to create a clean version of a paper while retaining the one from the teacher with edits and comments.

H.   Uses assessment results to plan and adapt instruction that addresses students' strengths, needs, and interests and that builds on students' current skills to increase media literacy

See Competency 11.G

RESOURCES

1. Abrams, M. H. ed. *The Norton Anthology of English Literature*. 6th ed. 2 vols. New York: W. W. Norton, 1993.

   A comprehensive reference for English literature, containing selected works from *Beowulf* through the twentieth century and information about literary criticism.

2. Adams, M. J. (2009). The challenge of advanced texts: The interdependence of reading and learning. In E. H. Hiebert (Ed.),

3. Alexander, P. A., & Jetton, T. L. (2000). Learning from text: A multidimensional and developmental perspective. In M. L. Kamil, P. B. Mosenthal, P. D. Pearson, & R. Barr (Eds.), Handbook of reading research (Vol. 3, pp. 285-310). Mahwah, NJ: Erlbaum.

4. Alvermann, D. E. (2002). Effective literacy instruction for adolescents. *Journal of Literacy Research, 34*(2), 189-208. Retrieved April 1, 2005, from http://archive.coe.uga.edu/lle/faculty/alvermann/effective2.pdf

5. Beach, Richard. "Strategic Teaching in Literature." *Strategic Teaching and Learning: Cognitive Instruction in the Content Areas*. Edited by Beau Fly Jones and others. ASCD Publications, 1987: 135–159.

   A chapter dealing with a definition of and strategic teaching strategies for literature studies.

6. Beck, I. L., McKeown, M. G., & Kucan, L. (2002). Bringing words to life: Robust vocabulary instruction. New York, NY: Guilford.

7. Beck, I. L., McKeown, M. G., & Kucan, L. (2008). Creating robust vocabulary: Frequently asked questions and extended examples. New York, NY: Guilford.

8. Brown, A. C. and others. *Grammar and Composition 3rd Course*. Boston: Houghton Mifflin, 1984.

   A standard ninth-grade grammar text covering spelling, vocabulary, and reading, listening, and writing skills.

9. Burmeister, L. E. *Reading Strategies for Middle and Secondary School Teachers*. Reading, MA: Addison-Wesley, 1978.

   A resource for developing classroom strategies for reading and content-area classes, using library references, and adapting reading materials to all levels of students.

TEACHER CERTIFICATION STUDY GUIDE

10. Carrier, W. and B. Neumann, eds. *Literature from the World*. New York: Scribner, 1981.

    A comprehensive world literature text for high school students, with a section on mythology and folklore.

11. Cheung, A., Slavin, R.E. (2012, April). The Effectiveness of Educational Technology Applications for Enhancing Reading Achievement in K-12 Classrooms: A Meta-Analysis. Baltimore, MD: Johns Hopkins University, Center for Research and Reform in Education.

12. Cline, R. K. J. and W. G. McBride. *A Guide to Literature for Young Adults: Background, Selection, and Use*. Glenview, IL: Scott Foresman, 1983.

    A literature reference containing sample readings and an overview of adolescent literature and the developmental changes that affect reading.

13. Coater, Jr., R. B., ed. "Reading Research and Instruction." *Journal of the College Research Association*. Pittsburgh, PA: 1995.

    A reference tool for reading and language arts teachers, covering the latest research and instructional techniques.

14. Common Core State Standards for English Language Arts and Literacy in History, Social Studies, Science, and Technical Studies, Appendix A.

15. Corcoran, B. and E. Evans, eds. *Readers, Texts, Teachers*. Upper Montclair, NJ: Boynton/Cook, 1987.

    A collection of essays concerning reader response theory, including activities that help students interpret literature and help the teacher integrate literature into the course study.

16. Cutting, Brian. *Moving on in Whole Language: The Complete Guide for Every Teacher*. Bothell, WA: Wright Group, 1992.

    A resource of practical knowledge in whole language instruction.

17. Damrosch, L. and others. *Adventures in English Literature*. Orlando, FL: Harcourt, Brace, Jovanovich, 1985.

    One of many standard high school English literature textbooks with a solid section on the development of the English language.

18. Davidson, A. *Literacy 2000 Teacher's Resource. Emergent Stages 1&2*. 1990.

19. Devine, T. G. *Teaching Study Skills: A Guide for Teachers*. Boston: Allyn and Bacon, 1981.

20. Duffy, G. G. and others. *Comprehension Instruction: Perspectives and Suggestions*. New York: Longman, 1984.

    Written by researchers at the Institute of Research on Teaching and the Center for the Study of Reading, this reference includes a variety of instructional techniques for different levels.

21. Fleming, M. ed. *Teaching the Epic*. Urbana, IL: NCTE, 1974.

    Methods, materials, and projects for the teaching of epics with examples of Greek, religious, national, and American epics.

22. Flood, J. ed. *Understanding Reading Comprehension: Cognition, Language, and the Structure of Prose*. Newark, DE: IRA, 1984.

    Essays by preeminent scholars dealing with comprehension for learners of all levels and abilities.

23. Fry, E. B. and others. *The Reading Teacher's Book of Lists*. Edgewood Cliffs, NJ: Prentice-Hall, 1984.

    A comprehensive list of book lists for students of various reading levels.

24. Garnica, Olga K. and Martha L. King. *Language, Children, and Society*. New York: Pergamon Press, 1981.

25. Gere, A. R. and E. Smith. *Attitude, Language and Change*. Urbana, IL: NCTE, 1979.

    A discussion of the relationship between standard English and grammar and the vernacular usage, including various approaches to language instruction.

26. Graham, S. and Perin. D. Writing Next: Effective Strategies to Improve Writing of Adolescents in Middle and High School, a Report to Carnegie Corporation of New York, Alliance for Excellent Education, 2007.

27. Hayakawa, S. I. *Language in Thought and Action*. 4th ed. Orlando, FL: Harcourt, Brace, Jovanovich, 1979.

28. Hook, J. N. and others. *What Every English Teacher Should Know*. Champaign, IL: NCTE, 1970.

    Research-based text that summarizes methodologies and specific applications for use with students.

29. Johnson, D. D. and P. D. Pearson. *Teaching Reading Vocabulary*. 2nd ed. New York: Holt, Rinehart, and Winston, 1984.

    A student text that stresses using vocabulary study in improving reading comprehension, with chapters on instruction components in the reading and content areas.

30. Kaywell, I. F. ed. *Adolescent Literature as a Complement to the Classics*. Norwood, MA: Christopher-Gordon Pub., 1993.

    A correlation of modern adolescent literature with classics of similar themes.

31. Kintsch, W. (2009). Learning and constructivism. In S. Tobias & M. Duffy (Eds.), Constructivist instruction: Success or failure? (pp. 223–241). New York, NY: Routledge.

32. Lenhart, A., Rainie, L, & Lewis, O. (2001, June 20). Teenage life online. (Available http://www.pewinternet.org/reports/toc.asp?Report=36)

33. Mack, M. ed. *World Masterpieces*. 3rd ed. 2 vols. New York: W. W. Norton, 1973.

    A standard world literature survey, with good introductory material on a critical approach to literature study.

34. McLuhan, M. *Understanding Media: The Extensions of Man*. New York: Signet, 1964.

    The most classic work on the effect media has on the public and the power of the media to influence thinking.

35. McMichael, G. ed. *Concise Anthology of American Literature*. New York: Macmillan, 1974.

    A standard survey of American literature texts.

36. Moffett, J. *Teaching the Universe of Discourse*. Boston: Houghton Mifflin, 1983.

    A significant reference text that proposes the outline for a total language arts program, emphasizing the reinforcement of each element of the language arts curriculum to the other elements.

37. Moffett, James and Betty Jane Wagner. *Student-Centered Language Arts K–12*. 4th ed. Boston: Houghton Mifflin, 1992.

38. Nelms , B. F. ed. *Literature in the Classroom: Readers, Texts, and Contexts*. Urbana, IL: NCTE, 1988.

    Essays on adolescent and multicultural literature, social aspects of literature, and approaches to literature interpretation.

39. Nilsen, A. P. and K. L. Donelson. *Literature for Today's Young Adults*. 2nd ed. Glenview, IL: Scott Foresman and Company, 1985.

    An excellent overview of young adult literature—its history, terminologies, bibliographies, and book reviews.

40. Perrine, L. *Literature: Structure, Sound, and Sense*. 5th ed. Orlando, FL: Harcourt, Brace, Jovanovich, 1988.

    A much-revised text for teaching literature elements, genres, and interpretation.

41. Piercey, Dorothy. *Reading Activities in Content Areas: An Ideabook for Middle and Secondary Schools*. 2nd ed. Boston: Allyn and Bacon, 1982.

42. Pooley, R. C. *The Teaching of English Usage*. Urbana, IL: NCTE, 1974.

    A revision of the important 1946 text that discusses the attitudes toward English usage through history and recommends specific techniques for usage instruction.

43. Probst, R. E. *Response and Analysis: Teaching Literature in Junior and Senior High School*. Upper Montclair, NJ: Boynton/Cook, 1988.

    A resource that explores reader response theory and discusses student-centered methods for interpreting literature. Contains a section on the progress of adolescent literature.

44. Pyles, T. and J. Alges. *The Origin and Development of the English Language*. 3rd ed. Orlando, FL: Harcourt, Brace, Jovanovich, 1982.

    A history of the English language; sections on social, personal, historical, and geographical influences on language usage.

45. Readence, J. E. and others. *Content Area Reading: An integrated approach*. 2nd ed. Dubuque, IA: Kendall/Hunt, 1985.

    A practical instruction guide for teaching reading in the content areas.

46. Robinson, H. Alan. *Teaching Reading and Study Strategies: The Content Areas*. Boston: Allyn and Bacon, 1978.

47. Roe, B. D. and others. *Secondary School Reading Instruction: The Content Areas*. 3rd ed. Boston: Houghton Mifflin, 1987.

    A resource of strategies for the teaching of reading for language arts teachers with little reading instruction background.

48. Rosenberg, D. *World Mythology: An Anthology of the Great Myths and Epics*. Lincolnwood, IL: National Textbook, 1986.

    Presents selections of main myths from which literary allusions are drawn. Thorough literary analysis of each selection.

49. Rosenblatt, L. M. *The Reader, the Text, the Poem. The Transactional Theory of the Literary Work*. Southern Illinois University Press, 1978.

    A discussion of reader response theory and reader-centered methods for analyzing literature.

50. Santeusanio, Richard P. *A Practical Approach to Content Area Reading*. Reading, MA: Addison-Wesley Publishing Co., 1983.

51. Shanahan, T., & Shanahan, C. (2008). Teaching disciplinary literacy to adolescents: Rethinking content-area literacy. Harvard Educational Review, 78 (1), 40–59.

52. Shepherd, David L. *Comprehensive High School Reading Methods*. 2nd ed. Columbus, OH: Charles F. Merrill Publishing, 1978.

53. Sutherland, Zena and others. *Children and Books*. 6th ed. Glenview, IL: Scott Foresman and Company, 1981.

    Thorough study of children's literature, with sections on language development theory and chapters on specific genres with synopses of specific classic works for child/adolescent readers.

54. Tchudi, S. and D. Mitchell. *Explorations in the Teaching of English*. 3rd ed. New York: Harper Row, 1989.

    A thorough source of strategies for creating more student-centered involvement in learning.

55. Tompkins, Gail E. *Teaching Writing: Balancing Process and Product*. 2nd ed. New York: Macmillan, 1994.

    A tool to aid teachers in integrating recent research and theory about the writing process, writing/reading connections, collaborative learning, and across the curriculum writing with practices in the fourth- through eighth-grade classrooms.

56. Wade, S. E., & Moje, E. B. The role of text in classroom learning. In M. L. Kamil, P.B. Mosenthal, P. D. Pearson, & R. Barr (Eds.), Handbook of reading research (Vol. 3, pp. 609-627). Mahwah, NJ: Erlbaum, 2000.

57. Warriners, J. E. *English Composition and Grammar*. Benchmark ed. Orlando, FL: Harcourt, Brace, Jovanovich, 1988.

    Standard grammar and composition textbook, with a six-book series for seventh through twelfth grades; includes vocabulary study, language history, and diverse approaches to writing process.

SAMPLE TEST

Section I: Essay Test

Given are several prompts reflecting the need to exhibit a variety of writing skills. In most testing situations, 30 minutes would be allowed to respond to each of the prompts. Some tests may allow 60 minutes for the essay to incorporate more than one question or allow for greater preparation and editing time. Read the directions carefully and organize your time wisely.

Section II: Multiple-Choice Test

This section contains 125 questions. In most testing situations, you would be expected to answer from 35–40 questions within 30 minutes. If you time yourself on the entire battery, take no more than 90 minutes.

Section III: Answer Key

How to Prepare for the Texas Educator Certification Test

Section I: Essay Test
Constructed-Response questions are given to assess the candidate's ability to explain content, apply knowledge, explain concepts, and determine the candidate's fundamental ability to disseminate and facilitate learning on an age appropriate level. For many candidates, this is the hardest aspect of the exam. The fundamental prompts may not look difficult, but they will be for those who have not had to explain them before. To be successful on the TExES educator certification constructed-response items, the candidate must be able to explain key concepts in a way that would facilitate learning, as well as exhibit the candidate's competency within the subject matter.

Section II: Multiple-Choice Test
Multiple choice questions can be presented in a variety of styles, most of them using syntax that differs from typical word order that the candidate is used to seeing in common texts. Read carefully to understand the question and look for the answer that best fits the question. Multiple choice questions may come in the following formats:

- Complete the statement
- Which of the following
- Roman numeral choices
- Questions containing 'Not', 'Except', or 'Least'
- Questions that include graphics, tables, or reading passages

Because MC questions are written with more grammatical correctness often the test questions can be difficult to comprehend at first glance.

Section I: Essay Prompts

Prompt A

Constructed Response Question 1: Literary Analysis

There are two thematically oriented passages with similar themes. Identify these themes and analyze any literary devices and writing techniques employed by the two authors. Plan to use 60–90 minutes. Your response needs to be grammatically coherent and adhere to conventional standards of English.

I, Too
By: Langston Hughes

   I, too, sing America.

   I am the darker brother.
   They send me to eat in the kitchen
   When company comes,
5 But I laugh,
   And eat well,
   And grow strong.

   Tomorrow,
   I'll be at the table
10 When company comes.
   Nobody'll dare
   Say to me,
   "Eat in the kitchen,"
   Then.

15 Besides,
   They'll see how beautiful I am
   And be ashamed—

   I, too, am America.

Source: *The Collected Poems of Langston Hughes* (Vintage Books, 2004).

To Kill a Mockingbird: Chapter 19

"You did all this chopping and hard work from sheer goodness, boy?"

"Tried to help her, I says."

Mr. Gilmer smiled grimly at the jury. "You're a mighty good fellow, it seems—did all this for not one penny?"

"Yes, suh. I felt right sorry for her, she seemed to try more'n the rest of 'em—"

"*You* felt sorry for *her*, you felt *sorry* for her?" Mr. Gilmer seemed ready to rise to the ceiling.

The witness realized his mistake and shifted uncomfortably in the chair. But the damage was done. Below us, nobody liked Tom Robinson's answer. Mr. Gilmer paused a long time to let it sink in.

Source: Lee, Harper. *To Kill a Mockingbird*. New York, 2010, pages 263–264.

Prompt B

The second constructed-response contains a student's draft response to an in-class writing task. You are to complete three assessment tasks regarding the draft.

Read the following writing assignment and student response closely.

In a ninth-grade English class, a teacher gives a 45-minute in-class writing assignment to assess students' skills in persuasive writing.

Read the prompt as well as the sample student response.

Prompt:

Think about one thing you would like to change about your school's sports program. Write a letter to the principal that explains the current sports policy, and make a case for what you would like to change or modify.

- State your position
- Organize a persuasive argument
- Support your position with specific details
- Pick your words wisely

Sample Response:

Dear Dr. Ramos,

I think our school's sports program is strong, but needs more independent sports, where kids can play without such strong completion all of the time. We have a lot of school spirit and our pep rallies are amazing and fun. We are known for our excellent skills on the football field and kids in our school where their Bears jerseys proudly. However, we do not have solitary sports, except for track and weightlifting.

Most of the kids who play in our sports program at school are in the 'jock' crowd and are very popular. They play football, baseball, soccer, and basketball. Many of the players play multiple sports, depending on the season, and use track or weightlifting as a way to train and stay in shape for the upcoming season.

I find myself surrounded by our high school's elite sports players when I am running track or lifting weights. And they bring completion with them. For example, in the weight-lifting room, some of the kids like to have contests for who can do the most reps, who can lift the most weight, and who can do the most chin-ups. I find this even on the track field, when players are joining me for winter track, for example. They want to make the best time, sprint the fastest, and throw shot-put the furthest. To me, this type of competitive arena takes the fun out.

I am an introvert. I enjoy doing sports without too much team interaction. Our school only offers track and weightlifting for my type of sports preferences. I think there are many students like me, who desire an exercise routine without having to be in heated competition, play in front of large crowds, or be popular. Many students, like myself, enjoy just playing the sport for the fun of it.

It would be cool if we added sports such as golf, archery, and yoga to our roster. Even though they may not become the most well-known sports in the school, or in the state for that matter, they will provide kids like me with a chance to succeed at a sport without feeling socially overwhelmed. Golf is a sport that takes strategy, and is also physically exerting. Some neighboring towns offer this sport, and the kids are bused to a local golf course to play every spring, a few times each week. Archery is not as well-known as golf, but it is also a potential sport for us to add to our school's sports program. It also requires strategy and great thought, while enjoying the fresh air with friends.

Thank you for reading my letter and taking my thoughts into consideration. Changing our sports program will enhance our school in many ways, and will reach kids like me, who just want to play for fun, and not to compete fiercely.

Sincerely,
Matthew Taloni

TASK 1
Identify one area of strength of the student's response and discuss how it assists the response's efficacy. Supply specific examples from the response to support your writing. Do not discuss the student's use of the conventions of standard written English.

TASK 2
Identify one are of weakness of the student's response and discus how it disrupts the response's overall efficacy. Supply specific examples from the response to support your writing. Do not discuss the student's use of the conventions of standard written English.

TASK 3
Describe one instructional activity that you would use to address the weakness of the student's response from Task 2. Discuss how the activity would address this particular weakness you found and why you think the activity would work.

Section II: Writing and Language Skills

Part A

Directions: Sentences 1–10 each contain four underlined words or phrases. If you determine that any underlined word or phrase has an error in grammar, usage, or mechanics, circle the letter underneath that underlined word or phrase. There is no more than one error in any sentence.

1. The volcanic eruption in Montserrat displaced residents of Plymouth <u>which</u>
 <u></u>   A
 felt that the <u>English government</u> <u>was</u> responsible for <u>their</u> evacuation.
                   B   C   D

2. When the <u>school district</u> privatized the school cafeteria, <u>us</u> students <u>were</u>
                 A   B   C
 thrilled to purchase more than soggy <u>French fries</u>.
                                               D

3. The homecoming <u>Queen and King</u> <u>were chosen</u> by the <u>student body</u> for
                        A   B   C
 <u>their</u> popularity.
 D

4. If the practical joke <u>was</u> <u>Cullen's</u> idea, then he <u>must</u> suffer the
                     A B   C
 <u>consequences</u>.
 D

5. She, not her sister, <u>is</u> the one <u>who</u> the librarian <u>has questioned</u> about the
                     A   B   C
 missing books, <u>*Butterfly's* Ball</u> and *The Bears' House*.
                   D

6. Jack told a <u>credulous</u> story about his trip <u>up the beanstalk</u> because each
         A   B
 child in the room <u>was convinced</u> <u>by his reasoning</u>.
                   C   D

7. My mother is a <u>Methodist</u>. She married a <u>Southern Baptist</u> and took <u>us</u>
               A   B   C
 children to the <u>First Baptist church</u> in Stuart.
                 D

8. When we moved from Jacksonville, Florida, to Little Rock, Arkansas, my
                                                 A   B

   Dad was promoted to store manager.
    C   D

9. "One of the burglar's had been already apprehended before his colleagues
                   A   B   C

   left the building," bragged the officer.
                D

10. Walter said that his calculator has been missing since last Monday
                 A   B   C

    responding to my question.
         D

Part B

Directions: Each underlined portion of sentences 11–20 contains one or more errors in grammar, usage, mechanics, or sentence structure. Circle the choice that best corrects the error without changing the meaning of the original sentence. Choice D may repeat the underlined portion. Select the identical phrase if you find no error.

11. Joe <u>didn't hardly know his cousin Fred</u>, who'd had a rhinoplasty.

    A. hardly did know his cousin Fred

    B. didn't know his cousin Fred hardly

    C. hardly knew his cousin Fred

    D. didn't know his cousin Fred

12. <u>Mixing the batter for cookies</u>, the cat licked the Crisco from the cookie sheet.

    A. While mixing the batter for cookies

    B. While the batter for cookies was mixing

    C. While I mixed the batter for cookies

    D. While I mixed the cookies

13. Mr. Brown is a school volunteer <u>with a reputation for twenty years service</u>.

    A. with a reputation for twenty years' service

    B. with a reputation for twenty year's service

    C. who has served twenty years

    D. with a reputation for twenty years service

14. Walt Whitman was famous for <u>his composition, *Leaves of Grass*, serving as a nurse during the Civil War, and a devoted son</u>.

    A. *Leaves of Grass*, his service as a nurse during the Civil War, and a devoted son

    B. composing *Leaves of Grass*, serving as a nurse during the Civil War, and being a devoted son

    C. his composition, *Leaves of Grass*, his nursing during the Civil War, and his devotion as a son

    D. his composition, *Leaves of Grass*, serving as a nurse during the Civil War, and a devoted son

15. **A teacher <u>must know not only her subject matter but also the strategies of content teaching</u>.**

    A. must not only know her subject matter but also the strategies of content teaching

    B. not only must know her subject matter but also the strategies of content teaching

    C. must not know only her subject matter but also the strategies of content teaching

    D. must know not only her subject matter but also the strategies of content teaching

16. **My English teacher, Mrs. Hunt, <u>is nicer than any teacher at school and is</u> the most helpful.**

    A. is as nice as any teacher at school and is

    B. is nicer than any other teacher at school and is

    C. is as nice as any other teacher at school and is

    D. is nicer than any teacher at school and is

17. **The teacher <u>implied</u> from our angry words that there was conflict <u>between</u> you and me.**

    A. implied ... between you and I

    B. inferred ... between you and I

    C. inferred ... between you and me

    D. implied ... between you and me

18. **There were <u>fewer pieces</u> of evidence presented during the second trial.**

    A. fewer peaces

    B. less peaces

    C. less pieces

    D. fewer pieces

19. **Mr. Smith <u>respectfully submitted his resignation and had</u> a new job.**

    A. respectively submitted his resignation and has

    B. respectively submitted his resignation before accepting

    C. respectfully submitted his resignation because of

    D. respectfully submitted his resignation and had

20. Wally groaned, "Why do I have to do an oral interpretation of "The Raven."

   A. groaned, "Why ... of 'The Raven'?"

   B. groaned "Why ... of "The Raven"?

   C. groaned "Why ... of "The Raven?"

   D. groaned, "Why ... of "The Raven."

Part C

Directions: Questions 21–100 pertain to various literary devices and content knowledge, and require a strong understanding of English Language Arts. Select one answer for each multiple-choice question.

21. The following passage is written from which point of view?

> As she mused the pitiful vision of her mother's life laid its spell on the very quick of her being—that life of commonplace sacrifices closing in final craziness. She trembled as she heard again her mother's voice saying constantly with foolish insistence: Derevaun Seraun! Derevaun Seraun!*
> * "The end of pleasure is pain!" (Gaelic)

   A. First person, narrator

   B. Second person, direct address

   C. Third person, omniscient

   D. First person, omniscient

22. The literary device of personification is used in which example below?

   A. "Beg me no beggary by soul or parents, whining dog!"

   B. "Happiness sped through the halls cajoling as it went."

   C. "O wind thy horn, thou proud fellow."

   D. "And that one talent which is death to hide."

23. Which of the following is not one of the four forms of discourse?

   A. Exposition

   B. Description

   C. Rhetoric

   D. Persuasion

24. Among junior-high school students of low-to-average reading levels, which work would most likely stir reading interest?

   A. *Elmer Gantry*, Sinclair Lewis

   B. *Smiley's People*, John LeCarre

   C. *The Outsiders*, S. E. Hinton

   D. *And Then There Were None*, Agatha Christie

25. "Every one must pass through Vanity Fair to get to the celestial city" is an allusion from a:

   A. Chinese folk tale

   B. Norse saga

   C. British allegory

   D. German fairy tale

26. Which teaching method would best engage underachievers in the required senior English class?

   A. Assign use of glossary work and extensively footnoted excerpts of great works.

   B. Have students take turns reading aloud the anthology selection.

   C. Let students choose which readings they study and write about.

   D. Use a chronologically arranged, traditional text, but assign group work, panel presentations, and portfolio management.

27. **Which term best describes the form of the following poetic excerpt?**

   And more to lulle him in his slumber soft,
   A trickling streame from high rock tumbling downe,
   And ever-drizzling raine upon the loft.
   Mixt with a murmuring winde, much like a swowne
   No other noyse, nor peoples troubles cryes.
   As still we wont t'annoy the walle'd towne,
   Might there be heard: but careless Quiet lyes,
   Wrapt in eternall silence farre from enemyes.

   A. Ballad

   B. Elegy

   C. Spenserian stanza

   D. Octava rima

28. **To understand the origins of a word, one must study the:**

   A. synonyms

   B. inflections

   C. phonetics

   D. etymology

29. **Which sonnet form describes the following?**

   My galley charg'ed with forgetfulness
     Through sharp seas, in winter night doth pass
     'Tween rock and rock; and eke mine enemy, alas,
   That is my lord steereth with cruelness.
   And every oar a thought in readiness,
     As though that death were light in such a case.
     An endless wind doth tear the sail apace
   Or forc'ed sighs and trusty fearfulness.
   A rain of tears, a cloud of dark disdain,
     Hath done the wearied cords great hindrance,
     Wreathed with error and eke with ignorance.
     The stars be hid that led me to this pain
     Drowned is reason that should me consort,
     And I remain despairing of the poet.

   A. Petrarchan or Italian sonnet

   B. Shakespearean or Elizabethan sonnet

   C. Romantic sonnet

   D. Spenserian sonnet

30. What is the salient literary feature of this excerpt from an epic?

> Hither the heroes and the nymphs resort,
> To taste awhile the pleasures of a court;
> In various talk th'instructive hours they passed,
> Who gave the ball, or paid the visit last;
> One speaks the glory of the English Queen,
> And another describes a charming Indian screen;
> A third interprets motion, looks, and eyes;
> At every word a reputation dies.

A. Sprung rhythm

B. Onomatopoeia

C. Heroic couplets

D. Motif

31. What were two major characteristics of the first American literature?

A. Vengefulness and arrogance

B. Bellicosity and derision

C. Oral delivery and reverence for the land

D. Maudlin and self-pitying egocentrism

32. Arthur Miller wrote *The Crucible* as a parallel to what twentieth-century event?

A. Sen. McCarthy's House un-American Activities Committee hearing

B. The Cold War

C. The fall of the Berlin Wall

D. The Persian Gulf War

33. Latin words that entered the English language during the Elizabethan Age include:

A. *allusion*, *education*, and *esteem*

B. *vogue* and *mustache*

C. *canoe* and *cannibal*

D. *alligator*, *cocoa*, and *armadillo*

34. Which of the following is not a characteristic of a fable?

A. Animals that feel and talk like humans

B. Happy solutions to human dilemmas

C. Teaches a moral or standard for behavior

D. Illustrates specific people or groups without directly naming them

ENGLISH LANG. ARTS & READING

35. **If a student has a poor vocabulary, the teacher should recommend first that:**

   A. the student read newspapers, magazines, and books on a regular basis

   B. the student enroll in a Latin class

   C. the student write words repetitively after looking them up in the dictionary

   D. the student use a thesaurus to locate synonyms and incorporate them into his or her vocabulary

36. **Which author did not write satire?**

   A. Joseph Addison

   B. Richard Steele

   C. Alexander Pope

   D. John Bunyan

37. **Which of the following was not written by Jonathan Swift?**

   A. A Voyage to Lilliput

   B. A Modest Proposal

   C. Samson Agonistes

   D. A Tale of a Tub

38. **Which is the best definition for diction?**

   A. The specific word choices of an author to create a particular mood or feeling in the reader

   B. Writing that explains something thoroughly

   C. The background or exposition for a short story or drama

   D. Word choices that help teach a truth or moral

39. **Which is the best definition of free verse or *vers libre*?**

   A. Poetry that consists of an unaccented syllable followed by an unaccented sound

   B. Short lyrical poetry written to entertain but with an instructive purpose

   C. Poetry that does not have a uniform pattern of rhythm

   D. Poetry that tells a story and has a plot

40. Which is an untrue statement about a theme in literature?

   A. The theme is always stated directly somewhere in the text.

   B. The theme is the central idea in a literary work.

   C. All parts of the work (plot, setting, mood) should contribute to the theme in some way.

   D. By analyzing the various elements of the work, the reader should be able to arrive at an indirectly stated theme.

41. Which is the least true statement concerning an author's literary tone?

   A. Tone is partly revealed through the selection of details.

   B. Tone is the expression of the author's attitude toward his or her subject.

   C. Tone in literature is usually satiric or angry.

   D. Tone in literature corresponds to the tone of voice a speaker uses.

42. Regarding the study of poetry, which elements are least applicable to all types of poetry?

   A. Setting and audience

   B. Theme and tone

   C. Pattern and diction

   D. Diction and rhyme scheme

43. Which of the following definitions best describes a parable?

   A. A short, entertaining account of some happening, usually using talking animals as characters

   B. A slow, sad song, poem or rose work expressing lamentation

   C. An extended narrative work expressing universal truths concerning domestic life

   D. A short, simple story of an occurrence of a familiar kind, from which a moral or religious lesson may be drawn

44. Which of the following is the best definition of existentialism?

A. The philosophical doctrine that matter is the only reality and that everything in the world (including thought, will, and feeling) is rightly explained exclusively in terms of matter

B. A philosophy that views things as they should be or as one would wish them to be

C. A philosophical and literary movement, variously religious and atheistic, stemming from Kierkegaard and represented by Sartre

D. The belief that all events are determined by fate and are hence inevitable

45. Which of the following is the best definition of imagism?

A. A doctrine teaching that comfort is the only goal of value in life

B. A movement in modern poetry (c. 1910–1918) characterized by precise, concrete images, free verse, and suggestion rather than complete statement

C. The belief that people are motivated entirely by self-centeredness

D. The doctrine that the human mind cannot know whether there is a God, an ultimate cause, or anything beyond material phenomena

46. Which choice below best defines naturalism?

   A. A belief that the writer or artist should apply scientific objectivity in his or her observation and treatment of life without imposing values or judgments

   B. The doctrine that teaches that the existing world is the best to be hoped for

   C. The doctrine teaching that God is not a personality, but that all laws, forces, and manifestations of the universe are God-related

   D. A philosophical doctrine professing that the truth of all knowledge must constantly be reexamined

47. The tendency to emphasize and value the qualities and peculiarities of life in a particular geographic area exemplifies:

   A. pragmatism

   B. regionalism

   C. pantheism

   D. abstractionism

48. The arrangement and relationship of words in sentences or sentence structures best describes:

   A. style

   B. discourse

   C. thesis

   D. syntax

49. Explanatory or informative discourse is:

   A. exposition

   B. narration

   C. persuasion

   D. description

50. The substitution of "went to his rest" for "died" is an example of a/an:

   A. bowdlerism

   B. jargon

   C. euphemism

   D. malapropism

51. A conversation between two or more people is called a:

    A. parody

    B. dialogue

    C. monologue

    D. analogy

52. "Clean as a whistle" and "easy as falling off a log" are examples of:

    A. semantics

    B. parody

    C. irony

    D. clichés

53. In literature, evoking feelings of pity or compassion is creating:

    A. colloquy

    B. irony

    C. pathos

    D. paradox

54. "I'll die if I don't pass this course" is an example of:

    A. barbarism

    B. oxymoron

    C. hyperbole

    D. antithesis

55. Addressing someone absent or something inhuman as though present and able to respond describes a figure of speech known as:

    A. personification

    B. synecdoche

    C. metonymy

    D. apostrophe

56. Slang or jargon expressions associated with a particular ethnic, age, socioeconomic, or professional group are called:

    A. aphorisms

    B. allusions

    C. idioms

    D. euphemisms

57. **When students are given an assignment that is new to them, which of the following should almost always be discussed?**

   A. What the students can expect to learn from doing the assignment.

   B. Whether the assignment will be graded in similar fashion to other assignments.

   C. Whether the students can expect to be tested on the material presented.

   D. The teacher's background with this type of assignment.

58. **Piaget's learning theory asserts that adolescents in the formal operations period:**

   A. behave properly from fear of punishment rather than from a conscious decision to take a certain action

   B. see the past more realistically and can relate to people from the past more than preadolescents can

   C. are less self-conscious and thus more willing to project their own identities into those of fictional characters

   D. have not yet developed a symbolic imagination

59. **How are middle and high school students most receptive to studying grammar and syntax?**

   A. Through worksheets and end-of-lesson practices in textbooks

   B. Through independent homework assignments

   C. Through analytical examination of the writings of famous authors

   D. Through application to their own writing

60. A high school classroom teacher is working with nonnative speakers of English. During class, students are asked to read aloud, and the teacher focuses on continuously correcting pronunciation errors. What has this teacher failed to take into account in regards to second language development?

   A. Reading skills must be established prior to learning the syntax of a language.

   B. The fastest way for a nonnative speaker is to imitate the way native speakers use the language.

   C. Students should never be asked to read out loud before they can read and comprehend grade appropriate texts silently.

   D. Nonnative speakers often understand what they are reading before they can accurately speak the language.

61. Which of the following is the least preferable strategy for teaching literature?

   A. Teacher-guided total-class discussion

   B. Small-group discussion

   C. Teacher lecture

   D. Dramatization of literature selections

62. Which event triggered the beginning of Modern English?

   A. Conquest of England by the Normans in 1066

   B. Introduction of the printing press to the British Isles

   C. Publication of Samuel Johnson's lexicon

   D. American Revolution

63. A middle school teacher gives her students a list of vocabulary words to use in their essay, intending for the list to act as a scaffold. If the students exhibit proficiency on a mastery level, which of the following would be the best 'next' step?

   A. Give the students advanced words, and more of them, to include in the next essay.

   B. Ask the students to work collectively to come up with a new list to use in the next essay.

   C. Ask students to use the same vocabulary words in the next essay as well.

   D. Give a new list of vocabulary terms and have them look up the definitions, then use them in the next essay.

64. Which of the following is not a technique of prewriting?

   A. Clustering

   B. Listing

   C. Brainstorming

   D. Proofreading

65. An English teacher observes that a 10th grade student seems very upset about the idea of having to write a research paper. The teacher explains to the class as a whole, that the best approach for completing the assignment is to break the larger project into smaller tasks. Which of the following actions exemplify this methodology?

   A. Having students write about a familiar topic, then contrasting it with the topic for the research paper.

   B. Writing a rough draft of the paper, then handing it to a fellow student for feedback and a critical evaluation.

   C. Finding at least two credible sources for the research paper's topic, and seeing which aspects they both agree on.

   D. Compiling a bibliography of sources relating to the topic.

66. Why was it determined that students should be placed in the least restrictive educational environment?

   A. Because placement in a 'least restrictive environment' would normalize children with disabilities, as opposed to being educated in isolation from others.

   B. Because it was determined that classrooms should no longer be restrictive to minorities or females.

   C. Because it would reduce the fiscal cost of providing additional classrooms.

   D. Because adopting the least restrictive policies would increase funding to the school for special education.

67. Which of the following should not be included in the opening paragraph of an informative essay?

   A. Thesis sentence

   B. Details and examples supporting the main idea

   C. A broad, general introduction to the topic

   D. A style and tone that grabs the reader's attention

68. What is the main form of discourse in this passage?

   "It would have been hard to find a passer-by more wretched in appearance. He was a man of middle height, stout and hardy, in the strength of maturity; he might have been forty-six or seven. A slouched leather cap hid half his face, bronzed by the sun and wind, and dripping with sweat."

   A. Description

   B. Narration

   C. Exposition

   D. Persuasion

69. In a crowded classroom with varying skill levels, how might the teacher best take advantage of the diversity of the learning styles?

   A. Separate the students by reading levels.

   B. Assess students individually, only, to mitigate potential anxiety for the students.

   C. Incorporate opportunities for multilevel interaction through reciprocal learning events.

   D. Assign students to learning centers for computer based learning.

70. When introducing a classic work of fiction to 8th graders, what is a significant factor in its presentation and study?

   A. Whether the student finds that he or she can relate to the material.

   B. Whether the material will include a test.

   C. The material must be drawn from modern fiction sources.

   D. Students must be able to read on grade level to be able to enjoy a classic work of literature.

71. Classroom rules, when established correctly, require the teacher to do which of the following?

   A. State the rules with a serious intent.

   B. Quickly establish authority in the classroom.

   C. Create as many rules as it takes to cover all of the possible issues that might arise.

   D. Explain why the rules are needed.

72. If a teacher wanted to obtain data from a criterion-referenced test, as opposed to a norm-referenced test, which of the following would offer that information?

    A. How much each student in the classroom already knows about a singular aspect of the subject.

    B. How much each student in the classroom knows about a singular aspect, as compared to other students on a national level.

    C. How much each student in the classroom knows as compared to other students in the district.

    D. How much each student in the classroom knows about a certain portion of the subject.

73. Which of the following activities is a feature of an accelerated program as opposed to an enrichment activity?

    A. Finishing an independent project.

    B. Participating in simulations, role playing, playing games.

    C. Taking an exam and receiving credit.

    D. Enrolling and completing a summer program.

74. Which of the following is not a theme of Native American writing?

    A. Emphasis on the hardiness of the human body and soul

    B. The strength of multicultural assimilation

    C. Indignation about the genocide of native peoples

    D. Remorse for the loss of the Native American way of life

75. Which of the following contains an error in possessive punctuation?

    A. Doris's shawl

    B. mother's-in-law frown

    C. children's lunches

    D. ambassador's briefcase

76. Which of the following would be the most significant factor in teaching Homer's *Iliad* and *Odyssey* to any particular group of students?

    A. Identifying a translation on the appropriate reading level

    B. Determining the students' interest level

    C. Selecting an appropriate evaluative technique

    D. Determining the scope and delivery methods of background study

77. A punctuation mark indicating omission, interrupted thought, or an incomplete statement is a/an:

   A. ellipsis

   B. anachronism

   C. colloquy

   D. idiom

78. When characterizing a student's creativity, which of the descriptors are most apt?

   A. The student's solution is applicable in many areas, not just one domain.

   B. The student's solutions, though seemingly unorthodox, upon further discovery prove sound.

   C. The student's solutions are a collection of false starts, some of which end up being relevant.

   D. The student's solutions do not deviate from the standard perspectives.

79. The technique of starting a narrative at a significant point in the action and then developing the story through flashbacks is called:

   A. in medias res

   B. octava rima

   C. irony

   D. willing suspension of disbelief

80. When seeking to improve academic performance, as well as motivation of students, which of the following strategies are most likely to succeed?

   A. Teachers appoint a liaison to work with the administration to create a 'best practices' set of rules.

   B. Teachers present material as a team, standardizing presentation, and mapping academic progress.

   C. Teacher collaboration to assess and monitor other classroom procedures offers successful solutions.

   D. The classroom teacher must utilize management techniques with which he is familiar and comfortable.

81. In a timed essay test of an hour's duration, how much time should be devoted to prewriting?

   A. 5 minutes

   B. 10 minutes

   C. 15 minutes

   D. 20 minutes

82. Which of the following sentences is properly punctuated?

   A. The more you eat; the more you want.

   B. The authors—John Steinbeck, Ernest Hemingway, and William Faulkner—are staples of modern writing in American literature textbooks.

   C. Handling a wild horse, takes a great deal of skill and patience.

   D. The man, who replaced our teacher, is a comedian.

83. The students in Mrs. Cline's seventh-grade language arts class were invited to attend a performance of *Romeo and Juliet* presented by the drama class at the high school. To best prepare, they should:

   A. read the play as a homework exercise

   B. read a synopsis of the plot and a biographical sketch of the author

   C. examine a few main selections from the play to become familiar with the language and style of the author

   D. read a condensed version of the story and practice attentive listening skills

84. For students learning the process of constructed response writing, what is the appropriate pedagogical process?

   A. independent writing (summative), guided writing (formative), model/shadowing

   B. Model/shadowing, guided writing (formative), independent writing (summative)

   C. Guided writing (formative), model/shadowing, independent writing (summative)

   D. Independent writing (summative), guided writing (formative), peer reviewed grouping

85. An aspect of the reflective practice methodology is exemplified in which of the following?

   A. The teacher limits the amount of peer review.

   B. The teacher should limit student input that challenges or questions established teaching practices.

   C. The teacher should allow peer review to take its natural course, offering very little framework to limit the problem solving process.

   D. The teacher should establish a safe environment that allows reflection to take place among an accepted practice that is applicable for all learning situations.

86. When establishing the best way to assist students with comprehension skills, a teacher should focus on which of the following techniques as an informational text is read aloud?

   A. Writing down questions as a text is read aloud

   B. Creating an outline

   C. Setting a purpose for reading

   D. Encouraging students to make predictions

87. Writing ideas quickly without interruption of the flow of thoughts or attention to conventions is called:

   A. brainstorming

   B. mapping

   C. listing

   D. free writing

88. A formative evaluation of student writing:

   A. requires a thorough marking of mechanical errors with a pencil or pen

   B. makes comments on the appropriateness of the student's interpretation of the prompt and the degree to which the objective was met

   C. requires the student to hand in all the materials produced during the process of writing

   D. involves several careful readings of the text for content, mechanics, spelling, and usage

89. Reading a piece of student writing to assess the overall impression of the product is:

   A. holistic evaluation

   B. portfolio assessment

   C. analytical evaluation

   D. using a performance system

90. Modeling is a practice that requires students to:

   A. create a style unique to their own language capabilities

   B. emulate the writing of professionals

   C. paraphrase passages from good literature

   D. peer evaluate the writings of other students

91. A teacher is planning a lesson on T.S. Eliot's "The Hollow Men" for his eleventh grade English class. This is an excerpt from the poem:

   > *The eyes reappear*
   > *As the perpetual star*
   > *Multifoliate rose*
   > *Of death's twilight kingdom*
   > *The hope only*
   > *Of empty men.*

   What strategy, of those listed below, best allows for identification and understanding of the word 'multifoliate'?

   A. Structural analysis

   B. Contextual analysis

   C. Graphophonic analysis

   D. Syntactical analysis

92. A teacher is working with a class that includes an ELL (English Language Learner) student. When assigning an informational essay to the class, which of the following techniques would assist the ELL in an understanding of the text?

   A. Have all students create an illustration of some part of the text that they found interesting.

   B. Have the class use a graphic organizer to write down main ideas in the article.

   C. Hand out a list of most often used sentence stems to the entire classroom to use.

   D. Provide a list of words to the ELL that are familiar synonyms to the words that he or she is likely to encounter in the article assigned.

93. An 8th grade English teacher notices that each day when she asks a couple of questions about the previous day's lesson, the same handful of students always answer. Which of the following would promote active engagement by a larger percentage of the students?

   A. Encouraging those who are not answering, to do so.

   B. Allowing all students to create two questions about the day's assignment, to be asked the next day.

   C. Giving a participation grade that is not dependent on the correct answer.

   D. Having students evaluate their peers' responses using a rubric

94. Which of the following indicators would suggest that a student has developed strong communication skills when placed in a small group to discuss a novel?

   A. Taking charge of the group and directing the conversation.

   B. Making comments that build upon statements made by others in the group.

   C. Asking questions of the group members that diverges from the topic of conversation.

   D. Asking whomever is talking to explain what they mean by their statements.

95. In a high school classroom, a teacher has had students complete rough drafts of an expository essay, and has placed them in pairs to peer review each other's work. As a guideline, what should the teacher have students read to discern first?

   A. Transitions

   B. Supporting details

   C. Biased language

   D. Varied sentence lengths

96. A ninth grade English teacher is attempting to develop strategies that will promote a reading community in his classroom. Which of the following would be the least effective way of accomplishing this task?

   A. Students bring in books from home to include in a classroom library.

   B. The teacher assigns book reports on books that are to be selected from a list.

   C. Students work with the teacher to create a list of favorite books to read.

   D. The teacher will institute a 'drop everything and read' program for thirty minutes each week.

97. **What best describes a type of formative evaluation for writing education?**

    A. Making careful readings of the text for mechanics, usage, spelling, and content

    B. Marking mechanical errors with a colored pen.

    C. Asks students to turn in all work pertaining to the writing assignment, including outlines.

    D. Teacher makes comments on the goals that are being met by the student as the student works.

98. **When utilizing a computer in the classroom for writing assignments, the teacher must be aware of which of the following drawbacks when writing on a computer?**

    A. The writer may be unable to focus on the details and become distracted by the technology.

    B. The ability of a computer to quickly correct mistakes, often automatically, takes away from the aspect of writing that calls for reflection.

    C. Spell check programs do not assist students in learning to spell correctly, or select proper grammatical choices in their writing.

    D. Students tend to overlook glaring errors on the page because of the print type.

99. **When attempting to introduce a unit on poetry to freshmen students in a regular classroom, which of the following is the most ineffective technique?**

    A. Students are encouraged to bring their favorite song lyrics to class to discuss poetic devices used.

    B. Students will bring in their favorite poems to read aloud to the class.

    C. Students will work in groups to try to apply poetic devices in creating a popular song.

    D. Students will work in groups to illustrate a given poem.

100. **A new teacher is experiencing his first ELL student and wonders what type of activity would help this student the most. Which of the following might be suggested?**

    A. Provide the ELL student with more opportunities to write in English.

    B. Provide opportunities for the class, as well as the ELL student, to listen to the language via various media.

    C. Provide a wide range of activities that promote exposure to the language in all of its various modes (speaking, writing, reading).

    D. Make an assignment requiring students to make oral presentations in front of the class.

Answer Key

1.	A	22.	B	43.	D	64.	D	85.	D
2.	B	23.	C	44.	C	65.	C	86.	A
3.	A	24.	C	45.	B	66.	A	87.	D
4.	A	25.	C	46.	A	67.	B	88.	B
5.	B	26.	C	47.	B	68.	A	89.	A
6.	A	27.	D	48.	D	69.	C	90.	B
7.	D	28.	D	49.	A	70.	A	91.	A
8.	C	29.	A	50.	C	71.	D	92.	D
9.	A	30.	C	51.	B	72.	D	93.	B
10.	D	31.	D	52.	D	73.	C	94.	B
11.	C	32.	A	53.	C	74.	B	95.	A
12.	C	33.	A	54.	C	75.	B	96.	C
13.	A	34.	B	55.	D	76.	A	97.	D
14.	B	35.	A	56.	C	77.	A	98.	B
15.	D	36.	D	57.	A	78.	B	99.	D
16.	C	37.	C	58.	B	79.	A	100.	D
17.	C	38.	A	59.	D	80.	C		
18.	D	39.	C	60.	D	81.	B		
19.	C	40.	A	61.	C	82.	B		
20.	A	41.	C	62.	B	83.	D		
21.	C	42.	A	63.	B	84.	B		

Rationales with Sample Questions

Prompt A Sample Essay Response

The common theme that unites "I, Too" by Langston Hughes and the excerpt derived from Harper Lee's *To Kill a Mockingbird* alludes to the struggle of equality. The theme of unfair or unequal treatment is evident in both pieces. Though Langston Hughes and Tom are both African American, and they have similar perspectives, the two texts are in different settings. Langston Hughes is asserting himself as being an American, and Tom is defending himself in the courtroom, to prove his innocence in the American court of law, before a jury. Both men have stories that should be heard and interpreted as two Americans speaking, not two inferiors. They are simply expressing themselves candidly. Both works use "I" in narrative form, representing singularity, and being outnumbered, by the "company" in Hughes' poem and the "jury" in Lee's story. Hughes and Tom are certainly Americans, but are not perceived as equal in the eyes of society during their time.

Both Tom and Hughes boldly use "I." They state their cases effectively. Hughes explains, in lines 1–7, that he is not welcome among guests. He is told to "eat in the kitchen, when company comes" (lines 3–4) as if he is not worthy, or as if he is invisible. He is not treated equally in the household, and is hidden or shamed. Tom's inequality is less poetic than Hughes' poem, but nevertheless, it is strongly similar. Tom states his innocence in a case very concisely, to the best of his ability, showing he is simply a nice man who wanted to do a favor. He states "I felt right sorry for her" because he is able to connect with others on a humane level and offer assistance when needed. Sadly, Mr. Gilmer mocks Tom and belittles his comments, "*You* felt sorry for *her,*" and oppresses Tom verbally in front of a courtroom jury, among others. The striking feeling of being an excluded outcast is the tone of both pieces.

The poem utilizes the first-person voice, and the excerpt from Lee's work is also a first-person account, from the mouth of Tom. Though Tom seems utterly defeated, as his verdict appears to be grim, Hughes' poem lightens toward the end. Hughes appears to be filled with hope, and the tone changes. "They'll see how beautiful I am, and be ashamed" (lines 16–17) demonstrates a feeling of empowerment. This is not the case in Lee's excerpt, since the diction that occurs at the end of the passage is unwaveringly gloomy, with word choices such as "mistake," "shifted uncomfortably," "nobody liked," and "damage done." This is a striking difference between the two pieces, as one turns to hope for the future, while the other meanders down a darker path.

Prompt B Sample Essay Response

TASK 1

A significant strength of the paper is the use of specific details to support the statements made. The student's claims are clearly made for why more solitary sports are critical for those who do not want to compete in popularity. He states he finds competition everywhere, "I find this even on the track field, when players are joining me for winter track, for example. They want to make the best time, sprint the fastest, and throw shot-put the furthest. To me, this type of competitive arena takes the fun out." Furthermore, when defending their compromise of offering just three new sports, the student also gives a meaningful manner, stating that this action could potentially "provide kids like me with a chance to succeed at a sport without feeling socially overwhelmed." By giving powerful, emotive examples the student demonstrates an awareness of how he feels and how this can help others in his situation at school.

TASK 2

One of the weaknesses in this response is the lack of attention to the specific audience. An effective argument targets the audience directly, Dr. Ramos, and uses diction and syntax that will appeal to the audience. In this response, some of the vocabulary is colloquial and perhaps not suited for the school principal. For example, he states pep rallies are "amazing and fun" in the first paragraph, which is too colloquial when addressing school administrators. Phrases such as "I think," and "It would be cool if" might be appropriate in comments in conversations and writing pieces directed to the student's peers, but they are not operative when addressing a principal.

TASK 3

To help Matthew, as well his fellow students, pay attention to audience and understand how diction and tone contribute persuasive writing, students could participate in an activity that helps them understand how to address different audiences on the same topic. First, I would have a verbal rehearsal skit, in which students would gather in teams of three or four students. Each student would represent a type of audience. For example, one or two students would be "peers," and the other student (or two) would be labeled "principal," or even "president" to denote roles of authority. The students could speak to one another in the proper tone, depending on their role. The peer could address the principal or president in a respectful tone, whereas the peer could address the other peer in an informal manner. This role-playing would prep for the upcoming written activity. The teacher could post a prompt that read: "Imagine you need a ride to the movies, and you have no way of getting there unless you ask someone. Write each person a one-paragraph in length request: your mother who may have to work that evening, your brother who is home from college, and your neighbor who is home with her young children but knows you are reliable."

This combination of activities will be even more effective if students are asked to share their responses with the class and analyze why the requests will or will not work. Through the role-playing and short writing activity, followed by a discussion, students will learn to select diction carefully, depending on the audience.

TEACHER CERTIFICATION STUDY GUIDE

Section II: Writing and Language Skills

Directions: In sentences 1–10, four words or phrases have been underlined. If you determine that any underlined word or phrase has an error in grammar, usage, or mechanics, circle the letter underneath the underlining. There is no more than one error in any sentence.

1. The volcanic eruption in Montserrat displaced residents of Plymouth <u>which</u>
                                                                                                        A

   felt that the <u>English government</u> <u>was</u> responsible for <u>their</u> evacuation.
                   B   **C**   **D**

The error is A: which
"Which" is a relative pronoun whose antecedent is "residents of Plymouth." This antecedent represents persons, not things. If the antecedent were a thing or things, then "which" would be correct. "Who" is the correct pronoun.

2. When the <u>school district</u> privatized the school cafeteria, <u>us</u> students <u>were</u>
                  A   **B**   **C**

   thrilled to purchase more than soggy <u>French fries</u>.
                                                     D

The error is B: us
"Us" is an object pronoun, not the needed subject pronoun. "We" is the right pronoun.

3. The homecoming <u>Queen and King</u> <u>were chosen</u> by the <u>student body</u> for <u>their</u>
                               A   **B**   **C**   **D**

   popularity.

The error is A: Queen and King
"Queen and King" are used as common nouns here and not as proper nouns naming a real sovereign such as Queen Elizabeth. Since the words "queen and king" are common nouns, they are not capitalized.

4. If the practical joke <u>was</u> <u>Cullen's</u> idea, then he <u>must</u> suffer the <u>consequences</u>.
                           A   **B**   **C**   **D**

The error is A: was
In a sentence beginning with "if" and expressing a condition, it is necessary to use the correct subjunctive forms: "If I were, if you were, if he/she/it were, if we were, if you were, if they were." The sentence here should read: "If the practical joke were Cullen's idea…"

5. She, not her sister, <u>is</u> the one <u>who</u> the librarian <u>has questioned</u> about the
                             A   **B**   **C**

   missing books, <u>*Butterfly's* Ball</u> and *The Bear's House*.
                          D

The error is B: is
The relative pronoun "who" is a subject pronoun, but the sentence requires the object form at this point, "whom."

6. Jack told a <u>credulous</u> story about his trip <u>up the beanstalk</u> because each
                    A   **B**

   child in the room <u>was convinced</u> <u>by his reasoning</u>.
                         C   **D**

The error is A: credulous
Only a person can be credulous, not a thing. It should read: "Jack told an incredible story about his trip…"

7. My mother is a <u>Methodist</u>. She married a <u>Southern Baptist</u> and took <u>us</u>
                         A   **B**   **C**

   children to the <u>First Baptist church</u> in Stuart.
                    D

The error is D: First Baptist church
The name of the church should be completely capitalized. It should read: "… the First Baptist Church."

8. When we moved from Jacksonville, Florida , to Little Rock , Arkansas, my
                                         A   B
   <u>Dad</u> <u>was promoted</u> to store manager.
    C   D

The error is C: Dad
"Dad" is a common noun, which is indicated by the possessive "my." "Dad" used as an actual name gets capitalized.

9. "One of the <u>burglar's</u> was <u>already</u> <u>apprehended</u> before his colleagues left
                    A   B   C
   the building ," bragged the officer.
              D

The error is A: burglar's
"Burglar" should be in the plural: "burglars." In this sentence, it is written as a possessive.

10. Walter said <u>that</u> his calculator <u>has been missing</u> <u>since</u> last Monday
                  A   B   C
    <u>responding to my question</u>.
              D

The error is D: responding to my question
The participle phrase ("responding to my question") modifies "Walter," not "Monday." The sentence should read: "Walter, responding to my question, said that his calculator has been missing since last Monday."

TEACHER CERTIFICATION STUDY GUIDE

Part B

Each underlined portion of sentences 11–20 contains one or more errors in grammar, usage, mechanics, or sentence structure. Circle the choice that best corrects the error without changing the meaning of the original sentence. Choice D may repeat the underlined portion. Select the identical phrase if you find no error.

11. Joe <u>didn't hardly know his cousin Fred</u>, who'd had a rhinoplasty.

    A. hardly did know his cousin Fred

    B. didn't know his cousin Fred hardly

    C. hardly knew his cousin Fred

    D. didn't know his cousin Fred

Answer C: hardly knew his cousin Fred
Using the adverb "hardly" to modify the verb creates a negative, and adding "not" creates the dreaded double-negative.

12. <u>Mixing the batter for cookies</u>, the cat licked the Crisco from the cookie sheet.

    A. While mixing the batter for cookies

    B. While the batter for cookies was mixing

    C. While I mixed the batter for cookies

    D. While I mixed the cookies

Answer C: While I mixed the batter for cookies
Answer A gives the impression that the cat was mixing the batter (it is a dangling modifier), B that the batter was mixing itself, and D lacks precision: It is the batter that was being mixed, not the cookies themselves.

13. Mr. Brown is a school volunteer <u>with a reputation for twenty years service</u>.

   A. with a reputation for twenty years' service

   B. with a reputation for twenty year's service

   C. who has served twenty years

   D. with a reputation for twenty years service

Answer A: with a reputation for twenty years' service
Answer B is a singular genitive ('s), C lacks the reputation part, and D lacks the genitive plural (s') that is necessary here.

14. Walt Whitman was famous for <u>his composition, *Leaves of Grass*, serving as a nurse during the Civil War, and a devoted son</u>.

   A. *Leaves of Grass*, his service as a nurse during the Civil War, and a devoted son

   B. composing *Leaves of Grass*, serving as a nurse during the Civil War, and being a devoted son

   C. his composition, *Leaves of Grass*, his nursing during the Civil War, and his devotion as a son

   D. his composition, *Leaves of Grass*, serving as a nurse during the Civil War, and a devoted son

Answer B: composing *Leaves of Grass*, serving as a nurse during the Civil War, and being a devoted son
To be parallel, the sentence needs three gerunds. The other sentences use both gerunds and nouns, which is a lack of parallelism.

TEACHER CERTIFICATION STUDY GUIDE

15. **A teacher <u>must know not only her subject matter but also the strategies of content teaching</u>.**

    A. must not only know her subject matter but also the strategies of content teaching

    B. not only must know her subject matter but also the strategies of content teaching

    C. must not know only her subject matter but also the strategies of content teaching

    D. must know not only her subject matter but also the strategies of content teaching

Answer D: must know not only her subject matter but also the strategies of content teaching
"Not only" must come directly after "know" because the intent is to create the clearest meaning link with the "but also" predicate section later in the sentence.

16. **My English teacher, Mrs. Hunt, <u>is nicer than any teacher at school and is</u> the most helpful.**

    A. is as nice as any teacher at school and is

    B. is nicer than any other teacher at school and is

    C. is as nice as any other teacher at school and is

    D. is nicer than any teacher at school and is

Answer C: is as nice as any other teacher at the school and is
When comparing one thing to others in a group, you need to exclude the thing under comparison from the rest of the group. Thus, you need the word "other" in the sentence.

17. The teacher <u>implied</u> from our angry words that there was conflict <u>between you and me</u>.

   A. implied ... between you and I

   B. inferred ... between you and I

   C. inferred ... between you and me

   D. implied ... between you and me

Answer C: inferred ... between you and me
The difference between the verb "to imply" and the verb "to infer" is that *implying* is directing an interpretation toward other people; *inferring* is deducing an interpretation from someone else's discourse. Moreover, "between you and I" is grammatically incorrect: After the preposition "between," the object (or disjunctive with this particular preposition) pronoun form, "me," is needed.

18. There were <u>fewer pieces</u> of evidence presented during the second trial.

   A. fewer peaces

   B. less peaces

   C. less pieces

   D. fewer pieces

Answer D: fewer pieces
"Less" is impossible in the plural, and "peace" is the opposite of war, not a "piece" of evidence.

19. Mr. Smith <u>respectfully submitted his resignation and had</u> a new job.

   A. respectfully submitted his resignation and has

   B. respectfully submitted his resignation before accepting

   C. respectfully submitted his resignation because of

   D. respectfully submitted his resignation and had

Answer C: respectfully submitted his resignation because of
Answer A eliminates any relationship of causality between submitting the resignation and having the new job. B changes the sentence and does not indicate the fact that Mr. Smith had a new job before submitting his resignation. D means that Mr. Smith first submitted his resignation, then got a new job.

20. Wally <u>groaned, "Why</u> do I have to do an oral interpretation <u>of "The Raven."</u>

   A. groaned "Why ... of 'The Raven'?"

   B. groaned "Why ... of "The Raven"?

   C. groaned "Why ... of "The Raven?"

   D. groaned, "Why ... of "The Raven."

Answer A: groaned, "Why ... of 'The Raven'?"
The question mark in a quotation that is an interrogation should be within the quotation marks. Also, when quoting a title that is styled in quotation marks (like the title of a poem or short story) within another quotation, one should use single quotation marks ('...') for the title of this work, and they should close before the final quotation mark.

Part C

Questions 21–100 pertain to various literary devices and content knowledge, and require a strong understanding of English Language Arts. Select one answer for each multiple-choice question.

21. The following passage is written from which point of view?

    As she mused the pitiful vision of her mother's life laid its spell on the very quick of her being—that life of commonplace sacrifices closing in final craziness. She trembled as she heard again her mother's voice saying constantly with foolish insistence: Dearevaun Seraun! Dearevaun Seraun!*

    * "The end of pleasure is pain!"

    (Gaelic)

    A. First person, narrator

    B. Second person, direct address

    C. Third person, omniscient

    D. First person, omniscient

Answer C: Third person, omniscient
The passage is clearly in the third person (the subject is "she"), and it is omniscient since it gives the character's inner thoughts.

22. The literary device of personification is used in which example below?

   A. "Beg me no beggary by soul or parents, whining dog!"

   B. "Happiness sped through the halls cajoling as it went."

   C. "O wind thy horn, thou proud fellow."

   D. "And that one talent which is death to hide."

Answer B: "Happiness sped through the halls cajoling as it went."
"Happiness," an abstract concept, is described as if it were a person.

23. Which of the following is not one of the four forms of discourse?

   A. Exposition

   B. Description

   C. Rhetoric

   D. Persuasion

Answer C: Rhetoric
Rhetoric is an umbrella term for techniques of expressive and effective speech. Rhetorical figures are ornaments of speech such as anaphora, antithesis, and metaphor. The other three choices are specific forms of discourse.

24. Among junior-high school students of low-to-average reading levels, which work would most likely stir reading interest?

    A. *Elmer Gantry*, Sinclair Lewis

    B. *Smiley's People*, John Le Carre

    C. *The Outsiders*, S. E. Hinton

    D. *And Then There Were None*, Agatha Christie

Answer C: *The Outsiders*, S.E. Hinton
The students can easily identify with the characters and the gangs in the book. S. E. Hinton has actually said about this book: "*The Outsiders* is definitely my best-selling book; but what I like most about it is how it has taught a lot of kids to enjoy reading."

25. "Every one must pass through Vanity Fair to get to the celestial city" is an allusion from a:

    A. Chinese folk tale

    B. Norse saga

    C. British allegory

    D. German fairy tale

Answer C: British allegory
This is a reference to John Bunyan's *Pilgrim's Progress from this World to That Which Is to Come* (Part I, 1678; Part II, 1684), in which the hero, Christian, flees the City of Destruction and must undergo different trials and tests to get to the Celestial City.

26. Which teaching method would best engage underachievers in the required senior English class?

    A. Assign use of glossary work and extensively footnoted excerpts of great works.

    B. Have students take turns reading aloud the anthology selection.

    C. Let students choose which readings they study and write about.

    D. Use a chronologically arranged, traditional text, but assign group work, panel presentations, and portfolio management.

Answer C: Let students choose which readings they study and write about
It will encourage students to react honestly to literature. Students should take notes on what they're reading so they will be able to discuss the material. They should not only react to literature but also experience it. Small-group work is a good way to encourage them. The other answers are not fit for junior-high or high school students. They should be encouraged, however, to read critics of works to understand critical work.

27. Which term best describes the form of the following poetic excerpt?

And more to lulle him in his slumber soft,
A trickling streake from high rock tumbling downe,
And ever-drizzling raine upon the loft.
Mixt with a murmuring winde, much like a swowne
No other noyse, nor peoples troubles cryes.
As still we wont t'annoy the walle'd towne,
Might there be heard: but careless Quiet lyes,
Wrapt in eternall silence farre from enemyes.

A. Ballad

B. Elegy

C. Spenserian stanza

D. Octava rima

Answer D: Octava rima
Octava rima is a specific eight-line stanza with the rhyme scheme *abababcc*.

28. To understand the origins of a word, one must study the:

   A. synonyms

   B. inflections

   C. phonetics

   D. etymology

Answer D: etymology
Etymology is the study of word origins. A synonym is an equivalent of another word and can substitute for it in certain contexts. Inflection is a modification of words according to their grammatical functions, usually by employing variant word endings to indicate such qualities as tense, gender, case, and number. Phonetics is the science devoted to the physical analysis of the sounds of human speech, including their production, transmission, and perception.

29. Which sonnet form describes the following?

My galley charg'd with forgetfulness,
Through sharp seas, in winter night doth pass
'Tween rock and rock; and eke mine enemy, alas,
That is my lord steereth with cruelness.
And every oar a thought with readiness,
As though that death were light in such a case.
An endless wind doth tear the sail apace
Or forc'ed sighs and trusty fearfulness.
A rain of tears, a cloud of dark disdain,
Hath done the wearied cords great hinderance,
Wreathed with error and eke with ignorance.
The stars be hid that led me to this pain
Drowned is reason that should me consort,
And I remain despairing of the poet

A. Petrarchan or Italian sonnet

B. Shakespearian or Elizabethan sonnet

C. Romantic sonnet

D. Spenserian sonnet

Answer A: Petrarchan or Italian sonnet

The Petrarchan sonnet, also known as the Italian sonnet, is named after the Italian poet Petrarch (1304–74). It is divided into an octave rhyming *abbaabba* and a sestet normally rhyming *cdecde*.

ENGLISH LANG. ARTS & READING 232

30. **What is the salient literary feature of this excerpt from an epic?**

> Hither the heroes and the nymphs resort,
> To taste awhile the pleasures of a court;
> In various talk th'instructive hours they passed,
> Who gave the ball, or paid the visit last;
> One speaks the glory of the English Queen,
> And another describes a charming Indian screen;
> A third interprets motion, looks, and eyes;
> At every word a reputation dies.

    A. Sprung rhythm

    B. Onomatopoeia

    C. Heroic couplets

    D. Motif

Answer C: Heroic couplets
A couplet is a pair of rhyming verse lines, usually of the same length. It is one of the most widely used verse forms in European poetry. Chaucer established the use of couplets in English, notably in the *Canterbury Tales*, using rhymed iambic pentameter (a metrical unit of verse having one unstressed syllable followed by one stressed syllable) later known as heroic couplets. Other authors who used heroic couplets include Ben Jonson, Dryden, and especially Alexander Pope, who became the master of them.

31. What were two major characteristics of the first American literature?

   A. Vengefulness and arrogance

   B. Bellicosity and derision

   C. Oral delivery and reverence for the land

   D. Maudlin and self-pitying egocentrism

Answer D: Maudlin and self-pitying egocentrism
This characteristic can be seen in Captain John Smith's work, as well as William Bradford, and Michael Wigglesworth's works.

32. Arthur Miller wrote *The Crucible* as a parallel to what twentieth-century event?

   A. Sen. McCarthy's House un-American Activities Committee hearing

   B. The Cold War

   C. The fall of the Berlin Wall

   D. The Persian Gulf War

Answer A: Sen. McCarthy's House un-American Activities Committee hearing
The seventeenth-century witch hunt in Salem, Massachusetts, gave Miller a storyline that was comparable to what was happening to persons suspected of communist beliefs in the 1950s.

33. Latin words that entered the English language during the Elizabethan age include:

   A. *allusion*, *education*, and *esteem*

   B. *vogue* and *mustache*

   C. *canoe* and *cannibal*

   D. *alligator*, *cocoa*, and *armadillo*

Answer A: *allusion*, *education*, and *esteem*
Since the English alphabet is based on the Latin one, which originally had 20 letters, consisting of the present English alphabet minus J, K, V, W, Y, and Z, answer B. is incorrect because of the word "vogue" (which is French in origin). "Canoe" is also French in origin, eliminating answer C. Cocoa, in answer D. is Spanish in origin. Although French and Spanish are based in Latin, the words most directly derived from Latin in these selections are those in answer A.

34. Which of the following is not a characteristic of a fable?

   A. Animals that feel and talk like humans

   B. Happy solutions to human dilemmas

   C. Teaches a moral or standard for behavior

   D. Illustrates specific people or groups without directly naming them

Answer B: Happy solutions to human dilemmas
Fables do not present a happy solution to a human dilemma. A fable is a short tale with animals, humans, gods, or even inanimate objects as characters. Fables often conclude with a moral, delivered in the form of an epigram (a short, witty, and ingenious statement in verse). Fables are among the oldest forms of writing in human history: They appear in Egyptian papyri from 1500 BCE. The most famous fables are those of Aesop, a Greek slave living in about 600 BCE. In India, the Panchatantra appeared in the third century BCE. The most famous modern fables are those of seventeenth-century French poet Jean de La Fontaine.

35. If a student has a poor vocabulary, the teacher should recommend first that:

   A. the student read newspapers, magazines, and books on a regular basis

   B. the student enroll in a Latin class

   C. the student write words repetitively after looking them up in the dictionary

   D. the student use a thesaurus to locate synonyms and incorporate them into his or her vocabulary

Answer A: the student read newspapers, magazines, and books on a regular basis
It is up to the teacher to help the student choose reading material, but the student must be able to choose where to search for material that will give him or her the reading pleasure indispensable for enriching vocabulary.

36. Which author did not write satire?

   A. Joseph Addison

   B. Richard Steele

   C. Alexander Pope

   D. John Bunyan

Answer D: John Bunyan
John Bunyan was a religious writer, known for his autobiography, *Grace Abounding to The Chief of Sinners*, as well as other books, all religious in their inspiration, such as *The Pilgrim's Progress*, *The Holy City, or the New Jerusalem* (1665), *A Confession of my Faith, and a Reason of my Practice* (1672), and *The Holy War* (1682).

37. Which of the following was not written by Jonathan Swift?

   A. *A Voyage to Lilliput*

   B. *A Modest Proposal*

   C. *Samson Agonistes*

   D. *A Tale of a Tub*

Answer C: *Samson Agonistes*
Samson Agonistes is a poem by John Milton. It was published in 1671 in the same volume as *Paradise Regained*.

38. Which is the best definition for diction?

   A. The specific word choices of an author to create a particular mood or feeling in the reader

   B. Writing that explains something thoroughly

   C. The background, or exposition, for a short story or drama

   D. Word choices that help teach a truth or moral

Answer A: The specific word choices of an author to create a particular mood or feeling in the reader
Diction refers to an author's choice of words, expressions, and style to convey his or her meaning.

39. Which is the best definition of free verse, or *vers libre*?

   A. Poetry that consists of an unaccented syllable followed by an unaccented sound

   B. Short lyrical poetry written to entertain but with an instructive purpose

   C. Poetry that does not have a uniform pattern of rhythm

   D. Poetry that tells the story and has a plot

Answer C: Poetry that does not have a uniform pattern of rhythm
Free verse has lines of irregular length and no uniform pattern of rhythm (but it does not run on like prose).

40. Which is an untrue statement about a theme in literature?

   A. The theme is always stated directly somewhere in the text.

   B. The theme is the central idea in a literary work.

   C. All parts of the work (plot, setting, mood) should contribute to the theme in some way.

   D. By analyzing the various elements of the work, the reader should be able to arrive at an indirectly stated theme.

Answer A: The theme is always stated directly somewhere in the text.
The theme may be stated directly, but it can also be implicit in various aspects of the work, such as the interactions among characters, symbolism, or description.

TEACHER CERTIFICATION STUDY GUIDE

41. Which is the least true statement concerning an author's literary tone?

   A. Tone is partly revealed through the selection of details.

   B. Tone is the expression of the author's attitude toward his or her subject.

   C. Tone in literature is usually satiric or angry.

   D. Tone in literature corresponds to the tone of voice a speaker uses.

Answer C: Tone in literature is usually satiric or angry
Tone in literature conveys a mood and can be as varied as the tone of voice of a speaker (see D), for example, sad, nostalgic, whimsical, angry, formal, intimate, satirical, or sentimental.

42. Regarding the study of poetry, which elements are least applicable to all types of poetry?

   A. Setting and audience

   B. Theme and tone

   C. Pattern and diction

   D. Diction and rhyme scheme

Answer A: Setting and audience
Setting and audience are important elements of narrative, but there are many poems in which the setting and audience are unimportant.

TEACHER CERTIFICATION STUDY GUIDE

43. Which of the following definitions best describes a parable?

    A. A short, entertaining account of some happening, usually using talking animals as characters

    B. A slow, sad song, poem or prose work expressing lamentation

    C. An extensive narrative work expressing universal truths concerning domestic life

    D. A short, simple story of an occurrence of a familiar kind, from which a moral or religious lesson may be drawn

Answer D: A short, simple story of an occurrence of a familiar kind, from which a moral or religious lesson may be drawn
A parable is usually brief and should be interpreted as an allegory teaching a moral lesson. Jesus's 40 parables are the model of the genre, but modern, secular examples exist, such as Wilfred Owen's *The Parable of The Old Man and The Young* (1920), or John Steinbeck's prose work *The Pearl* (1948).

44. Which of the following is the best definition of existentialism?

    A. The philosophical doctrine that matter is the only reality and that everything in the world, including thought, will, and feeling, can be explained only in terms of matter

    B. A philosophy that views things as they should be or as one would wish them to be

    C. A philosophical and literary movement, variously religious and atheistic, stemming from Kierkegaard and represented by Sartre

    D. The belief that all events are determined by fate and are hence inevitable

Answer C: A philosophical and literary movement, variously religious and atheistic, stemming from Kierkegaard and represented by Sartre
Even though there are other very important thinkers in the movement known as Existentialism, such as Camus and Merleau-Ponty, Sartre remains the main figure in this movement.

ENGLISH LANG. ARTS & READING

TEACHER CERTIFICATION STUDY GUIDE

45. Which of the following is the best definition of imagism?

A. A doctrine teaching that comfort is the only goal of value in life

B. A movement in modern poetry (c. 1910–1918) characterized by precise, concrete images, free verse, and suggestion rather than complete statement

C. The belief that people are motivated entirely by self-centeredness

D. The doctrine that the human mind cannot know whether there is a God, an ultimate cause, or anything beyond material phenomena

Answer B: A movement in modern poetry (c. 1910-1918) characterized by precise, concrete images, free verse, and suggestion rather than complete statement
The group known as the imagists was led by Ezra Pound at first, but he started the Vorticism movement and was replaced by Amy Lowell. Imaginsts rejected nineteenth-century poetry and were looking for clarity and exactness. Their poems were usually short and built around a single image. Other writers representative of the movement are Richard Addington, H.D. (Hilda Doolittle), F. S. Flint, D. H. Lawrence, Ford Madox Ford, and William Carlos Williams.

46. Which choice below best defines naturalism?

A. A belief that the writer or artist should apply scientific objectivity in his or her observation and treatment of life without imposing value judgments

B. The doctrine that teaches that the existing world is the best to be hoped for

C. The doctrine which teaches that God is not a personality, but that all laws, forces and manifestations of the universe are God-related

D. A philosophical doctrine which professes that the truth of all knowledge must always be in question

Answer A: A belief that the writer or artist should apply scientific objectivity in his or her observation and treatment of life without imposing value judgements
Naturalism is a movement that was started by French writers Jules and Edmond de Goncourt with their novel *Germinie Lacerteux* (1865), but its real leader is Emile Zola, who wanted to bring "a slice of life" to his readers. His saga *Les Rougon Macquart* consists of 22 novels depicting various aspects of social life. Authors writing in English who are representative of this movement include George Moore and George Gissing in England, but the most important naturalist novel in English is Theodore Dreiser's *Sister Carrie*.

ENGLISH LANG. ARTS & READING

47. The tendency to emphasize and value the qualities and peculiarities of life in a particular geographic area exemplifies:

   A. pragmatism

   B. regionalism

   C. pantheism

   D. abstract expressionism

Answer B: regionalism
Regionalism emphasizes and values the defining details of life in a particular geographic area. Pragmatism is a philosophical doctrine according to which there is no absolute truth. All truths change their trueness as their practical utility increases or decreases. The main representative of this movement is William James, who in 1907 published *Pragmatism: A New Way for Some Old Ways of Thinking*. Pantheism is a philosophy according to which God is omnipresent in the world; everything is God and God is everything. The great representative of this sensibility is Spinoza. Also, the works of writers such as Wordsworth, Shelly, and Emerson illustrate this doctrine. Abstract expressionism is one of the most important movements in American art. It began in the 1940s with artists such as Willem de Kooning, Mark Rothko, and Arshile Gorky. The paintings are usually large and nonrepresentational.

48. The arrangement and relationship of words in sentences or sentence structures best describes:

   A. style

   B. discourse

   C. thesis

   D. syntax

Answer D: syntax
Syntax is the grammatical structure of sentences.

49. Explanatory or informative discourse is:

   A. exposition

   B. narration

   C. persuasion

   D. description

Answer A: exposition
Exposition sets forth a systematic explanation of any subject. It can also introduce the characters of a literary work and their situations in the story.

50. The substitution of "went to his rest" for "died" is an example of a/an:

   A. bowdlerism

   B. jargon

   C. euphemism

   D. malapropism

Answer C: euphemism
A euphemism replaces an unpleasant or offensive word or expression with a more agreeable one. It also alludes to distasteful things in a pleasant manner, and it can even paraphrase offensive texts.

51. A conversation between two or more people is called a:

    A. parody

    B. dialogue

    C. monologue

    D. analogy

Answer B: dialogue
Dialogues are indispensable to dramatic work, and they often appear in narratives and poetry. A parody is a work that adopts the subject and structure of another work to ridicule it. A monologue is a work or part of a work written in the first person. An analogy illustrates an idea by means of a more familiar idea that is similar or parallel to it.

52. "Clean as a whistle" and "easy as falling of a log" are examples of:

    A. semantics

    B. parody

    C. irony

    D. clichés

Answer D: clichés
A cliché is a phrase or expression that has become dull due to overuse.

53. In literature, evoking feelings of pity or compassion is creating:

   A. colloquy

   B. irony

   C. pathos

   D. paradox

Answer C: pathos
A very well-known example of pathos is Desdemona's death in *Othello*, but there are many other examples of pathos.

54. "I'll die if I don't pass this course" is an example of:

   A. barbarism

   B. oxymoron

   C. hyperbole

   D. antithesis

Answer C: hyperbole
Hyperbole is an exaggeration for the sake of emphasis. It is a figure of speech that should not be understood literally. Hyperboles appear in everyday vernacular and in literature.

55. **Addressing someone absent or something inhuman as though present and able to respond describes a figure of speech known as:**

    A. personification

    B. synecdoche

    C. metonymy

    D. apostrophe

Answer D: apostrophe
An apostrophe addresses an absent person or something inhuman as though that person or thing were present and able to respond.

56. **Slang or jargon expressions associated with a particular ethnic, age, socioeconomic, or professional group are called:**

    A. aphorisms

    B. allusions

    C. idioms

    D. euphemisms

Answer C: idioms
An idiom is a word or expression that cannot be translated word for word in another language, such as "I am running low on gas." By extension, writers use idioms to convey a way of speaking and writing typical of a group of people.

57. **When students are given an assignment that is new to them, which of the following should almost always be discussed?**

   A. What the students can expect to learn from doing the assignment.

   B. Whether the assignment will be graded in similar fashion to other assignments.

   C. Whether the students can expect to be tested on the material presented.

   D. The teacher's background with this type of assignment.

Answer A: What the students can expect to learn from doing the assignment
According to many studies, students learn best when they are motivated. To be motivated, students must draw conclusions that are meaningful and worthwhile, leading toward larger goals instead of performance goals. By discussing *why* something is being done, and what they can gain from learning it, students will be more motivated to attempt something new.

58. **Piaget's learning theory asserts that adolescents in the formal operations period:**

   A. behave properly from fear of punishment rather than from a conscious decision to take a certain action

   B. see the past more realistically and can relate to people from the past more than pre-adolescents can

   C. are less self-conscious and thus more willing to project their own identities into those of fictional characters

   D. have not yet developed a symbolic imagination

Answer B: see the past more realistically and can relate to people from the past more than pre-adolescents can
According to Piaget, adolescents 12–15 years old begin thinking beyond the immediate and obvious and begin to theorize. Their assessment of events shifts from considering an action as "right" or "wrong" to considering the intent and situation in which the action was performed. Fairy-tale or other kinds of unreal characters have ceased to satisfy them, and they are able to recognize the difference between pure history and historical fiction.

TEACHER CERTIFICATION STUDY GUIDE

59. **How are middle and high school students most receptive to studying grammar and syntax?**

    A. Through worksheets and end-of-lesson practices in textbooks

    B. Through independent homework assignments

    C. Through analytical examination of the writings of famous authors

    D. Through application to their own writing

Answer D: Through the application to their own writing
At this age, students learn grammatical concepts best through practical application to their own writing.

60. **A high school classroom teacher is working with nonnative speakers of English. During class, students are asked to read aloud, and the teacher focuses on continuously correcting pronunciation errors. What has this teacher failed to take into account in regards to second language development?**

    A. Reading skills must be established prior to learning the syntax of a language.

    B. The fastest way for a nonnative speaker is to imitate the way native speakers use the language.

    C. Students should never be asked to read out loud before they can read and comprehend grade appropriate texts silently.

    D. Non-native speakers often understand what they are reading before they can accurately speak the language.

Answer D: Non-native speakers often understand what they are reading before they can accurately speak the language
Learning should focus on comprehension and formal accuracy, as well as usage.

ENGLISH LANG. ARTS & READING

TEACHER CERTIFICATION STUDY GUIDE

61. Which of the following is the least preferable strategy for teaching literature?

    A. Teacher-guided total-class discussion

    B. Small-group discussion

    C. Teacher lecture

    D. Dramatization of literature selections

Answer C: Teacher lecture
To engage students' interest, it is necessary that they be involved in the instruction; this can be through discussion or dramatization. A lecture is a much too passive technique to involve students of this age.

62. Which event triggered the beginning of Modern English?

    A. Conquest of England by the Normans in 1066

    B. Introduction of the printing press to the British Isles

    C. Publication of Samuel Johnson's lexicon

    D. American Revolution

Answer B: Introduction of the printing press to the British Isles
With the arrival of the written word, reading matter became mass produced, so the public tended to adopt the speech and writing habits printed in books, and the language became more stable.

63. A middle school teacher gives her students a list of vocabulary words to use in their essay, intending for the list to act as a scaffold. If the students exhibit proficiency on a mastery level, which of the following would be the best 'next' step?

   A. Give the students advanced words, and more of them, to include in the next essay.

   B. Ask the students to work collectively to come up with a new list to use in the next essay.

   C. Ask students to use the same vocabulary words in the next essay as well.

   D. Give a new list of vocabulary terms and have them look up the definitions, then use them in the next essay.

Answer B: Ask the students to work collectively to come up with a new list to use in the next essay
Scaffolding is, at best, a temporary framework to assist students toward the goal of being independent learners. Thus, once the skill has been mastered, the scaffold needs to be withdrawn. Having the students become responsible for providing their own vocabulary words not only withdraws the scaffold, but it encourages independent, as well as reciprocal, learning. None of the other answers meet these two criteria.

64. Which of the following is not a technique of prewriting?

   A. Clustering

   B. Listing

   C. Brainstorming

   D. Proofreading

Answer D: Proofreading
Proofreading cannot be a method of prewriting, since it is done on texts that have already been written.

65. An English teacher observes that a 10th grade student seems very upset about the idea of having to write a research paper. The teacher explains to the class as a whole, that the best approach for completing the assignment is to break the larger project into smaller tasks. Which of the following actions exemplify this methodology?

   A. Having students write about a familiar topic, then contrasting it with the topic for the research paper.

   B. Writing a rough draft of the paper, then handing it to a fellow student for feedback and a critical evaluation.

   C. Finding at least two credible sources for the research paper's topic, and seeing which aspects they both agree on.

   D. Compiling a bibliography of sources relating to the topic.

Answer C: Finding at least two credible sources for the research paper's topic, and seeing which aspects they both agree on
A larger task can often overwhelm a student, so breaking the task into smaller subtasks is a way of lessening a student's anxiety about a long term assignment. Both A and B involve creating the whole work first, and D is still a large task and may only serve to overwhelm the student further.

66. Why was it determined that students should be placed in the least restrictive educational environment?

   A. Because placement in a 'least restrictive environment' would normalize children with disabilities, as opposed to being educated in isolation from others.

   B. Because it was determined that classrooms should no longer be restrictive to minorities or females.

   C. Because it would reduce the fiscal cost of providing additional classrooms.

   D. Because adopting the least restrictive policies would increase funding to the school for special education.

Answer A: Because placement in a 'least restrictive environment' would normalize children with disabilities, as opposed to being educated in isolation from others
The idea of 'least restrictive' was based on the legislation that stated that the education of divergent learners, and learners with disabilities should only be segregated if necessary, and that permanent placement within a regular classroom setting would be of more benefit to all students. The legislation is based on P.L 94-142.

67. Which of the following should not be included in the opening paragraph of an informative essay?

   A. Thesis sentence

   B. Details and examples supporting the main idea

   C. A broad, general introduction to the topic

   D. A style and tone that grabs the reader's attention

Answer B: Details and examples supporting the main idea
The introductory paragraph should introduce the topic, capture the reader's interest, state the thesis, and prepare the reader for the main points in the essay. Details and examples, however, should be given in the second part of the essay to develop the thesis presented at the end of the introductory paragraph. This progression follows the inverted triangle method, consisting of a broad, general statement followed by some information, followed by the thesis at the end of the paragraph.

68. What is the main form of discourse in this passage?

   "It would have been hard to find a passer-by more wretched in appearance. He was a man of middle height, stout and hardy, in the strength of maturity; he might have been forty-six or seven. A slouched leather cap hid half his face, bronzed by the sun and wind, and dripping with sweat."

   A. Description

   B. Narration

   C. Exposition

   D. Persuasion

Answer A: Description
A description presents a thing or a person in detail and tells the reader about the appearance of whatever it is presenting. Narration relates a sequence of events (the story) through a process of discourse, in which events are recounted in a certain order (the plot). Exposition is an explanation or an argument within the narration. It can also be the introduction to a play or a story. Persuasion strives to convince either a character in the story or the reader.

69. **In a crowded classroom with varying skill levels, how might the teacher best take advantage of the diversity of the learning styles?**

    A. Separate the students by reading levels.

    B. Assess students individually, only, to mitigate potential anxiety for the students.

    C. Incorporate opportunities for multilevel interaction through reciprocal learning events.

    D. Assign students to learning centers for computer based learning.

Answer C: Incorporate opportunities for multilevel interaction through reciprocal learning events
Students who work within varying level environments all benefit. Those who are in the lower quartile may be motivated or encouraged by their peers, while those who are in the upper quartile will synthesize the material in a way that allows them to apply what they have learned.

70. **When introducing a classic work of fiction to 8th graders, what is a significant factor in its presentation and study?**

    A. Whether the student finds that he or she can relate to the material.

    B. Whether the material will include a test.

    C. The material must be drawn from modern fiction sources.

    D. Students must be able to read on grade level to be able to enjoy a classic work of literature.

Answer A: Whether the student finds that he or she can relate to the material
Many studies exist which indicate that students who are interested, and who feel that the material has some relevance to their lives will be motivated to learn a subject. Literature whose themes and relevancy to modern life are indicated by the teacher can play a significant factor in the successful completion of a unit of study.

71. **Classroom rules, when established correctly, require the teacher to do which of the following?**

    A. State the rules with a serious intent.

    B. Quickly establish authority in the classroom.

    C. Create as many rules as it takes to cover all of the possible issues that might arise.

    D. Explain why the rules are needed.

Answer D: Explain why the rules are needed
Classroom management is achieved by having a few rules that make sense to students. When students in this age group are given reasons for the rules, they are more likely to comply.

72. **If a teacher wanted to obtain data from a criterion-referenced test, as opposed to a norm-referenced test, which of the following would offer that information?**

    A. How much each student in the classroom already knows about a singular aspect of the subject.

    B. How much each student in the classroom knows about a singular aspect, as compared to other students on a national level.

    C. How much each student in the classroom knows as compared to other students in the district.

    D. How much each student in the classroom knows about a certain portion of the subject.

Answer D: How much each student in the classroom knows about a certain portion of the subject
Criterion-referenced tests determine the comprehension of a specific competency. These types of tests judge the student against the standard, and not against others in the state, nation, or district. Since the goal is to determine comprehension and knowledge, a group based performance (norm referenced) is not indicated. A is not the answer because it does not measure the student's gained knowledge, only knowledge that was preexisting.

73. Which of the following activities is a feature of an accelerated program as opposed to an enrichment activity?

    A. Finishing an independent project.

    B. Participating in simulations, role playing, playing games.

    C. Taking an exam and receiving credit.

    D. Enrolling and completing a summer program.

Answer C: Taking an exam and receiving credit
Students who take an exam and are able to receive credit for that class, or subject, are able to CLEP or skip out of that class. Thus, they have accelerated their learning process. The other options offer students enrichment activities designed to supplement learning.

74. Which of the following is not a theme of Native American writing?

    A. Emphasis on the hardiness of the human body and soul

    B. The strength of multicultural assimilation

    C. Indignation about the genocide of native peoples

    D. Remorse for the loss of the Native American way of life

Answer B: The strength of multicultural assimilation
Native American literature was first a vast body of oral traditions dating back to before the fifteenth century. The characteristics include reverence for and awe of nature and the interconnectedness of the elements in the life cycle. The themes often reflect the hardiness of body and soul, remorse for the destruction of the Native American way of life, and the genocide of many tribes by the encroaching settlements of European Americans. These themes are still present in today's contemporary Native American literature, such as the works of Duane Niatum, Paula Gunn Allen, Louise Erdrich, and N. Scott Momaday.

75. Which of the following contains an error in possessive punctuation?

    A. Doris's shawl

    B. mother's-in-law frown

    C. children's lunches

    D. ambassador's briefcase

Answer B: mother's-in-law frown
Mother-in-law is a compound common noun, and by convention the inflection should be at the end of the word (mother-in-law's frown).

76. Which of the following would be the most significant factor in teaching Homer's *Iliad* and *Odyssey* to any particular group of students?

    A. Identifying a translation on the appropriate reading level

    B. Determining the students' interest level

    C. Selecting an appropriate evaluative technique

    D. Determining the scope and delivery methods of background study

Answer A: Identifying a translation on the appropriate reading level
Students will learn the importance of these two works if the translation reflects both the vocabulary that they know and their reading level. Greece will always be foremost in literary assessments due to Homer's works. Homer is the most often cited author, next to Shakespeare. Greece is the cradle of both democracy and literature. This is why it is so crucial that Homer be included in the works assigned.

77. A punctuation mark indicating omission, interrupted thought, or an incomplete statement is a/an:

   A. ellipsis

   B. anachronism

   C. colloquy

   D. idiom

Answer A: ellipsis
In an ellipsis, a word or words that would clarify the sentence's message are missing, yet it is still possible to understand the sentence from the context.

78. When characterizing a student's creativity, which of the descriptors are most apt?

   A. The student's solution is applicable in many areas, not just one domain.

   B. The student's solutions, though seemingly unorthodox, upon further discovery prove sound.

   C. The student's solutions are a collection of false starts, some of which end up being relevant.

   D. The student's solutions do not deviate from the standard perspectives.

Answer B: The student's solutions, though seemingly unorthodox, upon further discovery prove sound.
With the exception of B, the other answers are common misconceptions about creative thinkers. Divergent thinkers typically arrive at their conclusions from different perspectives and angles.

79. The technique of starting a narrative at a significant point in the action and then developing the story through flashbacks is called:

   A. in medias res

   B. octava rima

   C. irony

   D. willing suspension of disbelief

   Answer A: in medias res
   As its Latin translation suggests, a narrative that begins in medias res begins "in the middle of things." An octava rima is a specific eight-line stanza of poetry with a rhyme scheme of *abababcc*. Irony is an unexpected disparity between what is stated and what is really implied by the author. Drama is what Coleridge calls "the willing suspension of disbelief for the moment, which constitutes poetic faith."

80. When seeking to improve academic performance, as well as motivation of students, which of the following strategies are most likely to succeed?

   A. Teachers appoint a liaison to work with the administration to create a 'best practices' set of rules.

   B. Teachers present material as a team, standardizing presentation, and mapping academic progress.

   C. Teacher collaboration to assess and monitor other classroom procedures offers successful solutions.

   D. The classroom teacher must utilize management techniques with which he is familiar and comfortable.

   Answer C: Teacher collaboration to assess and monitor other classroom procedures offers successful solutions.
   When teachers collaborate, share experiences, and assess one another on a routine basis, all are made stronger and benefit from the collaboration. New teachers often benefit from a veteran teacher's experience, while the veteran teacher can benefit by embracing new techniques and processes employed by the new teacher.

81. In a timed essay test of an hour's duration, how much time should be devoted to prewriting?

   A. 5 minutes

   B. 10 minutes

   C. 15 minutes

   D. 20 minutes

Answer B: 10 minutes
In the hour the students have to write the essay, they should not take more than 10 minutes prewriting. As the students prewrite, they should remember to have at least three main points and at least two to three details to support the main ideas.

82. Which of the following sentences is properly punctuated?

   A. The more you eat; the more you want.

   B. The authors—John Steinbeck, Ernest Hemingway, and William Faulkner—are staples of modern writing in American literature textbooks.

   C. Handling a wild horse, takes a great deal of skill and patience.

   D. The man, who replaced our teacher, is a comedian.

Answer B: The authors–John Steinbeck, Ernest Hemingway, and William Faulkner–are staples of modern writing in American literature textbooks.
Dashes should be used for amplification or explanation instead of commas when commas are used elsewhere in the sentence—in this case, within the dashes.

83. The students in Mrs. Cline's seventh-grade language arts class were invited to attend a performance of *Romeo and Juliet* presented by the drama class at the high school. To best prepare, they should:

   A. read the play as a homework exercise

   B. read a synopsis of the plot and a biographical sketch of the author

   C. examine a few main selections from the play to become familiar with the language and style of the author

   D. read a condensed version of the story and practice attentive listening skills

Answer D: read a condensed version of the story and practice attentive listening skills
By reading a condensed version of the story, students will know the plot and therefore be able to follow the play on stage. It is also important for them to practice listening techniques such as one-to-one tutoring and peer-assisted reading.

84. For students learning the process of constructed response writing, what is the appropriate pedagogical process?

   A. independent writing (summative), guided writing (formative), model/shadowing

   B. Model/shadowing, guided writing (formative), independent writing (summative)

   C. Guided writing (formative), model/shadowing, independent writing (summative)

   D. Independent writing (summative), guided writing (formative), peer reviewed grouping

Answer B: Model/shadowing, guided writing (formative), independent writing (summative)
Writing is a skill and as such must be presented in a logical manner, and in a manner which does not promote student anxiety or apprehension. Thus, showing the students how something is written, having them imitate the process, then guiding them through the process, culminating in independent attempts is the best method for acquisition of a new skill, in particular, writing.

85. **An aspect of the reflective practice methodology is exemplified in which of the following?**

    A. The teacher limits the amount of peer review.

    B. The teacher should limit student input that challenges or questions established teaching practices.

    C. The teacher should allow peer review to take its natural course, offering very little framework to limit the problem solving process.

    D. The teacher should establish a safe environment that allows reflection to take place among an accepted practice that is applicable for all learning situations.

Answer D: The teacher should establish a safe environment that allows reflection to take place among an accepted practice that is applicable for all learning situations.
Trust is the foundation upon which peer review and reflective practice must be built. B and C are useful only in a limited capacity, as creativity may be hampered. The classroom teacher must establish a set context upon which each assignment will draw, especially when peer interaction, reflection, or critique are involved.

86. **When establishing the best way to assist students with comprehension skills, a teacher should focus on which of the following techniques as an informational text is read aloud?**

    A. Writing down questions as a text is read aloud

    B. Creating an outline

    C. Setting a purpose for reading

    D. Encouraging students to make predictions

Answer A: Writing down questions as a text is read aloud
If a student is able to write down questions about what is being read, then comprehension must follow. This type of metacognition is evident when a relevant question is asked about the text that is read. C and D are used as pre-reading strategies.

87. Writing ideas quickly without interruption of the flow of thoughts or attention to conventions is called:

   A. brainstorming

   B. mapping

   C. listing

   D. free writing

Answer D: free writing
Free writing for 10 or 15 minutes allows students to write out their thoughts about a subject. This technique allows the students to develop ideas of which they are conscious, but it also helps them develop ideas that are lurking in the subconscious. It is important to let the flow of ideas run through the hand. If the students get stuck, they can write the last sentence over again until inspiration returns.

88. A formative evaluation of student writing:

   A. requires a thorough marking of mechanical errors with a pencil or pen

   B. makes comments on the appropriateness of the student's interpretation of the prompt and the degree to which the objective was met

   C. requires the student to hand in all the materials produced during the process of writing

   D. several careful readings of the text for content, mechanics, spelling, and usage

Answer B: makes comments on the appropriateness of the student's interpretation of the prompt and the degree to which the objective was met
It is important to give students numerous experiences with formative evaluation (evaluation as the student writes the piece). Formative evaluation will assign points to every step of the writing process, even though it is not graded. The criteria for the writing task should be very clear, and the teacher should read each step twice. Responses should be noncritical and supportive, and the teacher should involve students in the process of defining criteria and make it clear that formative and summative evaluations are two distinct processes.

89. **Reading a piece of student writing to assess the overall impression of the product is:**

    A. holistic evaluation

    B. portfolio assessment

    C. analytical evaluation

    D. using a performance system

Answer A: holistic evaluation
Holistic evaluation assesses a piece of writing as a whole. Usually a paper is first read through quickly to get a general impression. The writing is graded according to the impression of the whole work rather than the sum of its parts. Often holistic scoring uses a rubric that establishes the overall criteria for a certain score to evaluate each paper.

90. **Modeling is a practice that requires students to:**

    A. create a style unique to their own language capabilities

    B. emulate the writing of professionals

    C. paraphrase passages from good literature

    D. peer evaluate the writings of other students

Answer B: emulate the writing of professionals
Modeling has students analyze the writing of a professional writer and try to reach the same level of syntactical, grammatical, and stylistic mastery as the author whom they are studying.

91. A teacher is planning a lesson on T.S. Eliot's "The Hollow Men" for his eleventh grade English class. This is an excerpt from the poem:

> *The eyes reappear*
> *As the perpetual star*
> *Multifoliate rose*
> *Of death's twilight kingdom*
> *The hope only*
> *Of empty men.*

What strategy, of those listed below, best allows for identification and understanding of the word 'multifoliate'?

A. Structural analysis

B. Contextual analysis

C. Graphophonic analysis

D. Syntactical analysis

Answer A: Structural analysis
Structural analysis is the most effective way to analyze the prefix, and the root. Graphophonic requires a student to create a definition based on the sounds, and does not provide enough context for figuring out the meaning of the word. B is partially useful only in that the word, rose, offers some clues to the meaning of the word, but it does not offer enough context to come to a determination of its meaning. Syntactical analysis (D) is incorrect because this type of analysis will only determine that the word in question is being used as an adjective and nothing more.

92. A teacher is working with a class that includes an ELL (English Language Learner) student. When assigning an informational essay to the class, which of the following techniques would assist the ELL in an understanding of the text?

   A. Have all students create an illustration of some part of the text that they found interesting.

   B. Have the class use a graphic organizer to write down main ideas in the article.

   C. Hand out a list of most often used sentence stems to the entire classroom to use.

   D. Provide a list of words to the ELL that are familiar synonyms to the words that he or she is likely to encounter in the article assigned.

Answer D: Provide a list of words to the ELL that are familiar synonyms to the words that he or she is likely to encounter in the article assigned
The answer is D because the ELL is provided some context for the words that he or she is likely to encounter in the reading. Sentence stems (C) may be helpful when the ELL begins to write but it does not assist with comprehension in reading. (B) is incorrect because the student would have to already have an understanding of the content and context. (A) is incorrect because it does not perpetuate language development comprehension.

93. An 8th grade English teacher notices that each day when she asks a couple of questions about the previous day's lesson, the same handful of students always answer. Which of the following would promote active engagement by a larger percentage of the students?

   A. Encouraging those who are not answering, to do so.

   B. Allowing all students to create two questions about the day's assignment, to be asked the next day.

   C. Giving a participation grade that is not dependent on the correct answer.

   D. Having students evaluate their peers' responses using a rubric.

Answer B: Allowing all students to create two questions about the day's assignment, to be asked the next day
Having students create a bank of questions each day allows the teacher to use questions from students whom do not normally risk answering a question. Not only does this promote interaction, but it also creates an opportunity for students to create relevant questions, and adds one more evaluative model for a teacher to assess comprehension.

94. Which of the following indicators would suggest that a student has developed strong communication skills when placed in a small group to discuss a novel?

    A. Taking charge of the group and directing the conversation.

    B. Making comments that build upon statements made by others in the group.

    C. Asking questions of the group members that diverges from the topic of conversation.

    D. Asking whomever is talking to explain what they mean by their statements.

Answer B: Making comments that build upon statements made by others in the group
While many of the other answers may be indicators of someone who is able to communicate, (B) indicates that the student not only comprehends what is being said, but is also able to be a constructive listener. (C) is incorrect because students who diverge from the topic at hand are not effectively listening. (A) is incorrect because the student may be more interested in garnering attention without furthering the goal of the group, while (D) is incorrect because if someone is asking for a lot of explanation it is clear that they are not listening, or that there may be comprehension issues.

95. In a high school classroom, a teacher has had students complete rough drafts of an expository essay, and has placed them in pairs to peer review each other's work. As a guideline, what should the teacher have students read to discern first?

    A. Transitions

    B. Supporting details

    C. Biased language

    D. Varied sentence lengths

Answer A: Transitions
While all of these are good aspects to evaluate, the first to be evaluated should be the use of adequate transitions. If a student has used transitions, shifts from one idea to the next, then the student has internalized the concept of 'flow' and 'voice' within their writing. The other aspects must certainly be considered, but as a first evaluative assessment, (A) is the starting point.

96. A ninth grade English teacher is attempting to develop strategies that will promote a reading community in his classroom. Which of the following would be the least effective way of accomplishing this task?

A. Students bring in books from home to include in a classroom library.

B. The teacher assigns book reports on books that are to be selected from a list.

C. Students work with the teacher to create a list of favorite books to read.

D. The teacher will institute a 'drop everything and read' program for thirty minutes each week.

Answer C: Students work with the teacher to create a list of favorite books to read
(C) is the least likely technique to improve or promote a sense of community as it is teacher-centric rather than student-centric. Students are motivated and readily participate on a larger percentage when there has been active participation in the process. Additionally, (D) is a type of modelling behavior where the teacher actively promotes reading for enjoyment, and it opens up a ready platform for a dialogue about reading, thus motivating reluctant readers to attempt reading more frequently.

97. What best describes a type of formative evaluation for writing education?

A. Making careful readings of the text for mechanics, usage, spelling, and content.

B. Marking mechanical errors with a colored pen.

C. Asks students to turn in all work pertaining to the writing assignment, including outlines.

D. Teacher makes comments on the goals that are being met by the student as the student works.

Answer D: Teacher makes comments on the goals that are being met by the student as the student works
In formative evaluation the teacher continues to give insight to the student on those goals that are being met, thus supporting behaviors and skills that are wanted, and focusing on achieving the goal rather than focusing on those skills that are lacking.

98. When utilizing a computer in the classroom for writing assignments, the teacher must be aware of which of the following drawbacks when writing on a computer?

   A. The writer may be unable to focus on the details and become distracted by the technology.

   B. The ability of a computer to quickly correct mistakes, often automatically, takes away from the aspect of writing that calls for reflection.

   C. Spell check programs do not assist students in learning to spell correctly, or select proper grammatical choices in their writing.

   D. Students tend to overlook glaring errors on the page because of the print type.

Answer B: The ability of a computer to quickly correct mistakes, often automatically, takes away from the aspect of writing that calls for reflection. One of the largest components of learning to write is to take the time to consider what will be written. Because of various social media interactions, the quick aspect of the computer to automatically correct problems, the contemplation factor is removed, and the process of revising may break down.

99. When attempting to introduce a unit on poetry to freshmen students in a regular classroom, which of the following is the most ineffective technique?

   A. Students are encouraged to bring their favorite song lyrics to class to discuss poetic devices used.

   B. Students will bring in their favorite poems to read aloud to the class.

   C. Students will work in groups to try to apply poetic devices in creating a popular song.

   D. Students will work in groups to illustrate a given poem.

Answer D: Students will work in groups to illustrate a given poem
Students may enjoy illustrating a poem, but it does not facilitate or accomplish the goal. The goal is to encourage students to learn to appreciate poetry and to try to write their own poems. Allowing students to bring in poems that they already like, or song lyrics they are familiar with, are better methods for promoting interest and motivating students to attempt the new skill.

100. A new teacher is experiencing his first ELL student and wonders what type of activity would help this student the most. Which of the following might be suggested?

    A. Provide the ELL student with more opportunities to write in English.

    B. Provide opportunities for the class, as well as the ELL student, to listen to the language via various media.

    C. Provide a wide range of activities that promote exposure to the language in all of its various modes (speaking, writing, reading).

    D. Make an assignment requiring students to make oral presentations in front of the class.

Answer D: Make an assignment requiring students to make oral presentations in front of the class
While this may be initially a difficult assignment, the ELL student will benefit from hearing the language and thus understand phonologically the differences in the sounds. Correlations and contextual meanings of words are understood when heard and viewed, than when read.

Interested in dual certification?

XAMonline offers over 50 TExES study guides which are aligned and provide a comprehensive review of the core test content. Want certification success on your first exam? Trust XAMonline's study guides to help you succeed!

TExES Series:

Principal 068
ISBN: 9781607874546

Chemistry 7-12 240
ISBN: 9781607873792

Core Subjects 4-8 211
ISBN: 9781607874560

Core Subjects EC-6 291
ISBN: 9781607874553

English as a Second Language (ESL)
ISBN: 9781607873877

English Language Arts and Reading 4-8
ISBN: 9781581977721

English Language Arts and Reading 7-12
ISBN: 9781607873785

Pedagogy and Professional Responsibilities EC-12
ISBN: 9781607874362

Pedagogy and Professional Responsibilities EC-12 Bonus Edition PPR EC-12, THEA, Generalist 4-8
ISBN: 9781607873150

Life Science 7-12 238
ISBN: 9781607873761

Mathematics 4-8 115
ISBN: 9781607871118

Mathematics 7-12 235
ISBN: 9781607873747

Mathematics-Science 4-8 114
ISBN: 9781581979480

Physical Education EC-12 158
ISBN: 9781581976205

Reading Specialist 151
ISBN: 9781581979411

School Counselor 152
ISBN: 9781581977196

School Librarian 150
ISBN: 9781581979404

Science 4-8 116
ISBN: 9781581972979

Social Studies 4-8 118
ISBN: 9781581976618

Don't see your test? Visit our website: www.xamonline.com

www.ingramcontent.com/pod-product-compliance
Lightning Source LLC
Chambersburg PA
CBHW080536300426
44111CB00017B/2743